CONTENTS

PREFACE

The intentions for this book have evolved during its writing. There was a stage when an objective review of the history of Sonoma Valley since 1960 seemed essential. Setting the record straight on what was reported in the local newspaper as opposed to what Bob claims really happened also seemed a worthy crusade.

But with time it became more than obvious that the key element of Bob's Cannard's life is his unique point of view, and total conviction that it is the right one.

This is not a comprehensive biography or a fair and balanced review of local politics; it's a simple memoir. One person's recollections of his public existence, from his point of view, mellowed and refracted by time.

SONOMA'S LAST PIONEER

"A LIFE WELL LIVED"
by Tom Whitworth

Whitworth & I with the Sonoma Valley Historical Society - Sonoma, California

Sonoma Valley Historical Society
P.O. Box 861
Sonoma, CA 95476
(707) 938 1762
www.vom.com/depot

Whitworth and I
P.O. Box 545
Vineburg, CA 95487
(707) 939 3760
www.whitworthandi.com

Library of Congress Control Number: 2005928202

Produced by Whitworth and I
Book design and production: T.W.Whitworth
Project Management: J.L.Chandler

ISBN 0-9771655-0-7

Printed and bound in China

10 9 8 7 6 5 4 3 2 1

Dedicated to Bob Cannard's wife Edna.

ACKNOWLEDGEMENTS

This book would not have been possible without the funding and support of the Sonoma Valley Historical Society and its Board of Directors. The author would also like to thank Jeri Lynn Chandler, who created the book's structure, carried out research, completed much of the word processing and guided us through the printing and publishing process. Bob Cannard's own huge collection of documents and memorabilia, and the photograph collections of various members of his family have provided many of the visual references. T.W.W.

When you start a book of this nature you have in mind to record events in your life that you think may be of interest and value to your family and friends. This is not what really happens. It becomes the ultimate ego trip. All of the little things that have happened piled on one another plus hundreds of pictures and newspaper articles and dozens of small honors give greater appearance to the whole than is really there.

Man is not a humble being. Humility is rarely seen. One might as well confess to being vain because no one would believe otherwise anyway. However, if I had my life to live over again, I probably would not do much differently. Hopefully I would correct some of the errors and refrain from wasting time. I could have accomplished much more if I had not spent time in idle pleasures.

This is not all bad because the qualities that make you vain are also the ones that make you productive and valuable as a public animal. To be beneficial to others one must overcome shyness and give of yourself. The good book says not to hide your talents under a bushel.

As you read these pages and enjoy the pictures you might get the impression that I acted alone on many of these projects. Nothing could be farther from the truth.

People and newspaper accounts focused on me because I usually put forth the idea. There were nearly always many people working on the project at hand with me. Many public officials at various public meetings would make the snide remark that they were honored that Mr. Cannard was here with his staff. I had many devoted fellow workers.

In Kenwood ours was one of a dozen young families that had similar ideas about the community. In pulling the Chamber of Commerce out of bankruptcy, there were always at least a dozen fellow members that could be counted on. It would have been impossible without the devoted work of Treasurer Jerry Jolly. I was just one of three or four people who put together the campaign that saved the open space around the Vallejo Home.

On every other environmental project there were always the few who could be counted on to face the opposition. In many cases I was the spokesperson, but there were always others to back me up.

So as you read these pages, remember that there were a group of citizens who were more concerned about the future livability of Sonoma Valley than the money in their pockets. The opposition was often the group that was out for the fast buck.

Throughout my life I have participated in many events, sometimes in the lead and often following others. The idea as often came from the group as from myself. When I came to Sonoma Valley, I was determined to have an effect on the future. I quickly learned the history and the family background of a lot of people. It seemed so natural to me. There were people still living who knew General Vallejo. Most of the heads of the Italian families were immigrants like my father. These people came here between 1890 and 1930, the latter part of my childhood and at about the same time my father immigrated.

During my short stay in Santa Rosa, I interviewed a dozen people who worked for Luther Burbank. My mother had

It did not take long to become part of the fabric of Sonoma Valley. Within a short time lots of people thought of me as an old timer and sought me out for information about the valley and its history. Most of these people had lived here longer than I and should have known the answer to their own questions. Today people stop me on the street nearly every day for information about Sonoma. Many people think I was born here.

There developed around me a group that had similar ideas for our future. I have been fortunate to be one of a large number of people who have marched to the same tune. These were conservative, family-oriented people with very basic American values that evolved from the Frontier Spirit.

Many were astute business people or agriculturists, but that did not prevent them from helping their neighbors on short notice, people more interested in having good schools than joining social clubs. Some were devoutly connected to their churches, more than a few were Orthodox Jews. Some were very wealthy, and there were many with few resources as well. There were Democrats and Republicans, a true mix of the kind of people who made America great.

Bob Cannard
Sonoma, Calif.
Summer 2005

INTRODUCTION

In the accepted historical sense, Robert Hiatt Cannard of Sonoma, California, is not a pioneer, but he sure looks like one. Tall, strong, weather beaten, afraid of nothing. He has done the things that pioneers did – moved his family from east to west, built log cabins, made furniture, grown his own produce, reared and butchered his own food animals.

He can "do anything," claiming that if he can figure it out in his mind, he can do it in practice. He has the pioneer's mentality of adaptability, inventiveness, self-sufficiency, determination, and utter confidence in his ability to surmount any obstacle. He is beholden to no one. He also happens to be self-opinionated and presumptuous, but views these as virtues. He is immensely generous, having given away in time, money, food and trees, about a third of his life to his community, as did his father before him.

That these characteristics have played out a century late makes him that much more interesting. Whether he is the last of such types remains to be seen, but probably not, because his six strapping and accomplished sons are not that different from their father.

He has a presence that goes beyond size. It's that hard to define set of characteristics that imbue a few with an air of natural authority. Such a quality is inclined to attract as much envy as admiration.

He doesn't trade in opinions too much, because to him opinions are kind of tentative. People with authority talk facts, and he is brimming over with them on every subject you can imagine—although they incline toward the practical rather than intellectual.

He is an old style Republican—the type that *really* believes in less goverment and more personal responsibility. At the same time he is adamant that continuous contact with the natural world is integral to a balanced mind. So he is an ardent environmentalist too, and by default deeply suspicious of city folks, especially when they move to the country and try to bring the city with them, as they have increasingly done in recent years.

He is a fierce protector of rural eccentricity and the agricultural heritage that has defined Sonoma Valley. He was at the heart of the only event in Sonoma's checkered history that managed to make it to the front page of the Wall Street Journal. For decades, unwanted chickens had been dropped off—usually in the dead of night—somewhere on Sonoma's big central plaza, home to City Hall, the duck pond, a music amphitheatre, various commemorative monuments and a children's park. The chickens quickly made it their home and became the favorites of tourists, locals and some Plaza retailers, roosting in trees and nesting in chic retail establishments. But after decades or so of peaceful coexistence, a small child was chased, and of all horrors, pecked by a scraggly plaza rooster, prompting the mother to threaten the City with a lawsuit. On the advice of attorneys and excited by the opportunity to make real decisions that impacted people's lives, the Council immediately voted to banish the birds. This provoked an outcry from locals who considered the birds to be at least representative of the city's independent spirit and rural heritage—certainly as important as the bear on the state flag, and possibly symbolic of freedom itself, the way some of them told it.

The most vocal and visible of these protestors, of course, was Bob Cannard, and not only because of his height, booming voice, and take-charge attitude. He has, since birth, rarely been without a bunch of his own chickens and considers them one of the mainstays of a happy and healthy life. Just a few years before, a newcomer to his residential neighborhood had officially complained that Bob's roosters crowed in the early morning and woke him up. Bob response was "that's what roosters do!" He won the point, and kept his birds. Efforts to keep the plaza chickens, even with Bob's promise to find non-aggressive roosters, have so far failed, and the ban remains in place.

It may have seemed a trivial issue. Who really cares if a few chickens no longer strut the public areas of a small rural town, particularly if that town is now a style-setter in world renowned "Wine Country", which has even transcended the definite article?

But it was not a trivial issue to Bob. It cut at the very heart of what he believes, that the present and future are logical extensions of past experience, and if you break the links, the continuum of life is harmed.

For the same reason he has crusaded for far greater preservation of historic buildings and celebration of local history, for protection of the valley's water resources, for building new homes one at a time, with individual character, not in groups on big expanses of compacted and leveled ground. He has proposed plans to anticipate traffic problems with bypasses and rail links, to anticipate residential growth with the creation of satellite towns.

All this would have taken proactive planning and wresting power away from the city bureaucrats, county planners and state government. While not an insurmountable problem to Bob, such a course of action has been rejected by successive bands of elected officials who have remained merely reactive to the developers, who are only too willing to impose their profit-driven notions of what the area should look like.

True to his nature, Bob has more often than not taken matters into his own hands. He's done privately what the establishment would or could not do, and the evidence is apparent everywhere you look, in the form of thousands of shade trees, protected and restored buildings, a commemorative fountain, institutions like the Chamber of Commerce, events like the Ox Roast and the Vintage Festival. Sometimes, the evidence is not there to see. Like the hundreds of houses that would have covered the huge public green space near the center of town if it hadn't have been for Bob's ability to rally and motivate like-minded people, fight city hall, and win.

He still claims "the voice of reason has never been heard in this valley," and yet despite setbacks, is wildly optimistic for the future. He's not in the least bitter toward past opponents (at least those still living), perhaps with the single exception of the local newspaper and its owners. The feeling is presumably mutual as evidenced by the Sonoma Index-Tribune's pattern of alternately deriding Bob's actions or comically avoiding mentioning his role in events altogether. None of this is surprising to Bob, because he has not changed his original opinion that California offers a home to the descendants of malcontents and ne'er-do-wells.

If you try to imagine the way Charlton Heston as Moses might deliver the line "the voice of reason has never been heard in this valley," you will begin to get an idea of how Bob's everyday voice sounds a lot of the time. For his mind to automatically search out and assemble as many memorized facts as possible (to give force to his next sentence), he needs to be in neutral space. Being in it requires him to focus on some point above and behind you, which gives him the look of someone giving a speech during normal conversation. But the results can be spectacular when his synapses release a stream of synergistically linked facts that would leave any search engine in the dust.

In the summer of 2004, Bob and I attended a meeting of the directors of the Sonoma Valley Historical Society. We were to give them a progress report on this book. First, Bob was asked to explain to the board members how funds for the project had come to exist. The simple answer would have been that his Vallejo Association (a local preservation foundation) had provided funds to the Historical Society, some of which was earmarked for this book. But that wouldn't be Cannard's style at all. He paused, leaned back, folded his arms, thought for a moment, smiled, and began.

The story Bob related started with the origins of Sonoma and the state of California. It progressed to his scheme to foil the intentions of grasping developers by kicking out Sonoma's rubber-stamp council in a bold election maneuver, and a deal to help elect a state senator in return for a promise of state funds to buy the land around the home of California's last Mexican commandant, M. J. Vallejo. This allowed for a public park and the creation of a winery in Vallejo's name, as a tribute to the county's agriculture and to boost the infant varietal wine industry. Somehow an opera was involved, too, and finally, Bob's own attempt to restore Vallejo's daughter's mansion as a theme museum for public benefit, a plan that was squelched by "vindicative city schemers."
Appropriate names, places, dates and times spilled out effortlessly as he wove the threads together and concluded with the sale of the house and winery, thereby coming up with the funds for, among other things, this book.

Other people might study history for enlightenment, but Bob studies history in order to place himself in it. His every act is the latest installment of a bigger story, stretching back as far as his memory allows, and usually a lot further. It's almost as if knowing history gives him ownership of it, all of it.

The history of his America stars the pioneer. The gritty individualist, utterly self-dependent and independent, moving westwards with his family, creating true freedoms at a frontier level, freedoms that 'The Declaration' had only intellectualized.

Forty-five years ago Bob arrived in Sonoma Valley, California from Pennsylvania, and seized the opportunity to determine his own destiny at a similarly local frontier level. Sometimes that meant fighting for what he wanted, sometimes for his community, frequently both, and always to protect natural resources. People didn't always know quite which, and that sometimes got him bad press, but it didn't trouble Bob too much. If America struggles with its identity, he doesn't. He knows that the power of this country lies in its individual and collective spirit of self-reliance, something he practices every day. His ability to directly connect himself to a history replete with vivid characters who were self-sufficient, self-motivated, built their own homes, grew their own food, raised families – all against enormous odds, provides him with a personal sense of purpose, and a personal sense of responsibility to do the same.

At the end of the Historical Society presentation, one of the board members said that shortly after he had arrived in town thirteen or fourteen years before, he'd been invited to an ox roast. It had been one of Bob's impromptu larger-than-life events to publicize a successful bid for a local council seat, announced only days before the election.

> "It was at your barn Bob. Sure enough there was an ox roasting over a huge pit, and barrels of apples, and mountains of food and wine. You had invited everyone in the city, everyone! Hundreds of people were there, all new to us, and I talked to you with my two boys. You gave them each a tree, and told them how to plant it, just like that. They never forgot that ox roast, and neither did I."

Another member of the Society's board related that he lived in a mobile home park, and that if it hadn't been for the efforts of Bob and a few like him some years back, there'd be no rent control and he would be in serious trouble. "So I'd like to say a big thank you, Bob."

I was reminded that we were meeting at the Chamber of Commerce, itself an institution saved from bankruptcy by Bob's personal efforts thirty-five years before. One way or another, everyone in the building had been affected by Bob's presence in Sonoma Valley.

When he arrived in California, it wasn't just with the idea that he would find a new environment with opportunity for himself and family to thrive in a much warmer climate than Pennsylvania's. It was to find a place that could be his frontier—if not geographically, then socially. A place, maybe, where his ideas could have an influence on the way society worked out. Sonoma Valley contained a rural agricultural community, conservative like himself, with growth headed its way and a services infrastructure to build. The challenge of preserving the values of a rural community with great historical significance, while at the same time enjoying the benefits of growth, appealed to him no end.

Life back east in Pennsylvania, in an older community with its social conventions and landuse issues long established and its successes and failures well studied, had prepared him for such challenges. He was also an accomplished botanist, horticulturalist, environmentalist, historian, cook, woodworker, farmer, butcher, bird breeder, trader in old coins and other antiques, and insurance salesman. Above all, he was a promoter, of himself, his ideas, and any business that needed a boost. Where does this all come from?

Ask Bob Cannard for a blessing on a meal, and he will rise straight up to his full six feet one inches, grip the top of the family's speaking staff, and with eyes wide open and a broad grin, invoke the spirit of the natural world.

"Life comes from the sun, to the plants, to the good food, to the good wine, to the table, to family and to good friends...to the goodness of life. May we all enjoy the goodness of life."

It's his celebration of the dead certainty that good things follow a cycle you can trust absolutely. And he would know, because in his words he has "a few drops of the pure blood." By some happy accident of birth he has a rare ability to sense the infinite continuum of life just as profoundly as he feels its present moment. The effect is to produce an overwhelming sense of destiny, tranquility, confidence, and rightness. And it accounts for his uncanny ability to sense the future before it happens.

"At a very early age, I realized that I was different from the other kids on the block. If I thought about something, I could usually find a way to make it happen."

Since then, Bob Cannard has made a lot happen, even though his personal aspirations have rarely extended beyond his visible horizon.

Cannard's pioneer reverence for the natural order of things is a driving force. His blueprint for a happy and fulfilled society features five simple points. Everyone must grow something they eat (in a window box if necessary), keep three chickens, and not buy new if used will do. If you're not sure who to vote for, make it the youngest candidate because they have to live with their mistakes for the longest time. And finally, support education to the nth degree.

If you can get over the chicken thing, it's not a bad ethos at all, although it might not fit too well with a society that wants to enjoy surfing its own economic wave. To Bob, this would be no more than a detail, a minor hurdle to get over.

And if you think he's stuck in the past, consider that he thinks one of the great tragedies of recent years was that the 1976 Bicentennial wasn't used as an opportunity to rewrite *all U.S. law* in a fresh and dramatic "rebirth of a nation." He has consistently reinvented himself so why can't the nation? A radical society evolving with every new challenge needs people like him. Pioneers did not intellectualize a new strategy for surviving a hostile environment; they figured it out right away from experience and instinct.

Bob Cannard is a remarkable man. Remarkable as much for the way he memorializes his rich experiences in nearly eighty years, as for what he has achieved, which by anyone's measurement is considerable.

When Bob Cannard arrived in Northern California's Sonoma Valley in 1959, there were four small wineries, a population of 17,000, and a mixed agricultural economy. Today, there are more than fifty wineries, few other agricultural ventures, a thriving tourist industry, a large retired population, wealthy escapees from San Francisco and commuters to San Francisco, as well as an ill-defined group that claim some right to its unique character either through longevity, land ownership or commercial monopoly. Many in this latter group enjoy their status as a result of the nineteenth century manifest destiny that disenfranchised anyone with a claim dating prior to 1846, (when the "Bear Flaggers" rejected Mexican rule and claimed California a republic,) or by killing anyone who had the misfortune to be native Californian. Others owe theirs to the murky politics of the first sixty years of the twentieth century, which allowed the land and water incorporation deals affecting the public to be done very much in private. Explosive growth and dramatic change in the social profile of the wine country north of San Francisco means Sonoma Valley has not been without growing pains, as one self interest group or another has fought to either shape it in their image, not change it at all, or allow "market forces" to do their worst or best, while all the time trying to squeeze their slice of the profits from the increased desirability of whatever has emerged.

And through it all, the valley has remained exquisitely beautiful. Vines have replaced dairy herds and orchards, and the burgeoning metropolis of Santa Rosa to the north has only managed a limited foray into the rolling hills and narrow valley. San Francisco and its Marin County suburbs stay remotely to the south. The railroad has long disappeared, along with the springs and year-round streams, but the roads remain narrow, and everywhere there are wildflowers and trees, nourished by the hot California sun by day yet cooled pleasantly by Bay winds at night. It is so wonderful that many of its residents have taken to spending their vacations in Italy's Tuscany—which looks pretty much the same as Sonoma Valley but with real Tuscan villas as opposed to modern knock-offs.

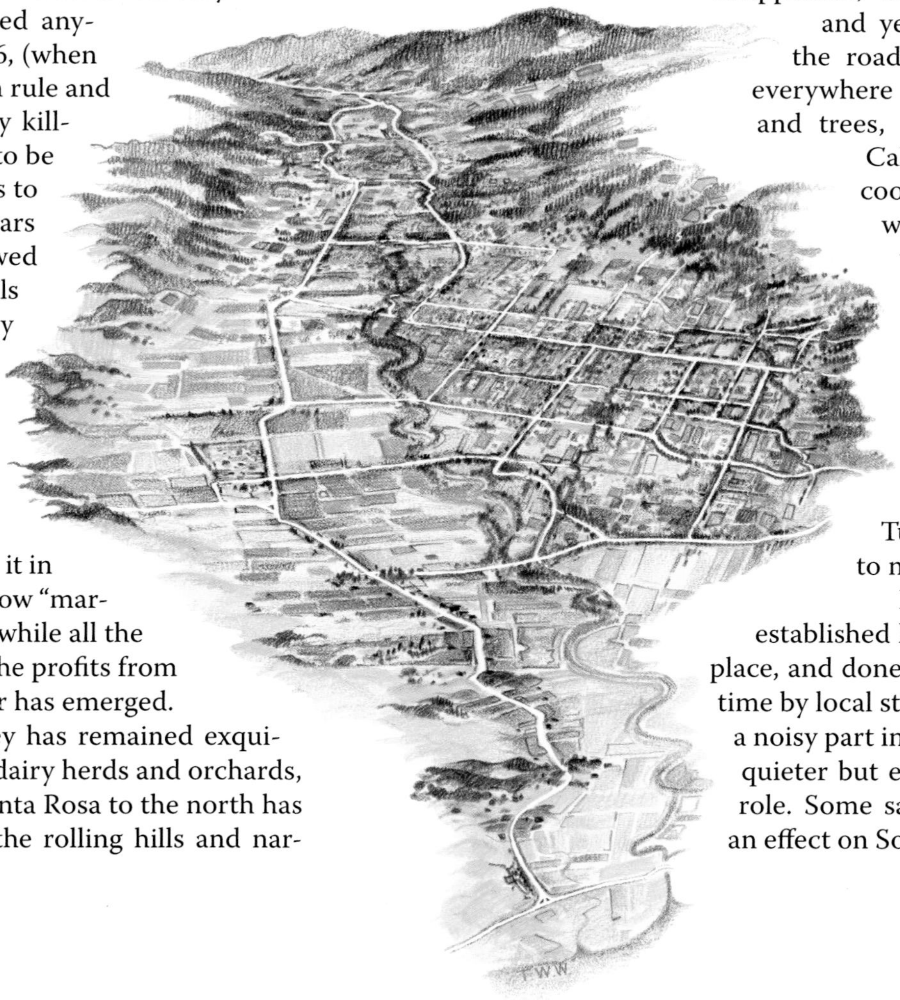

Bob Cannard has firmly established his place in this unique place, and done so in a relatively short time by local standards. He has played a noisy part in its public affairs, and a quieter but equally effective private role. Some say he has had as great an effect on Sonoma Valley as anyone since its founder, Mariano Vallejo - of whom Bob himself is an avid and knowledgeable student.

He has taught its horticultural students, funded and run its business associations and institutions, helped build its wine industry, served in elected and appointed offices and acted as informal watchdog on the excesses of people not as dedicated as he to guardianship of the natural resources inherited by all. He has made generous contributions to the celebration of its cultural heritage and invented some of it himself. He has built his own memorials to its history for the benefit of all.

He was perhaps drawn inexorably to the City of Sonoma because it has been a powerful magnet to the people and forces that shaped the west, and represents a symbolic finishing line for the race to colonize North America.

There have been few important events since Bob's arrival in the valley (some 114 years after the raising of the Bear Flag,) in which he has not had a direct or indirect hand, so his recollection is a valid, but not necessarily unbiased, view of its recent history. This is not unusual in Sonoma Valley, with more than it fair share of iconoclasts who have difficulty in agreeing with each other on what happened yesterday, and where gossip is more treasured than mere facts.

The local newspaper, headed by the same family for a few generations now, is so excruciatingly "establishment" that some think it cannot be relied on for accuracy, or at least fairness, perhaps with the exception of high school sports results and the time of church services. Its editors have also enjoyed something of a feud with the subject of this book—hardly the basis for factual reporting of his deeds or misdeeds. In fact, if you were to read *The Sonoma Valley Story* by ex-editor and now deceased Robert Lynch, you would think that Bob Cannard had never existed. In his apparently exhaustive history of the City and Valley, the name Cannard never appears. It is more than just an accidental omission, especially when you consider that from the mid-1960s through the1970s, and then again in the early 1990s, Bob's name is rarely absent from every issue. The reasons may become apparent in the chapters of this book. But given that Bob Lynch was a newspaperman, the omission of Cannard's name from his purported "Sonoma Story" throws some doubt on the likelihood of a legacy of balanced reporting.

Many of the characters that could have corroborated Bob's memory have either passed on, or have been reluctant to talk about controversial events. And Bob has rarely been involved in anything but controversial events, mostly because he is the kind of man that needs to have a hand in his own destiny, control of his own surroundings and a sharp awareness of his own place in its history. The way he characterizes his own life fits neatly with his sweeping perspective of the pioneer in the wider history of America. . . . .

America's Pioneer Spirit was conceived in the British Isles and Northern Europe. The discontent and turmoil following the Reformation resulted in a major break from the bondage of the Middle Ages. This, on top of the practice of

elections of kings by the Vikings and the formation of the guilds in England, expanded man's drive to determine his own future and that of his children. The political and religious upheaval that resulted in the beheading of King Charles I in 1649 accelerated the emigration to America.

The first permanent English settlement in America occurred at Jamestown, Virginia in 1607. Those settlers had a Royal Charter; their goal was profit. Many that came after, such as the Pilgrims in 1620 and the Puritans in 1631, emigrated for religious freedom. They had strong views on how their settlements should be organized.

The New England settlements were highly organized and laid out by strict design. Whole groups of people would move together into the wilderness and lay out a town. These newer towns provided places for immigrants as well as further protection to the older towns on the coast. Settlers leap-frogged across Massachusetts until they ran into the Berkshire Mountains.

Further south in New York, the Dutch had settled on Manhattan Island and then advanced up the Hudson River to the Albany area. They settled a strip of land along the river perhaps sixteen to twenty miles wide. Their houses, farms and towns are still evident. Kingston, New York has an old Dutch section that could be a town in Holland.

The English took over New York before William Penn received Pennsylvania for debt from the Crown in 1681. Penn settled Pennsylvania at Philadelphia as a proprietary colony. There were other settlers along the Atlantic Coast: Roger Bacon in Rhode Island, the Swedes in New Jersey, and Lord Baltimore in Maryland. These comprised the main settlements in the middle colonies and New England. In the South, Oglethorpe settled in Georgia as an experiment.

By the late 1600s, everything was in place for the great leap forward that the settlers, farmers and general working class would make in the next two centuries. The two major migrations from Europe that followed pushed the boundaries of coastal communities westward and over the first mountains.

First were the Germans, including many Hugue-

nots, who followed William Penn into Pennsylvania and settled in the river valleys of the Delaware, Schuylkill and Susquehanna. These were stouthearted fellows who probably sustained a higher percentage of casualties from the Indians than any other group of settlers. They did not intend to be pushed out. They would sacrifice their lives if necessary so their sons and daughters could live and farm. They remain today as the Pennsylvania Dutch.

The Irish and the Scotch-Irish that also came at this time had the guts, gumption and grit to push over the first mountains. These people had suffered so much in Europe before they came. The survivors of this persecution were some of the toughest people that ever lived. I don't think anything in the world today begins to compare with what they went through.

The Germans and Scotch-Irish came to the port of Philadelphia beginning about 1700 to 1720. As I have said, the Germans migrated to the river valleys to farm. The Scotch-Irish moved a little further up the valleys to the foothills. They were fiercely independent people who were not going to have anyone tell them how to live in their new land. With a Bible in one hand and a long gun in the other, they kept ahead of the settlements and lived as best they could.

The character of these people can best be illustrated with the story of one family. The parents of Daniel Boone came to America about 1720. They moved up the Delaware River to a place near where Redding, Pennsylvania stands today. This was a very remote and dangerous location at the time. There were several Indian tribes in the area ruled by the Iroquois in upstate New York. Daniel was born at the family's homestead in 1734 and spent the first twelve to fourteen years of his life there. He was a good friend to many Indians and learned woodcraft better than any Indian that ever lived. By the time he was twelve years old, he was doing all the hunting for the family.

As the number of Irish and Scotch-Irish coming into Philadelphia increased, many of them moved west in Pennsylvania and then south into western Virginia and the Carolinas on the eastern side of the Allegheny Mountains. The Boone family decided to do the same. They settled on a hard scrabble farm in western Carolina.

The pattern had been set: never be closer than ten or twenty miles from your nearest neighbor. No sense in being crowded.

About 1755, Daniel heard stories about the land west of the mountains. He decided to go take a look. At the time a fierce frontier war was going on between the English and the French and Indians for control of the Ohio Valley. That didn't seem to have bothered Daniel Boone. He had been a scout under George Washington when General Broddock was defeated and killed by the Indians and French.

Daniel Boone was not the first white man to visit Kentucky; he might have been the second or third. The story is too well known to retell of the incredible trials of the immigrants who followed Boone into Kentucky through the Cumberland Gap and their problems after they got there. But there is much more about Boone that is not so well known.

After Kentucky became too crowded for him, he moved west again. His next move was to the banks of the Missouri River a few miles upstream from where it joins the Mississippi River. His son and grandson were with him. Lewis and Clark on their expedition to the Pacific visited him at his cabin. He continued to hunt and trap until the end. Making two trips to the Yellowstone after he was eighty years old, hunting and trapping to build an estate for his family. This was after Lewis and Clark returned but before the era of the mountain men who came a decade later. He died in1820 at the age of eighty-six in bed, after surviving hundreds of escapes and near death by the Indians.

This Scotch-Irish family's history does not end there. Kit Carson, whose mother was a Boone, was the guide and scout for the pathfinder John C. Fremont as he made two major expeditions into the west. He traipsed up and down California several times and visited Sonoma, California on occasion. This Boone family's story spans about a hundred years and the breadth of the country from the Atlantic to the Pacific Ocean.

Your Sincere friend
C. Carson

Twenty-seven of the thirty-three members of the party that raised the Bear Flag in Sonoma on June 14, 1846, were of Scotch-Irish decent. Manifest Destiny had been completed. Thank the Scotch-Irish for leading the way.

The resourcefulness and independence of the people who struck out into untried territory are the cornerstones of the pioneering spirit that made the settlement of this vast country possible. The Scotch-Irish families relied entirely on themselves as they moved over the mountains ahead of the settlements. They had to grow everything, hunt everything, make everything they used and needed. The conditions they encountered were extreme and the work was hard. They cleared trees and planted what they needed around the stumps. They built their cabins and protected themselves from the Indians. They were fiercely independent and valued their privacy. If too many neighbors moved in, they simply packed up and moved further west to more free land. No one told them what they could or could not do.

There was a tempering influence to this indepen-

dence. The New Englanders and Pennsylvanians who were structured and organized in their communities also came west. The New Englanders crossed the Berkshires into New York then south through New York and Pennsylvania and west by way of the Ohio River. These people brought the idea of organized towns and the rule of law. The people living there at the time mostly made up these laws. The combination of the independent Scotch-Irish, the organized New Englanders, the Pennsylvanians and a smattering of Royalists from Virginia and Carolina tidewater combined to establish the pattern that continued until we became a nation from the Atlantic to the Pacific.

The founding fathers on the Atlantic Coast spearheaded the Revolution that gave us freedom from England. These intellectuals wrote the Declaration of Independence and the Constitution, but the individual freedom and personal independence we enjoy today comes from those people who moved west and relied on themselves in doing so. As the new territories became states and these people sent representatives to Congress, the national assembly began to incorporate their views. Congress was not dominated again by intellectuals for another 150 years.

During the twentieth century the same spirit pushed the frontier of every area of human endeavor beyond the scope of anything envisioned at the founding of the nation. Advances in medicine, science, education, social concerns and the push for foreign democracy are all the result of the unshackling that the American pioneer spirit gave to the world. The pioneer tolerated only a little government. He and his neighbors relied on themselves. His motto was "the least government is the best government."

Today the pendulum has swung again. There is a segment of the population that is undermining the pioneer spirit that built America. The leaders of this movement believe that the government should solve all of our problems. "Don't rely on yourself—let the government take care of you from the cradle to the grave—we can spend your money better than you can." I believe they do this simply to get votes and keep poor people in bondage. We all know there is corruption in big government, big business and big labor. If the person who works for a living will follow the simple rule of paying his union dues and voting Republican, he can have it both ways. The union will keep his income up and the Republicans will keep his taxes down. This is the only way the working person will ever get ahead.

This point of view comes from never having had to struggle to create something from scratch. We have become so separated from the lifestyles and values that settled this country that we've forgotten what truly made this country great. I firmly believe that progressive views are the greatest threat to the future of America. We are in danger of becoming a nation of people who are led around by the nose. The resulting federalism has become so pervasive that you can't go to the toilet without wondering if you are not breaking some law. Federalism will destroy the

Pioneer Spirit.

Every person who works for a living must join together. The only check on Federalism is reduced spending by government and that means reduced taxes for everybody. The rich will get richer but so will the poor. Fifty percent of all taxes are now paid by less than ten percent of the people. Taxes are harder on the other ninety percent. Taxes on poor people prevent them from climbing the ladder of success.

It is only natural that the poorest of the ninety percent who pay taxes want the most in return for their money. If they could keep some of their tax money, they would not ask the government to take care of them. The spirit of independence is not dead but is being strangled by Federalism. The only effective weapon of those ninety percent, who might not be able to influence with the dollar, is to vote.

RHC January 16, 2004 Hilo, HI

It's not unusual for people with firm convictions to award to the opposition evil motivations for holding opposing views. It makes their own beliefs seem less selfish.

But although Bob ostensibly ascribes all social ills to liberals and federalists, there's an implication that it's more to do with people who don't "work" for a living, or "who have never had to struggle to create something from scratch."

Yet Bob comes from a family that never really struggled, even during the depression. And it has been his choice to assume a practical rather than intellectual existence. Maybe he truly believes that the person who rises at five to milk cows in a freezing barn has a greater right to determine the country's direction than the person who rises at five to drive a subway train or write computer code.

Once you buy into the idea that adversity produces character, you're bound to believe that your kind of adversity is the best kind. And if adversity doesn't exist, then maybe you create it, to sharpen your wits.

This cartoon was put on the Cannard refrigerator door thirty-five years ago, not so much as a reminder, more as the unofficial family coat of arms.

In a country that is on the cutting edge of just about everything, everyone is a pioneer of sorts. Bob Cannard is the big and noisy variety. And if our lives are products of genetic code reacting to experience, then the magical combination that made Bob be what he is, and do what he has, is evidence enough that untold treasures of potential exist within us all.

"Sweet are the uses of adversity, which like the toad, ugly and venomous, wears yet a precious jewel in his head. And this our life, exempt from public haunt, finds tongues in trees, books in the running brooks, sermons in stones, and good in everything."   Wm. Shakespeare.

CHAPTER ONE

WITH ROOTS FIRMLY PLANTED

Robert H. Cannard was born on May 31, 1926, at the family home in the town of Danville in central Pennsylvania. It was a Monday. His father, Sidney George Cannard, as a respected local community leader, was at the time giving the official Memorial Day address in Memorial Park, and was thus absent, as were his six siblings, ushered out of the house and off to the park in the care of the eldest daughter Sarah, then ten years old, and brother George who was twelve. Mary was seven, twins Tom and John six, and Jim just three.

His mother, Frances was small, quiet, calm and retiring. Bob was large, noisy, and stayed that way. This turned out to be a useful attribute in a household of seven siblings, six older and subsequently one younger (Ed), all of whom Bob has continued to consider his intellectual superiors. His size afforded him a more significant voice in family affairs than his years warranted, but he has always striven to support his physical presence with knowledge. Knowledge, and the weight it provided to opinion and argument, was highly valued in the Cannard household, where participation in debate and conversation was encouraged and expected at every meal. It is why Bob today enjoys listening to or reading another man's opinion—"even if he is wrong."

The Cannards were impressive thinkers, led by Sidney Cannard, who was forty-eight years old when Bob was born, and by then a man of independent means. In fact, although Sidney had an office in downtown Danville, he went to it infrequently, and Bob never actually saw his father work.

Sidney was an English immigrant, born in 1878 to devout Methodists—his ancestors had toured the country with the Methodist evangelical founder John Wesley— in the village of Pucklechurch in Gloucestershire, a few miles to the north of the port city of Bristol, in the west of England. Sidney's father, Bob's grandfather George, was a hostler who took care of the horses and mules used extensively in the coalmines of that area, and also a champion grain cutter with the scythe. (George's great grandson, the younger Bob Cannard of organic farming fame who farms to the west side of Sonoma Valley on Sobre Vista, has by all accounts inherited that skill and is a similar expert with the two-handed long-blade scythe.) George Cannard probably cared for the pit ponies at the mine established in 1848 by Handel Cossham in the nearby village of Parkfield, and the huge working shire horses that abounded on local farms.

Sidney was born at Pendenis House, an impressive manor built in Elizabethan times by the influential Denis family that provided accommodation to William III on his return to Bristol from the Battle of the Boyne in Ireland.

The village was prominent in much earlier Saxon times and the scene of the murder of Edmond, a young Saxon King of Wessex. Edmond's son was some years later crowned in nearby Bath Abbey as King of Northumbria, Mercia, East Anglia and Wessex uniting all these kingdoms to become the first King of all England.

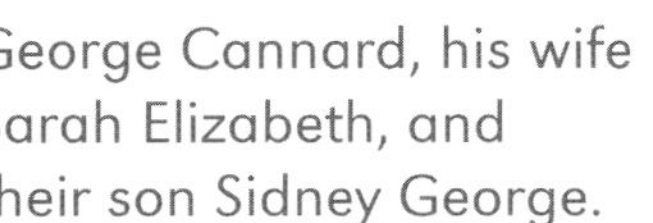

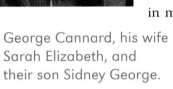

George Cannard, his wife Sarah Elizabeth, and their son Sidney George.

It was important in these hard times for every member of a family to be productive, and Sidney played his part. Almost every day, he carried milk to peddle on the streets of Bristol, eight miles away, a bucket in each hand and a cream can on his head. He retained this balancing skill throughout his life, and Bob remembers that even with severe heart problems, Sidney could proudly carry a bucket of chickenfeed on his head all the way down the garden to the chicken pen at the age of sixty-three.

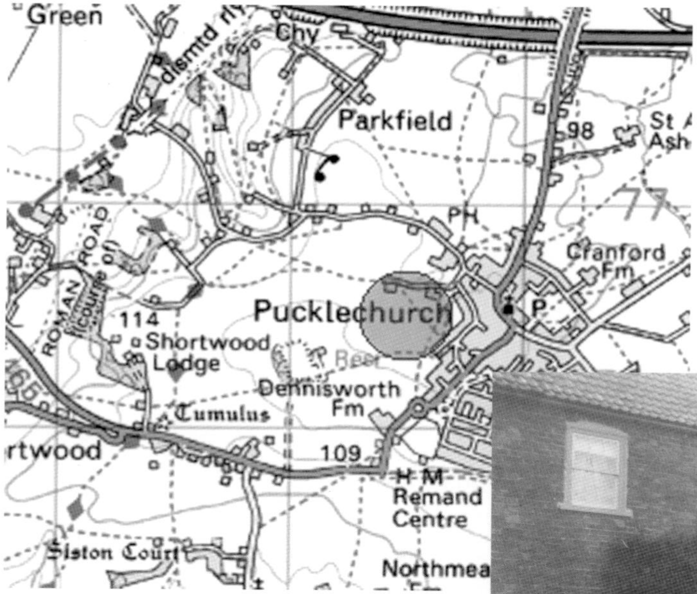

The young Sidney's formal education at the local village school (or perhaps the Handel Cossham mine school) would have ended at the age of twelve or thirteen when he became apprenticed to a flour mill near Bristol to learn the trade of millwright. He developed an intense intellectual curiosity and began to feed his great interest in mathematics, astronomy and the new science of electricity, by reading every published scrap of information he could find on the subjects.

Pucklechurch Rank, Gloucestershire, England. Sidney Cannard's sister Beatrice and her husband are to the left of the children.

Two years later, in 1893, England was in the grip of a great social panic caused by a deep economic depression. The burden of maintaining a fragmented global empire, over speculation in industrial expansion, and production of goods for which insufficient markets existed (but for which there was plenty of competition from other industrialized nations) had left the country hugely over-extended, and its currency vastly over-valued.

An impoverished rural England could never offer Sidney an opportunity to exploit the engineering skills and knowledge he was rapidly acquiring, and it was during this difficult time that Sidney decided to emigrate. America, although suffering a similar depression, offered greater hope for the future with land available for settlement and abundant natural resources. The U.S. economy, despite inflation, deflation, high unemployment, uncertainty regarding adoption of gold or silver standards, and wild stock market fluctuations, was growing. And it could still provide the funds to exploit scientific discovery to the advantage of industries more than ready to feed the country's population expansion. This huge economic engine was slowed but would never stop its forward momentum.

Living and working near the largest port in the west country with its transatlantic shipping trade would have the effect of making the far shores of America seem closer and more attainable to young Sidney.

The decision to leave England was probably helped by visits from relatives living in the United States. One of these visitors was Frances Hiatt, who enjoyed European tours, once as a young girl and again as a teenager, meeting Sidney on both occasions. She was the daughter of an old respected American family, and one of her aunts by marriage was a distant cousin of Sidney's. Frances lived in Danville, Pennsylvania with her aunt, her own mother having died during Frances' birth. Whether Sidney knew then that he would later marry Frances is unclear, but the die was cast.

Sidney was intelligent enough to see that the future of industry depended on harnessing the productive power of electricity. He began corresponding with Thomas Edison, and the six-year, long-distance relationship provided Sidney with superior scientific knowledge and a distinct competitive advantage. His future career would benefit from an ability to engineer the application of electricity to a heavy mechanized

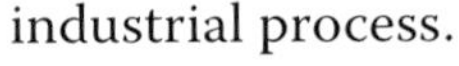

industrial process.

By 1899, Sidney was twenty-one, an established millwright, skilled, self-educated, confident and ambitious. He had absorbed his parents' convictions, was deeply religious and full of compassion. Judging by his photograph he was handsome, too. He made arrangements to live with his cousin in Danville, and left England for the New World.

When he got off the boat, he had one gold sovereign in his pocket. His son Bob has the coin in his collection today.

It's hard to imagine that Sidney George Cannard could be anything but successful, and successful he was.

Danville was perfectly primed for Sidney's talents. It was founded in 1792 by William Montgomery and his son Daniel on the northern banks of the Susquehanna at the site of what had been Montgomery Landing—a trading post. They established woolen, grist and sawmills to meet the needs of and to help grow the local agricultural economy.

The river and the canal system developed by Daniel Montgomery played key roles in the settlement of the town of Danville, which began to boom in the mid-1800s. The Montgomerys were also responsible for pioneering the use of anthracite coal to heat the county's residences.

With huge deposits of ore in the surrounding hills, all the ingredients were in place for an iron industry to develop. Although the manufacturing process was perfected by other industrialists, it could not have occurred without the transportation system, coal, and ready labor supply created by the efforts of the Montgomery family in general, and Daniel in particular.

First iron furnaces and forges, and then iron mills, which converted the base metal into Danville's greatest contribution to America's economy, the T-rail. Until 1845, rails for the railroads racing across America were imported from England at great cost. Instead Danville imported the talent to make them in the form of John Foley and William Hancock, expert ironworkers from England. In just a few years, Danville would claim five blast furnaces, four foundries, and three rolling mills producing T-rails.

By 1899, the great iron-manufacturing boom was giving way to steel, and the numerous iron works had been consolidated into two trusts. But the industry would survive for another thirty years with improved productivity, provided by conversion from steam power to electrical power.

Fortuitously then, Sidney George Cannard arrived in Danville with just the right credentials at just the right time.

111, Ash Street, Danville.

With his letters from Thomas Edison under his arm, he interviewed for a vacancy at the Foley Iron Company. It didn't hurt that Edison was himself working on the installation of electric street lights in Sunbury, fifteen miles away, and in his letters had offered Sidney his advice. Sidney was hired—to convert the entire plant from steam to electric power.

This he did, and fourteen years later he was able to sell his acquired stock interests in the company, leave the senior engineering job, marry Frances, the niece of his cousin by marriage, and become a vice president of the Prudential Insurance Company, with responsibility for a large territory in central Pennsylvania. They moved into a modest home overlooking the town.

Sidney had relentlessly pursued his many interests

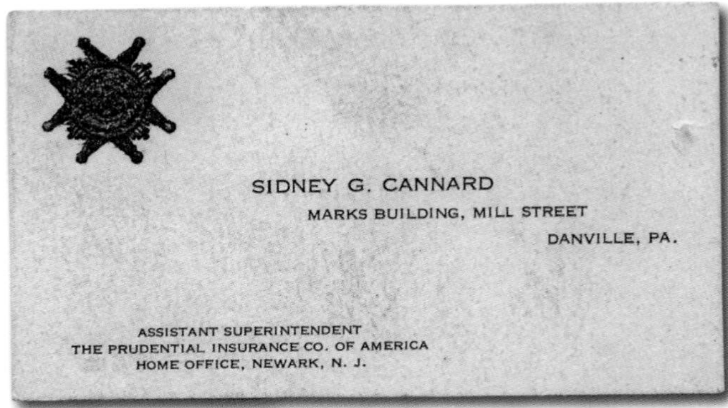

SIDNEY G. CANNARD
MARKS BUILDING, MILL STREET
DANVILLE, PA.

ASSISTANT SUPERINTENDENT
THE PRUDENTIAL INSURANCE CO. OF AMERICA
HOME OFFICE, NEWARK, N. J.

Mary, Mother, George,
twins Tom & John, Father and Sarah.

including astronomy and math, and could scale astronomic movement—an amazing feat for an amateur armed with nothing more than a fourth grade education. He formed a club to study Shakespeare's works and memorized most. His ability to quote great passages of the Bible at any time was unparalleled; he mastered several languages and never failed to meet his personal goal to learn one new fact every single day. It was also his habit to give 20 percent of his income to charitable causes.

Sidney was too old to serve in the U.S. Army in France during World War I, and instead enlisted in the Home Guard.

By the end of the war, in 1918, Frances and Sidney's family had grown with the births of George, Sarah and Mary. The United States was in the grip of a frightening flu epidemic. In the next eighteen months, more than a million people would die. Sidney, urged by his great compassion, spent all that time tirelessly transporting medical people and driving sick people to and from care, day and night.

P. M. G. O. Form No. 66.

REGISTRATION CERTIFICATE.

To whom it may concern, Greetings:

THESE PRESENTS ATTEST, That in accordance with the proclamation of the President of the United States, and in compliance with law,

Sidney George [illegible]
(First name.) (Middle name.) (Last name.)

111 Ash [illegible]
(No.) (Street or R. F. D. No.) (City or town.) (County.) (State.)

has submitted himself to registration and has by me been duly registered this 12 day of Sept., 1918, under the supervision of the Local Board designated on the back hereof.

[illegible], Registrar.

3—6172

(Place stamp of Local Board on back of this card.)

The strain of the effort proved too much. Just forty-one years old, Sidney suffered a major heart attack from which he never fully recovered. He would continue in his position with Prudential, but was never able to attend his office on a regular basis again.

However, the family grew when twins John and Tom arrived, with another brother Jim following shortly after. And Sidney's community activities continued unabated. He mastered one Masonic lodge and chartered another, served as

Mary, John, Jim, George, Tom and Sarah
Frances, Ed, Bob and Sidney.

trustee and president on the boards of several institutions, and was a sought-after speaker for any and every civic and religious function. Which is why he was speaking at Danville's Memorial Day celebration the day Bob was born in 1926.

The Methodist Church and religion were central to my father's life. He felt compelled to train all the young ministers in the area (Methodist or not) in his opinion of the proper direction. He and a couple of others kept two Methodist churches functioning during the Depression. With his compelling interest in the church, it became a guiding activity for the family. We always attended Sunday school and church services, participating in all the various activities. Mother's Day, Children's Day, Harvest Home and all the other religious holidays called for the attendance of the entire family. I was involved in singing, acting and recitations of all kinds. And even though the family sat all together in the second pew from the front, my mother rarely joined us. She preferred to take a seat in the small room at the rear of the organ, where she claimed the music sounded better.

I never knew my father to go to work. His income was from investments he had made earlier in life. He spent his time going to his club, to civic functions or the church. He was very mechanically inclined, often tinkering in his shop making innovations for functions around home. He seemed to feel he needed to be the first to have new inventions – refrigerator, electric stove, washing machine and any other gadget that came along. He built the first radio in the area and listened to the surrender of Germany on November 11, 1918. He read several papers a day, including two from England. He even had one radio tuned constantly to the BBC to get the hourly news 'from home.' We heard Big Ben strike several times a day—usually at dinnertime.

Frances and her boys

We had frequent guests and great discussions around the dinner table. All were encouraged to participate. We were all expected to be able to substantiate any position we took. My mother rarely sat at the table with us, and I seldom saw her eat. She preferred to be in the background, making sure everyone had what he or she needed.

My father was a highly intelligent and curious man, but his primary interests were in directions that I had little interest in.

The fact is, Bob's interests were those of his mother, and therefore not at the forefront at family gatherings. Frances had been allowed by the good fortunes of her family to enjoy those European tours, and to follow her own desires with her education. She had studied the natural sciences and was teaching botany at the local high school when she agreed to marry Sidney. They had lived in the same home for fourteen years before getting married, and one assumes that their interest were satisfyingly complementary, albeit very different.

The aunt who had raised Frances was a strict Christian—no smoking or drinking—and although she was encouraged to be socially confident, Frances preferred to stay in the background. In retrospect, to Bob, she was not at all the product of her sophisticated social environment, but instead the pure and simple evolution of a human being having a perfect bond with her natural environment. Nothing mystified her. She accepted life in all its forms for what it was. Bob is convinced that there was "pure blood" in his mother—from her Welsh ancestry—and that it has passed on to him and his sons. It represents oneness with the natural world, and a certainty that human existence is interwoven with that of plants and animals and any living thing on earth. Immortality derives from the acceptance that the atoms comprising our physical make-up are indestructible and will go on to create other forms of life—even chickens—in infinite variety and for infinity. It grants the believer a great sense of belonging and lessens the need to ponder the deep interrogative metaphors that drive so many into unnamed anxiety—Why are we here, what does it all mean, where are we going?

Joseph Hiatt was a successful mining engineer who once operated an assay office in Cripple Creek with partner William "Wild Bill" Hickock. He was living in Colorado with his wife Frances Mary "Fanny" Cope, and their four children when Fanny died giving birth to Bob's mother, also Frances. The distraught Joe immediately brought his family back east by train, and the children were subsequently raised by relatives.

Joe returned west and there are suspicions that he started another family in the Seattle area. He remained remote from youngest daughter Frances, apparently blaming her for the death of his wife Frances. She in turn rejected him. The two were briefly united when Frances reluctantly agreed to share the job of nursing him during the last weeks of his life as he succumbed to "black lung". She refused to accept her legacy from him, and shares he left in trust to her remained unclaimed until late in her own life.

The younger Frances is seen here with siblings (clockwise from bottom left) John Jay, great aunt Elizabeth, Beth, George, Harriet and aunt Sarah.

While not entirely at odds with the ethos of the day, these feelings would be necessarily subjugated—at least in the Cannard household—to its Methodism, intellectual philosophy and scientific enquiry.

But Bob's closeness to his mother and her ways shaped him to a far greater degree, and it is why today the irresponsible removal of a tree prompts outrage in him equal to what one might expect at the removal of a human life.

His mother didn't know how to grow plants and rear poultry and tend sickness simply because she had studied, she knew it instinctively. She was remarkably clairvoyant. She would sense when local people were ill or in need, and take to them what they needed without being asked or informed. She would just appear at their door with the appropriate food, or kind words or natural remedies. It wasn't just an occasional phenomenon, it was a permanent fixture in her life, which seemed subjugated to the interests of both her immediate family and the broader community. During the particularly tough years of the Depression, Bob's mother, sisters, and family friend Vi would spend evenings at home making warm comforters for those in need—as many as three per evening. And Vi would deliver them the following day, with Frances' directions on where they would be needed most.

> *No one in distress ever passed my mother without being helped, and no one was allowed to suffer in her presence. I can recall that during the worst years of the Depression, my mother and I would take baskets of vegetables to the poor people that lived along the railroad tracks in makeshift shacks. They would hear us coming. Ragged barefoot children would come out of the bushes and run towards us, grabbing from the baskets and scraping potatoes down over their teeth to cram raw food into their stomachs without even chewing. It made a great impression on me as a child, and I have never forgotten the empty looks on those faces.*

If you live in Sonoma Valley, you may have been the recipient of a similar generosity from her son, who has done his best to make sure the specter of hunger is never experienced again—"if he has anything to do with it."

Frances had the same sensitivity towards plants as she did towards people, and she was a consummate interpreter of nature.

> *My mother had a sense of perception of plants that went far beyond what anyone could see. She taught me this understanding, and I am still amazed that other people do not see in a plant what I do. My earliest memories are of being in the garden with my mother. I can remember the scent of the flowers. I remember every spring when the robins arrived, she would stand motionless, her outstretched palm holding strands of wool and string for nesting material. The birds would come and take them with no sign of fear, landing first on the rose arbor and then on her hand. My mother knew individual birds, and they would return to our garden, year after year.*

At two years old, Bob had his own favorites—usually the most fragrant flowers such as dianthus (pinks), mignonettes and lilies of the valley, rather than the most vivid—and every year he would receive seeds and a new plant for his birthday and on other special occasions.

Frances, with Bob constantly at her side, took care of the household's extensive garden with its flowers, fruits and vegetables, and from it came almost all the family food, with enough left over for a host of neighbors and needy local people. If a passerby admired a particular plant, they would soon find it planted in their own garden. Baskets of seasonal flowers went to the church every week, and Bob took on the responsibility for keeping the displays fresh. His mother taught him all the basics of horticulture, a passion that has driven him ever since. Together they made wine, cordials, juices and jams from every conceivable fruit. They canned fruit and vegetables, dried herbs and corn in big bunches, and filled the root cellar. Bob learned how to keep bees and make honey.

Bob's father and twin brothers listened to opera on the radio on Sunday evenings—not the typical interest of a young boy. So it became Bob and his mother's habit to take long walks through the neighborhoods and local countryside, or trips to the Presbyterian Church on those Sunday evenings. And on these walks, she passed on her knowledge of every tree and plant native to Pennsylvania, and every tree and plant growing in the gardens of their neighbors. She could name them all by genus, species and common name; soon Bob could do the same, and insists today that he could teach you the trick—"easy."

It was during these intimate strolls with his mother that Bob developed his bond with the natural world, the world so central to her existence. He avidly absorbed the information, and his senses became similarly attuned to the infinite variety of textures, shapes, colors, patterns and scents of all growing things as the seasons slowly changed around him. He began to unconsciously assemble and index this wealth of experience into a personal and unique library of knowledge.

I was walking with my mother in Powder Mill Hollow one spring morning when I noticed this very wonderful smell. My mother told me to follow the smell, and about a quarter mile further we came to a rose growing wild in an old homestead garden.

My mother said it was a sweet briar (Rosa excelsa). The species had been brought from Europe by the early settlers.

She took a cutting, rooted it and planted it in our garden. I smelled it and enjoyed it as long as I lived in the family home. I have a sweet briar rose in my garden in Sonoma.

When Bob describes the singular smell of a specific flower, or the taste of a particular variety of fruit, there is a fine tuning in his words and syntax that provides a clue to the breadth of this knowledge, and the ecstasy that must have been a part of its gathering.

Another of Bob's lifelong interests, birds, developed just as early. Again, one of his earliest memories is of watching baby chicks in a box that sat near a cast iron kitchen stove.

I kept and raised chickens since my earliest days. The first money I remember earning was from raising a large bird—either an Indian Game or Cornish rooster. Sold it to a neighbor for Thanksgiving. Probably spent the money at the circus!

He was fascinated by all birds and as a young teenager raised and sold canaries, learning all the tricks of the trade. He has never lost his affection for canaries and raised a large number of them years later at his nursery in Kenwood, California, as an attraction for customers. "They were singing most of the time."

Growing up, Circus Day was the biggest day of the year for Bob. One of the major circus companies would come to the area every year. Ringling Bros., Barnum & Bailey, Hagenbaum & Wallace, and others less well known would visit the nearby bigger towns of Sunbury, Wilkes-Barre, and Williamsport, with announcements being made well before in the local papers.

We would plan and talk about it for months in advance of our trip. How we would get there, what we would see, what we would do, what the cost would be and every imaginable thing that could happen. The circus went on rain or shine. Even if it was cloudy we would hunt for a little blue in the sky and say if the there were enough blue to make a pair of Dutchman's breeches that it would clear up and we would have good weather.

Together with his brother Ed, Bob would start by studying every animal they expected to see, reading about them in a large natural history book that he still has today. The family called the volume, a work by a British explorer, "the Monkey Book." By the time they had examined the illustrations and researched the habits of every creature, excitement was running high. When the great day finally arrived, they would be up at daybreak and off to the circus field.

The circus would pull into town by railway at night or very early in the morning and begin to unload everything that was needed. An empty field was transformed in a couple of hours into a bustling sensation. The horses and elephants did much of the heavy work.

Watching the tent go up was one of the most fascinating things a boy could watch. Three or four burly men with great wooden mallets around one big stake, hitting alternately, would soon drive it several feet in the ground. The main poles were put into the huge white flapping big top, and it was pulled upright by teams of men hired locally for the day. Thick guy ropes from the tops of the poles were secured on the big corner stakes and tightened up. The shorter poles holding out the sides of the enormous tent were put in next, and all the rest of the ropes attached to the sides were looped around their stakes and the whole thing took shape as they were drawn tight. When the long flags high up at the top of the main poles streamed out in the wind, it was a marvelous sight, marvelous.

About ten o'clock that morning, the circus parade would begin. All of the animals in their painted and gilded rolling cages were pulled through town by horses or elephants to the circus grounds. The whole town turned out to see the parade. It was almost as good as the circus itself—no charge and everyone had a chance to see everything. The cages were finally pulled into a great circle under the enormous tent.

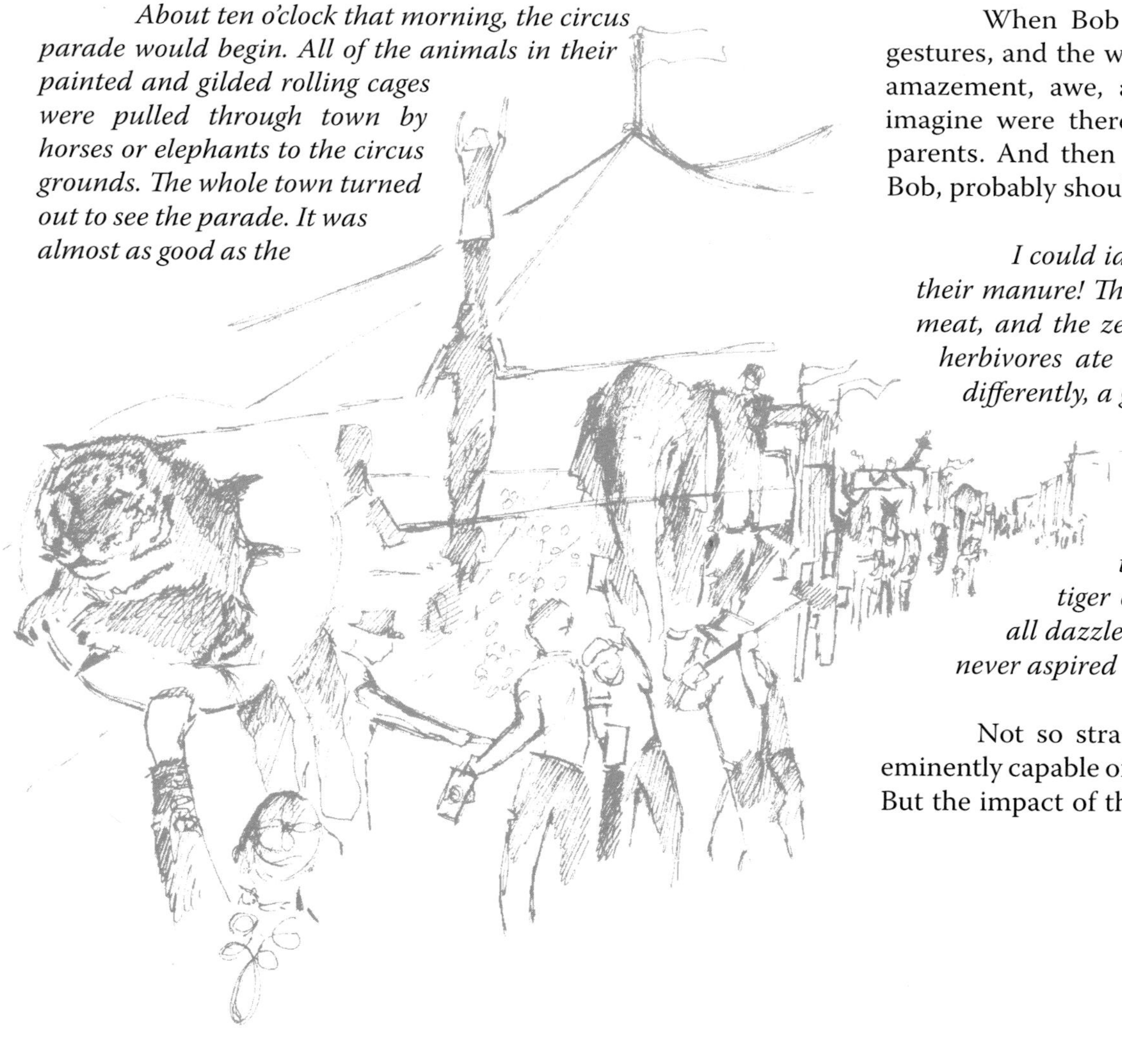

When Bob tells this story, his arms wave in grand gestures, and the wide-eyed look on his face shows the same amazement, awe, and breathless excitement that one can imagine were there when he first related the event to his parents. And then comes a bigger surprise, which knowing Bob, probably shouldn't be...

I could identify many of the animals by the smell of their manure! The monkeys ate much fruit, the big cats got meat, and the zebras, elephants, rhinos, horses, and other herbivores ate hay. The manure of all of them smelled differently, a good education for a boy always interested in the food chain.

The show itself was always grand. The big John Phillip Sousa-style band with the colorful uniforms, the high wire and trapeze, the bareback riding, the lion and tiger exhibition, and the elephant performance all dazzled a boy in love with the circus. Strangely, I never aspired to work for or be part of the circus.

Not so strange really, when you realize that Bob is eminently capable of creating his own circus wherever he goes. But the impact of these wonderful days stayed with him, and he did bring the circus to Sonoma Valley, California, in one of his grand publicity stunts to promote interest in, of all things, the Chamber of Commerce.

But no influence has been as strong as that of his mother and her natural abilities. She was an instinctive genius with all forms of growing—the soil, birds, poultry, animals, trees, flowers, and plants. Frances, with the family's help, grew much of their food. They canned, dried, and preserved produce to sustain the family's diet and provide great variety throughout the year, even preserving eggs in the summer for winter use by storing them in crocks of water glass. The family also made fruit flavorings and essences, sugars and syrups.

[Note: Water glass is a substance that consists usually of the silicate of sodium and is found in commerce as a glassy mass, a stony powder, or dissolved in water as a viscous syrupy liquid. It is used especially as a cement, as a protective coating and fireproofing agent, and in preserving eggs. Merriam-Webster]

Growing, cooking and eating food has remained a lifelong passion for Bob, and he never uses a recipe.

I always have said that when I have eaten something once or twice, I can cook something so similar that you could not tell the difference.

Growing up, when I visited the neighboring kitchens—mostly Pennsylvania Dutch—I would straightaway guess what was in each pot without going near the stove, and I was usually right. This led to an invitation to help myself to a taste of whatever I had identified. "Bobby," they would then say, "how did you like it?" My reply would be that I forgot to taste it, which of course would lead to another taste. Worked every time, and great innocent fun for all of us it was. This is when I began to learn to cook. By the time I was six or seven, I would get up early on Saturday and Sunday mornings, scramble some eggs, make toast on a long-handled fork over a fire in the cast iron stove, and with homemade jam and milk, feast to my heart's content. I learned to cook well because I like to eat well.

It was about this time that observation of the poultry raised by his mother and him led Bob to make the confident assertion in a loud voice to the entire family at the dinner table, that a chicken's reproductive organs were on its head. There were snickers and raspberries from his older brothers, but his father gave him the opportunity to explain how he had figured it out. In the family tradition of reasoned argument, Bob began "Observation will affirm that I am correct" and went on to explain how he had seen the rooster grab the hen at the back of the neck as he climbed on her back, mistaking the attempt to maintain balance as the sexual act itself.

The misunderstanding that gave the rest of the family so much amusement must have been quickly corrected and it wasn't long before he was breeding and rearing all kinds of birds. Except for the brief time he was in the services during World War II, Bob has raised chickens for eggs and meat every

year since. As a youngster, he particularly liked pigeons because they were so tame and easy to keep. At one time or another he raised Pouter pigeons, Tumblers, Fantails, Rollers, and of course Homers. For a few cents, the Greyhound bus drivers would take a basket of birds south and release them wherever they stopped—Harrisburg, Lancaster, York, or even Baltimore. In all the years Bob raised pigeons, he only lost one bird, all the others returning safely to his "loft" in Danville. He also caught wild pigeons, selling them to clubs for ten cents a bird, and sometimes baked or roasted them over an open fire with a few baked potatoes for the kids in the neighborhood, putting on quite a feast.

In the early summer of 1938, Bob had a visit from a stranger to Danville. He was particularly interested in Bob's flock of English spangled game chickens.

"When I asked around about chickens, someone told me to talk to you. You got some?"

"Sure," said Bob, who raised them to sell for around fifty cents each and had a flock of twenty or thirty birds.

"What about roosters?" the stranger asked.

"I have a few," was Bob's reply.

"Do they fight?"

"Well, yes, but I don't want them to kill each other."

The Light Brahma has always been a great favorite of Bob's, perhaps because it is one of the largest and most imposing breeds.

"Put a couple together. Let me see."

Bob did as he was asked, and of course the two roosters fought like hell until Bob pulled them apart. The stranger was well satisfied.

"I'll take 'em all," the stranger said.

"No, but I could sell you some," offered Bob.

"How much?"

When Bob hesitated, the man took the initiative. "I'll give you five dollars for every rooster you got."

That was an offer tough to refuse. Bob sold the stranger five birds and he returned two weeks later for another pair—and an order for as many roosters as Bob could supply for the next year.

It was a well-known fact that East Coast Mafia bosses took summer outings in the Pocono Mountains at Pittston just a short distance to the north. They were well-publicized events and, by all accounts, attended by droves of FBI agents and newspapermen. Bob was aware of the likely destination of his English game roosters, but he continued supplying them for the next three summers.

Until enlisting in 1943, he also raised roosters for Sam Marks, who had a large poultry farm. Bob had a deep fascination for chicken breeding, perhaps in reaction to his embarrassing error at the family dinner table years before when he had claimed that a chicken's sex organs were on its head. He became a considerable expert, and never failed to win first prize for his birds at the local fair. He was an avid reader of Poultry Press and American Poultry Magazine, a publication he has now been taking for over seventy years. He experimented with cross breeding and, from White Rock and White Cornish breeds, developed a bird that grew fast and plump—eight or nine pounds in just three months. He gave the idea to Walter Meek who went on to become one of the largest chicken producers in the East. Bob believes that his special cross formed the basis for Meek's success and subsequently for that of poultry farmers all across the country. He knew from practical experience everything there was to know about poultry.

With a 99.9 percent certainty, I could incubate a bunch of eggs in a homemade incubator in the kitchen in Allenwood, and know that the chicks would be popping out of their shells on Easter Sunday morning right as the boys were having breakfast—did it several times.

What appealed to me was the science. I caponized two roosters in 2003 for the Plaza flock—first time in thirty years. Charlie Umstead taught me how when I was thirteen on a farm just outside of Danville. They grow bigger, heavier and more tender, you know. The rate of conversion of food to animal increases, too. I would probably choose a Sussex or Dorking breed for the best possible eating. You can easily get them up to ten or eleven pounds. Even the feathers are high in protein. And they will decompose to make fine compost. By the way, I consider composting to be one of nature's major miracles, along with photosynthesis.

From these beginnings, Bob's affection for and delight in birds has prompted him to keep not just poultry, but a huge variety of other species, from pheasants—Ring-neck, Golden, Lady Amherst, and many exotic varieties—to canaries, finches, cockatiels, budgerigars and parrots, including Blue Amazons, Double Yellowheads, and Senegals. He has also been known to keep a few wild turkeys.

Many a landlady, in response to faint sounds of chirping, clucking, or pecking, has asked Bob, "What's that I hear upstairs, young man?"

And once, in Montgomery, Pennsylvania, when Bob's wife Edna was ill and the doctor was called, the doctor went to wash his hands in the bathroom and found boxes full of young bantam and pheasant chicks.

"I've seen a lot of strange things in my time," he remarked, "but this is the first time I've seen chickens raised in a bathroom."

Bob just loves all manner of caged and wild birds and has a compulsion to rear them. He returned from Hawaii in 2002 with fertile eggs from a breed of wild poultry new to him, which he intended for the foundation of a new flock for Sonoma Plaza. He raised a small flock from the original eggs but never pursued installing them on the Plaza. Instead, he gave the birds to his son Bobby. If you have ever wondered why it's a common sight to see huge flocks of non-native wild turkeys in the hills on the west side of Sonoma Valley, well...

The foundation for these lifelong interests and amazing skills in growing and rearing were established through Bob's closeness to his mother in those early years. As he has said, he had little interest in or experience of his father's work. However, to find the roots of his business acumen and enterprising spirit, we need to look no further than across the street from the family home to the Sherwood Grocery Store.

"Aunt Em" Linker-Sherwood, a Pennsylvania Dutch Jewish woman, had broken ground on March 17, and opened the general store in September 1929. Only a few weeks later, Wall Street crashed initiating the Great Depression. She was then forty-seven, and her husband Jack sixty-one. He had been the best core maker at the local iron foundry but had become disabled.

The Sherwood grocery store and day market thrived through the Depression, and Em always managed to buy a new Buick every year. She priced her products carefully—loose

Em Sherwood

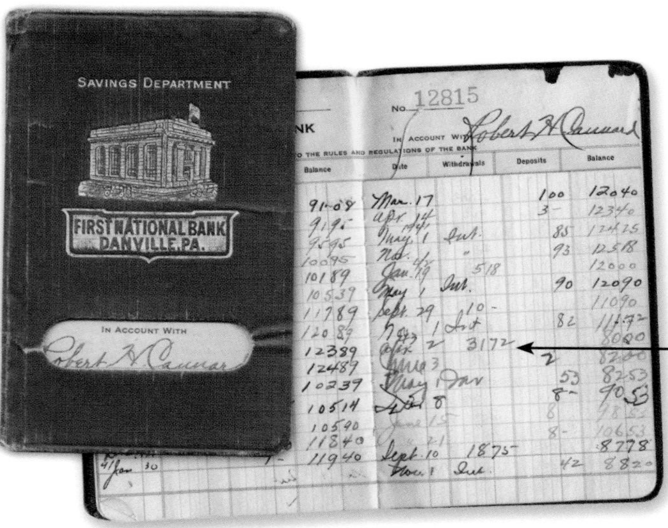

Bob's earnings at the store slowly add up, and he makes a rare purchase - an eighth grade graduation suit

meal, crackers, beans, cookies and meat sliced to order—with the help of Sydney Cannard's math skills. Em provided local customers with true service, fresh produce, and the finest prepared food value you could find locally. Dinner, salad, dessert, and coffee was forty cents on weekdays and fifty on Sundays, when she served as many as sixty diners.

Selling other ready-to-eat foods, like baked beans by the quart, allowed her to make up in volume what couldn't be made on the margin. And when the economic situation eased, she was quick to offer the few luxuries that people could afford—Aunt Em's ice cream was the very best around.

Em was likeable and kind. She would never let poor people go hungry—freely extending credit and rarely expecting payment. She had become a close friend of Frances Cannard, and Bob became a frequent visitor to the store. By the time he was seven or eight, he was working there in the winter months on Fridays after school and on Saturdays, emptying wastebaskets, sweeping the sidewalk, and trimming the waste from vegetables. (There was no valuable refrigeration space for humble veggies in those days.) Later he learned to kill and clean the chickens for Sunday dinners.

One Saturday morning Bob had the idea that the trimmings and other rejected wilted vegetables could be sold to make perfectly good soup, especially if customers also went to the local butcher who was happy to provide free soup bones. Aunt Em agreed to let Bob try, and soon he had filled a few bags with five or six pounds of trimmings mixed with wilted celery, turnips, or carrots—whatever couldn't be sold as fresh. At five cents a bag, they were sold out in an hour, and Bob was already taking orders for more. Aunt Em remarked, "You'll never go hungry Bobby." And of course, he never has.

Within a week, his hand-pulled express wagon with wooden wheels and sideboards was loaded with twenty-five bags, and he had a regular delivery route. In another week, he needed a second wagonload. Pretty soon he was taking orders for full bags of "good" as well as wilted produce, and twenty-five to fifty cents a week was being recorded in his bankbook.

Bob continued to work for Em, and they became close friends. Bob took on more and more responsibilities, and Em came to depend on him. By the time he was twelve or thirteen, he was working on weekday evenings and at weekends. He did the weekly store "walkthrough," taking stock and figuring out what had been sold, and then Em would pick him up from school to take their weekly order to the wholesaler. He was trusted enough to act as cashier on Sunday evenings.

Bob liked the work and found it easy. He enjoyed listening to stories from Uncle Jack, who sat in a corner of the store and smoked cigars. Jack would try and get Bob to sneak the best Cuban imports for him, but more often than not Aunt Em would say "just give him the two-fers"—the much inferior two for a nickel, domestic King Edwards.

Jack Sherwood was five when the 1873 financial panic struck the United States, and he could remember that a nickel was all Danville's "bone pickers" got for scavenging a hundred pounds of old newspapers, rags, or bones. Maybe the two-fers tasted about the same as those salvaged bits.

But Jack did get to enjoy the results of the frequent fishing trips taken by Em, her dogs, and Bob in the Buick. The heavyset Em would sit in her ever-present folding chair on the banks of the Susquehanna River, Chillisquaque Creek, or whatever river, stream, or lake they had chosen, with her dog on a blanket by her side. She would watch for hours as Bob fished. Em Sherwood never touched a fishing pole—or reel or bait or lures, but "she loved to fish," and loved to eat the fish "we" caught, skinning and frying up the sunfish or green rock bass really crisp, bones and all, for herself, Bob, and Uncle Jack.

Some weeks they fished every day, driving up to seventy-five miles to the chosen river. If it rained, Em sat in her folding chair wearing a poncho to cover her, the chair, and her dog—either Brownie, Tarzan, or Poocher. She would watch Bob and his friends fish for hours, always taking the fish "we caught" home to Uncle Jack. Em insisted on taking her folding chair even in the rowboat, and on one occasion, Em's weight pushed the legs of the chair outwards, which sprung the boat's planks so that Bob had to "row like hell to reach the shore before the boat sank. I would have had to rescue Em, the dog, the chair, and Eddie Fisk—and we were in fifteen feet of swift-flowing water."

Fortunately, Bob was strong on the oars, having spent many hours with Em's nephew Johnnie Linker trolling for walleye, or as they then called them, "Susquehanna Salmon."

Although a good and likeable friend and a fine photographer, Eddie Fisk was more than a little gullible—what Em called a "dopic." On a fishing trip to Canada with Em and Bob, he had gone outside the cabin to relieve himself. It was a clear starlit night, but when he returned, Eddie claimed that it was raining and pointed to his wet legs and shoes as evidence. He was told it was a cloudless night but insisted that it was raining, not realizing that he had met the call of nature a little too close to a tree and "got his own back."

On a night fishing expedition on Chillisquaque Creek with Bob and Johnnie, Eddie couldn't understand why he didn't get even a hint of a bite when the other two were pulling in catfish one after another. The other two encouraged him to freshen his bait, but Eddie was convinced that wasn't the problem and sat quietly all night, watching the end of his pole intently. But the bite never came. It was only when the sun came up in the morning and they began to pack their gear that they could see why. Eddie's first and only cast in the dark had gone flying over the low branch of a tree growing right there at the edge of the creek, and his bait still hung, some five hours later, suspended a good six feet above the surface of the water.

> *The three of us were fishing along the river. Eddie wasn't doing so well, and he went back to the car for a drink or something. While he was gone, I followed up on a bad smell we'd all noticed and found an old deerskin a few hundred feet away through the undergrowth. I took a good-sized piece of it to show Johnnie, and we tied it, hair and all, on Eddie's hook and cast his line back into the river. When Eddie came back, Johnnie said, "You better check your bait Eddie; I think you could have something there." Eddie wound his line in. "What's this?" he says, holding up the deerskin. "Why Eddie," I told him, "You hooked a waterdog, and that's a piece of his tail." Well, in no time at all, Eddie got himself off to the Danville Morning News and showed them the evidence. They took a picture of Eddie and the waterdog's tail and had it in the paper the following day. We didn't stop laughing for a week!*

Bob always loved being close to water, fishing, swimming, or hunting for tadpoles and minnows after a picnic. During the summer months, the family moved to their small second home, Riverside Farm, across the river to the south of Danville, where the opportunities to immerse himself in the local wildlife were all around.

His interest in agriculture grew, and he became more familiar with the Dreer's seed catalog and old agricultural almanacs than he did with school textbooks.

Bob was particularly fond of a retired dentist who sold apples and berries from his small orchard and experimented with crossing blackberries and raspberries to produce loganberries. Bob remembers the oval holes in the side of his Model T truck that you leaned through to reach whatever was inside. His mother frequently consulted Doctor Echroff on garden problems, taking Bob along for the walk, and Bob was forever asking if he could go up to Doc Echroff's for berries.

He asked Doc if he would teach him how to graft. The doctor showed him, insisting that lots of practice was needed but that he would set Bob up with a suitable exercise. He knew that every year Bob's mother would get a crate of pineapples for the pear-pineapple butter that was a Cannard family favorite, so he asked Bob if he would like to grow pineapples. Bob replied that of course he would. Pretty soon the doc had him cutting scions from apple trees and taking them up into the wood to graft them on to the pine trees, and back he came with pine shoots to graft on to apple trees. Doc said, "Keep at it, it might work," and showed him how to make protective grafting wax from beeswax and linseed oil.

> *My god, I must have made 5,000 grafts in the course of the next year. The woods were festooned with apple grafts, and of course, not one of them took. But I'll tell you what. I became an incredible expert at grafting.*

By this method of practical trial and error, Bob learned every imaginable country craft. He would take his bees to the blossoms of particular fruit trees to make honey with distinct fragrance and flavor. He became an expert at making scrapple in a butcher's kettle, and he reared "Florida swamp chickens" (frogs) in the springhouse, feeding them corn meal.

At that time, children who lived in the country went to school for just seven months of the year—two months less than in the towns—so that they could help out with all the farm chores. With everything that Bob seemed to pack into his life, you would not think he had sufficient time for school at all. He did manage to fit it in somehow, although he wasn't known for his academic achievements. "I varied between being a poor, to a very poor student." It was a situation tolerated by his parents and teachers alike, possibly because it was well known how industrious he was outside of school, but more likely because the Cannard family was held in such high local esteem; his brothers and sisters were usually at the top of their classes. Besides, Bob did brighten his classroom with fresh flowers every day. He got the leads in school plays because of his confident speaking voice, although his acting was poor, and he could only recall the lines by staring at the vases of flowers near the stage.

"Don't you worry about Bobby," people would say. "He will do OK."

In 1936, at the age of ten, Bob got his introduction to politics. In the presidential elections that year, the Democratic candidate Franklin D. Roosevelt was running as the apparent underdog against Governor Alfred Landon of Kansas, picked to win by every major newspaper. As an active and deeply committed Republican, Bob's father, of course, supported Landon and never failed to assert at every opportunity that no intelligent person could possibly vote for Roosevelt. In the Cannard household, Bob's sister Sarah, who had just graduated from Penn State University, was the lone dissenter, arguing that political philosophy was unimportant in the face of dire social problems such as the 25 percent unemployment, and that only Roosevelt offered any worthwhile solutions.

There was great optimism on both sides, but it was the posters in support of Landon that Bob and his brother Jim were instructed to distribute around Danville. Within a couple of weeks, they had posted many hundreds on windows, doors, walls, and fences all over town. Each poster featured a large sunflower—the state flower of Kansas—with "LANDON & KNOX" (Knox being the vice presidential running mate) printed in the center of the flower. But within a very short time, Danville's Democratic Party committee had covered the centers with their own "LAND ON THE ROCKS WITH LANDON AND KNOX" stickers. The local Republicans printed more correct centers and Bob and Jim were dispatched to cover up the offending messages.

Roosevelt won the election, and there was great consternation in the Cannard household (with the exception of Sarah). This was short-lived as Roosevelt introduced a flurry of programs to help the unemployed (WPA, PWA, CCC, etc.), although despite these programs, he never earned the respect of Bob's father. In particular, Sidney strongly opposed Secretary of Agriculture Henry Wallace's policy of destroying food in order help support prices. At a time when so many people were hungry, thousands of tons of potatoes were dyed and dumped into Long Island Sound and millions of pigs were killed and plowed under.

His father pushed Bob gently towards the arts and encouraged him to take piano lessons with the nuns at the Sacred Heart Villa school. It was a practice of the academy to have the students display their improving musical talents at various times through the year at recitals, to an audience of proud parents. In order to protect the children from the numbing effects of stage fright, the nuns would place them behind a screen, hidden from the audience, and call for them to perform when it was their turn in the program.

Well, Bob did not show the same natural talent with the piano that he had rearing chickens, but one of the other students was something of a prodigy on both the violin and the piano. So, with the promise of a stick of bologna, Bob "persuaded" fellow student George to play in his place at the piano behind the screen. On each of the two occasions that George reluctantly agreed—giving fine performances "as Bob"—he was duly given, as promised, a five-cent stick of bologna. When telling this story, Bob is more impressed with the size of the bologna stick that you could buy for five cents in those days (it was an impressive one and one-half inches thick and four inches long), than he is concerned with the deception. He points out that he also rewarded himself with one. Anyhow, George was happy, the nuns were happy, and Bob was happy. Of course his father was delighted, although Mr. Cannard did remark to the nuns, "Bob seems to play so much better here than at home."

After that remark, it didn't take the nuns long to figure out what was going on, and Bob's musical career came to an abrupt end.

If Bob didn't gain as much as he might from formal education, he certainly made up for it from informal private tutoring. This came, as he frequently points out, from women who themselves were born well before 1880. It is why, he claims, "I'm a link to the past" usually going on to add, ever conscious of his place on time's continuum, "and my sons are a link to the future."

The Cannard's good neighbor Viola Young was the

most notable of his informal teachers. Even her birthday was part of the history lessons she gave—April 18, 1875, one hundred years to the day after the great midnight ride of Paul Revere at the time of the tumultuous birth of the nation. How fitting that the grandson of Paul Revere, Lieutenant Warren Revere from the USS Portsmouth anchored in San Francisco Bay, should be assigned to replace California's bear flag with the American flag on Sonoma Plaza in early July 1846.

Viola Young was raised on a country farm and in a town house, with strict adherence to religious principles, her father having been one of the founders of Danville's Trinity Methodist church in 1869. She graduated from the Kelso Academy for Teachers at sixteen and taught in a country school for twenty-five dollars a month. In her early twenties, she met and was courted by a young lawyer from Danville, agreeing to marry him and move to where he worked in New York City, where he practiced.

Mentor and tutor Vi Young, who advised Bob to wear his new testament in his breast pocket. After all, it had saved the lives of Civil War Soldiers.

Sadly for Viola, her mother considered New York to be a den of iniquity and corruption at least on a level with Sodom and Gomorra and refused to allow her to go. With her father deceased, and her mother insisting that Viola respect her religious upbringing and "honor thy mother," the accepted custom of the day, the engagement was broken. Viola stayed at home in Danville and took care of her mother until she died twenty-five years later. Viola instead became secretary to the manager of a silk mill conglomerate, and after twenty years, the financial manager of a shirt factory. She "adopted" Bob as the son she never had and tutored him on a regular basis from the time he was five years old. She started by teaching him to read, and as he says today, "If it hadn't have been for Vi Young, Bill Cole and I would never have made it out of first grade." He pauses, " I think I may have been dyslexic, you know. It's possible."

It was his friend Bill Cole's grandfather who had first hired Viola to tutor Bill's father, and thirty years later Bill himself. Bill went on to build the family hardware business into a chain of regional home improvement stores. Bob and he remain friends, and when Bob makes his spring and fall visits back east, he stays at Bill Cole's hunting lodge five miles south of Danville.

Viola was also

treasurer at the Cannard family's church, and Bob joined her to count the coins from the offertory on a Sunday evening after the service. Sorting and identifying scarce coins became a passion with Bob and prompted his lifelong interest in numismatics. In return for the pleasure, Bob took sole charge of Viola's big garden and chickens.

Bob devoured Viola's stories. In 1778, during "the great runaway" on the west branch of the Susquehanna River, Indians had raided the farm next door to her father's, just a few miles out of Danville on the road to Milton. The neighbor Mrs. Kurry ran to the nearby creek with her two children and hid in a hollow sycamore log. By the time the Indians had burned the crops, house, and farm buildings, a spider had woven a web across the end of the hollow tree trunk, and the hiding place went undetected when the Indians came looking for them. Unfortunately, Mr. Kurry had been killed.

Bob speculates that the incident might have been one of the reasons Viola's father voted for Andrew Jackson as president, considering the latter's vehement stance towards Native Americans. Years later, Bob's wife, Edna, painted a picture of the creek where some of the Kurrys hid that day and gave it to him for his birthday. It hangs in their living room today.

Vi regaled Bob with her accounts of the historical heritage of the United States. Her personal recollections and those passed down by her father, born in 1806, gave Bob close to first person accounts of the majority of presidents and important statesmen of the country up to that time. The accounts were not always in accordance with the history books.

> *The American history taught in the schools then was written by Ivy League professors. To them, anything that occurred west of Cambridge, Massachusetts, was less than important. They reluctantly agreed that a few significant things happened, but considered that if these new westerners had any sense, they would have stayed at home.*

From these early accounts, Bob grew to hold immense respect for the tall slender immigrants from Scotland and Ireland (they were never short and stout) and their early descendents. These were people who, with bible in one hand and long gun in the other, became the pioneers that dominated the move west, outfighting Indians with superior woodcraft and the determination born of suffering in their native lands. "The Scotch-Irish were at the forefront of every new frontier from the Atlantic to the Pacific."

In Bob's eyes Daniel Boone was an exemplary representative of this group. Born not far from where Bob grew up, Boone survived many adventures to walk cross-country to Yellowstone Park at the age of eighty-two.

Mrs. Raver, ninety years old and another favorite neighbor of the Cannards, had actually been across the plains by covered wagon in 1850 when she was only five. She vividly remembered floating in the wagon across rivers. Her parents were also Danville Methodists, this time from Wales, who decided to seek their fortunes in the West. Reaching western Nebraska in the late fall, and well aware of the disaster that befell the Donner party in the California Sierras, they chose to wait until spring for the mountain crossings and built a temporary sod hut on the plain.

One day in the early spring, when her father was away on a hunting trip to stock up for the rest of the journey, a party of Sioux Indians rode up to the hut and began to terrorize the family. Mrs. Raver's mother was boiling fat for soap on a fire outside the hut, and with the children beside her, the only thing she could think to do was hurl the hot fat at the Indians with a large ladle. It was enough to send the Sioux packing, apparently no match for the enraged pioneer mother.

And pack is exactly what Mrs. Raver's mother did as well as soon as her husband returned. She refused to go another step west and they headed back to Danville right away.

Mrs. Raver married a Welshman who "liked a nip," according to Viola Young, who lived across the street from the old lady. When Mr. Raver got drunk, she said, his wife would chase him through the house and upstairs, beating on him with the broomstick, until he would leap from the roof across to a neighbor's house in order to escape her fury. To this day, Bob remains amazed that a man, especially a drunken Welshman, could make such a jump. "It was quite a way," he laughs.

In her old age, Bob took care of Mrs. Raver's garden, and she was sustained by twice-daily visits from Bob's mother, Frances, whose own father had also "gone west" from Danville. Joseph Hiatt and his young wife had gone by train to St. Louis, and then across the plains to Colorado by covered wagon, taking seven days to reach the Rocky Mountains once the range first came into view. They eventually settled in Idaho Springs, Colorado.

Joseph Hiatt was a prospector and miner, employed by a British mining company to carry out geologic surveys throughout the West. When he found coal, he claimed it for his employers, but if he turned up anything else, he was free to stake his own claim. For work and for pleasure, he and his brothers walked Colorado, Utah, Nevada, parts of California and the northwest states. After working one particular drift, Joseph and his brother Jim emerged from the entrance and Jim was promptly attacked by a grizzly bear. Fortunately both men were carrying sprags, short timbers used to stop mine cars, and they managed to beat the bear to death, but not before Jim had been badly bitten on the shoulder.

Memorial Park, Danville. Where his Father was giving the Memorial Day address the day Bob was born, and where he recieved informal history lessons from veterans.

When Joseph's wife Fanny died during the birth of Bob's mother Frances in 1889, her father returned east by train with the ten-day-old infant and four other children. Theirs was to be the last train across the Johnstown Bridge in southwestern Pennsylvania on May 31, hours before it was caught up in the greatest flood disaster in the history of the United States.

Years later, an aunt of Bob's mother tried to persuade her friend Bertha, who lived down by the Susquehanna River (and who was in the habit of carrying her furniture upstairs before the spring floods) to move up the hill and out of the flood zone. Bertha's reply has always amused Bob: "Why ever would I want to do such a thing? I'd always have to walk uphill to go home!"

And so Bob received his education, one way or another, from his mother, Aunt Em, Vi Young, Mrs. Raver, and a whole host of older men, some of them veterans of Gettysburg, who liked nothing better than to fill young Bob Cannard's head with firsthand accounts and gory details of the Civil and Spanish American wars.

Much of the history that fills Bob's head today, and his convictions about the forces that shaped modern America, derives from his interrogations of Danville's veterans, who spent the twilight of their lives in Memorial Park with its majestic ancient trees and reminders of wars past. Through their tales, Bob grew to understand that transcontinental industrialization and the mechanization of agriculture could never have taken place without these terrible events. The country lost hundreds of thousands of able-bodied men, but those that remained had witnessed what great feats could be accomplished on the field of battle through teamwork, training, and discipline. Bob was particularly impressed by the way the organization and cooperation skills gained in wartime was applied in peacetime. As a result, the potential offered by such great Industrial Revolution inventions as the John Deere plow and McCormick reaper would be realized across the country's vast agricultural heartland, and the Colt revolver would provide a measure of protection for the pioneers.

Despite his public education and private tuition, Bob still thought of himself as the dumbest of the Cannard family. As far as he can remember, all of his siblings were at the top of their classes at school, or close to it. Sarah considered Ed to be the most intelligent. The twins reckoned Bob to be pretty stupid, but although they were five years older, he was every bit as tough as them, and probably more so.

Demonstrating his toughness was a means for Bob to draw level with his siblings. Climbing higher in the tree to pick cherries than anyone else dared go was one way he showed his fearlessness. That was a relatively safe demonstration, but he wasn't always as smart. Like when he decided to parachute from the barn roof.

I should think I was around eleven or twelve years old. I borrowed a sheet from home and tied strings to the corners. I had some experience from flying kites and knew enough to use thin strips of bamboo to spread the sheet out so that it would catch the air as soon as I jumped. I suppose the barn roof was about thirty feet up, but the ground underneath was soft and grassy.

There was a good crowd watching—I believe they expected me to break something.

Anyway, off I jumped with the parachute held above me. But it never caught the air and I came down with quite a crash. There were some horrified looks from the neighborhood kids, but I think they were impressed too. It hurt like hell, but I never let on, and somehow hobbled home.

I may not have had a childhood typical of many today, with TV and nothing to do most of the time. Those were simpler times with the Depression limiting what anyone could do. Even so, there were always plenty of things for us children to be involved in. My father was not actively working. My mother took care of the house, the garden, and most of the problems in the neighborhood, and my two older sisters were a great help to my mother. During my early childhood, our family did a lot of things together, and so the highlights of the year tended to be centered on various family activities.

There were many activities that occupied our time. Some of the most memorable highlights to me include such things as children home for the summer, the first new potatoes and peas, picking cherries and the first apple pie. A ten-mile trip to the Delong Museum at Washingtonville where they had some Lindberg artifacts, and any visit to or from relatives. There was the Sunday school picnic, the fall and winter holidays, and all the special food that went with them like mince pies, plum puddings, and cans full of wonderful cookies. Looking at the sky through the telescope, learning the planets and constellations, and my father calculating the next eclipse. Getting worms, minnows, and night crawlers for bait, and fishing with Em Sherwood. Collecting butterflies, moths, and insects and learning the twenty-five orders and what differentiates one from the other. I know most of them today...Diptera, Hymenoptera, Lepidoptera, Coleoptera... Picking wild berries, strawberries, and black raspberries. Gathering walnuts and butternuts and saving the hulls for dye. Watching the clouds and swallows, identifying all the birds and wild flowers, and working in the garden. Taking care of the chickens and gathering the eggs. Smelling everything—good and bad. Gathering bittersweet and black alder and various club mosses, teaberry, and partridge berry

Art Young, Ray Beiswanger, Melvin Diehl and Bob.

for winter terrariums. Foot races in the street—Art Young always won. Boxing. I was considered the 'Great White Hope' and was nicknamed 'Two Ton Tony' after Tony Galento who knocked Joe Lewis down twice but lost. Going to the circus was a big day. Never went to the movies.

The days were full from morning 'til night. I never once heard "I'm bored, there is nothing to do" from any of my family or friends. Reading was a big thing for the whole family. I was also a champion at marbles, although Art Young was darned close to me. I won hundreds of glass marbles in contests with local kids, jars of them I had. I was unbeatable at short distances. I could make a hit every time. Glass marbles were one of my treasured possessions. Twelve migs equaled a peewee, and fifteen migs equaled a glass marble, so you can tell how good I was.

Bob was not always well behaved, and although he wasn't easily led, he could get into trouble because he "liked to accommodate people." Ray Beiswanger, for example. Ray was from a less fortunate family, and he only weighed thirty-nine pounds when he was six years old. He would get fed at Bob's home on the way to school, and they would run home for a sandwich at recess. Ray would also get an apple at the end of the day but still seemed to suffered from malnutrition. They were hard times.

At Easter time when they were in the third grade, Bob took a nickel with the intention of buying a chocolate creme egg for their teacher, Alice McVeigh. But Ray had a better plan.

"I know where we can get a hyacinth in a pot—it's on a back porch. If we give that to Miss McVeigh, and you know she likes plants, we can get two marshmallow eggs, one each, with the nickel."

Bob agreed, and Ray took him down the alley where the hyacinth sat on the back porch. While Bob kept watch, Ray went over the fence and reappeared minutes later with the hyacinth, which he handed to Bob. They took it to Bob's mother who said, "Well, it's a little gone, but maybe it'll be OK. Where did you get it?" Ray quickly answered that he got it for a nickel, and they left for school where they handed over the plant to Alice McVeigh. Later they bought and enjoyed their two marshmallow eggs. Deal done.

Well, it turned out that Alice McVeigh recognized the hyacinth because it was off her own back porch. She cornered the two miscreants the next day in the cloakroom, confronted them, and they soon admitted stealing the plant. Hitting just the right chord, their teacher offered, "If you promise to never do such a thing again, I won't say any more about it." They promised, and she never said a word, much to Bob's relief.

CHAPTER TWO

INDEPENDENCE & THE GROWING YEARS

In January of 1939, Bob's mother suffered a debilitating stroke. She spent long months in hospital, and then at home with part and full-time nursing. Her speech was limited, yet when she and Bob were in the garden, their connection had become so profound that the merest gesture on her part would provide all the direction that was necessary for Bob to prune, plant or graft whatever was in her mind. In March 1941, she died. Bob was fourteen years old at the time and recalls his older brother Tom telling him early in the morning while he was still in bed that "mother died last night." He was not distraught or filled with remorse at the news, and thinks now that he just fell back into his pillow with a sigh and a "sinking feeling."

She had been confined to a wheelchair since her stroke, and so the family had begun to make adjustments. At the time of his mother's death, Bob had already taken over many of the gardening and kitchen chores, and brother Jim also did cooking and baking until he went into the service. They did have a housekeeper, but she was "not much of a cook." Bob's father and younger brother Ed would handle the shopping, and the older boys would wash the dishes, while older sister Mary supervised the housecleaning and clothes washing. Time spent gaining various cooking skills began to pay off for Bob. Because of his abilities, the older twins, Tom and John, soon approached him to provide them with a steady supply of root, birch, and ginger beer. They would provide the ingredients and bottles, and Bob would make the beer, demanding an appropriate "cut" of the production. Because of his unique talents and his size, his brothers rarely challenged him and usually acceded to his demands for an increasing share.

He was treated as an adult by everyone, and in addition to school, growing produce, rearing birds, cooking for the family and working for Em in the store, he worked for a Danville feed company, driving to Baltimore once a week for supplies. By the time he went to high school, he could turn his hand to anything practical and was able to establish a unique niche for himself. He was left alone to decide which classes he would attend for general education and agriculture. It was tacitly accepted that grades would be based on the family reputation, not Bob's performance, and in return, he would be relied on to handle some of the school's maintenance jobs. He had free run of the school and looked after shop equipment, helped in the agriculture department, and changed the light bulbs in the gym. The agriculture teacher relied on Bob to drive a team of students to his farm orchard thirty miles away to pick apples and pears—it's where he learned the art of fruit tree pruning.

When the United States joined World War II, a lot of things were simply allowed to happen. Everyone was urged to do what he or she could to help out, while eyes were turned the other way. Today Bob believes he would have been better off with a strong mentor at that time.

Bob didn't work hard in school but listened intently to everything. In math and physics he played a mind game with himself, converting scientific problems into verbal word puzzles, then talking himself through them mentally until he had the solution.

His size made him a natural for sports, and he became "the enforcer" in basketball and football, physically taking out the most skilled players on the opponent's team, and making himself the target of their anger, so that his teammates could score while he was chased for revenge. Frequently, they could hardly turn out enough for a team, and Bob played both offensive and defensive tackle, with no substitutes available. He was a better strategist than most and could usually be relied on to knock his man down. To Bob, it was purely a mental game.

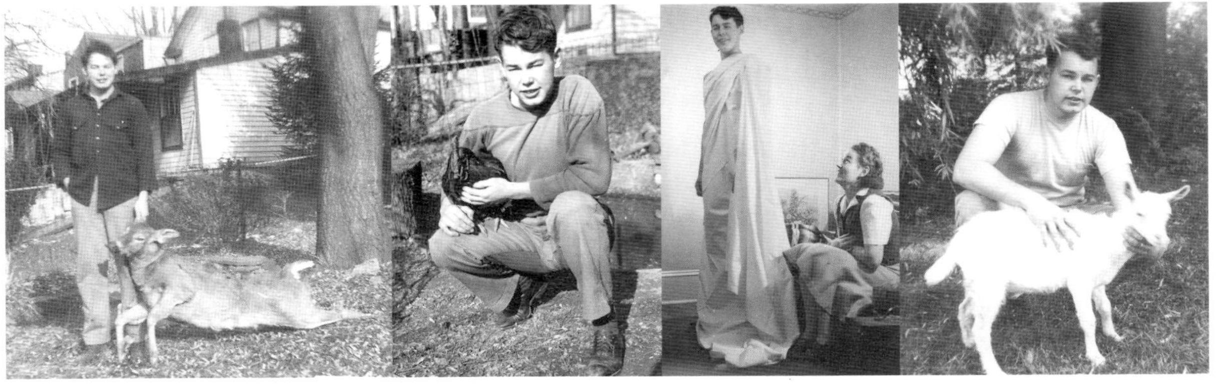

In his freshman and

sophomore summers, he took a job working for a seventy-seven-year-old farmer for ten dollars a month. He learned butchering anytime they would let him try, and soon he could not only tackle any animal but also make sausages, head cheese, pudding, canned loins, "and anything else you care to name."

Having spent so many summers in and around the Susquehanna River and its tributaries, Bob had become a terrific swimmer. He doesn't remember when he learned; he remembers that he could always swim.

In 1941 he decided to become a lifeguard and took the certification tests with ease. They included a requirement to be able to stay afloat for several hours in a swimming pool. Of course, not one to miss an opportunity to showboat, Bob decided to make it a full six hours, during which he enjoyed the attention of all the girls he had set up to bring him soda pop and sandwiches as he floated around the pool. "You float like a cork, Cannard!" remarked the instructor, who promptly gave Bob his Senior Lifeguard's certificate. "I was as

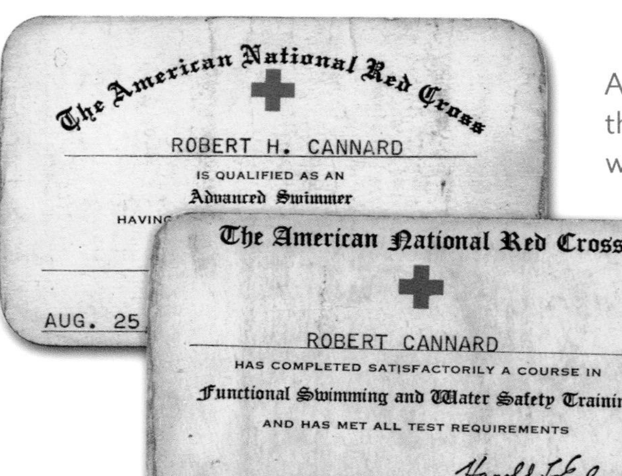

The American National Red Cross
ROBERT H. CANNARD
IS QUALIFIED AS AN
Advanced Swimmer
HAVING
AUG. 25

The American National Red Cross
ROBERT CANNARD
HAS COMPLETED SATISFACTORILY A COURSE IN
Functional Swimming and Water Safety Training
AND HAS MET ALL TEST REQUIREMENTS
AUG. 13, 1943
(DATE)
Harold F. Enlows
DIRECTOR, FIRST AID, WATER SAFETY AND ACCIDENT PREVENTION

All the girls wanted their photo taken with the lifeguard.

comfortable in the water as I was in bed."

Before too long, Bob was the resident lifeguard at the Sunnybrook swim club just outside Danville—a magnet for the local young people. He also became an indispensable assistant to the owner, Jerry Lewis. In the summer, he did the landscaping, pool maintenance, and anything else needed, in addition to his duties as lifeguard. He worked such long hours that he took to sleeping in the room above the clubhouse, situated at the side of the pool.

Thirteen miles away in Milton, Edna Taylor and her parents had moved to their new home in Pennsylvania from Long Island. She and a new friend decided to bike (Yes, it was thirteen miles!) to the Sunnybrook swim club. Bob was soon joking around with the newcomers. Edna didn't think a whole lot of the brash young Cannard, and it was her besotted friend who willingly gave her address to Bob. Although they corresponded a few times, it wasn't long before he crushed her by asking for Edna's address. The friend was furious, but Bob and Edna became close, and their relationship strengthened through the summer of 1942.

Edna Taylor

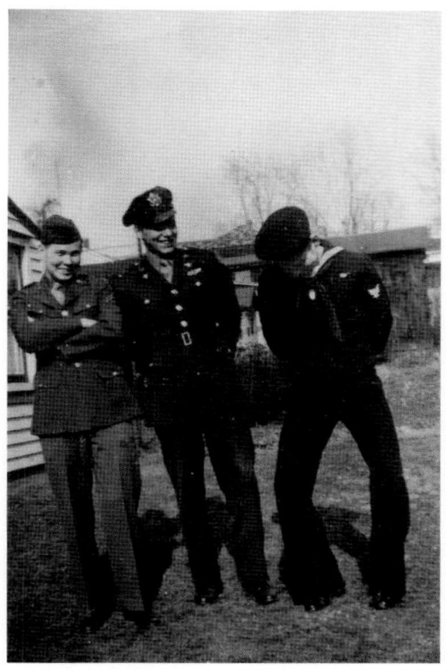

Tom, Jim and John home on leave in 1943

In December 1941, Japan had bombed Pearl Harbor, and the United States mobilized itself for war with a total and all-consuming commitment. Bob's older brothers volunteered right away. Tom, who would later become a physician, joined the army as a medic. Jim went into the air force and saw plenty of action as a B24 bombardier in the Fifteenth Air Force stationed in Italy. His plane was shot down over the Ploesti oil fields, and he spent time as a POW. John joined the navy medical corps and served in the Pacific at Iwo and Okinawa. He later went on to become a psychiatrist.

George, the oldest son, had a strange experience. He was working in Washington, DC, and heard that the president would draw the names of the first hundred men to be drafted in a public ceremony on the White House lawn. He had a compelling premonition that he would be on the list and went to the ceremony. Sure enough, his name was drawn, and being the only person drawn who was present, received hearty congratulations. At his subsequent medical, he was classified 4F because of tuberculosis. He returned to Danville for treatment and never served overseas.

By then in his late sixties, Bob's father served on the War and Mobilization Board. Women and children at home knitted socks and folded bandages.

Too young for active service, Bob did everything he possibly could to contribute at home. At school, he and others built model airplanes—Allied and Axis—to the plans provided by the air force, using any raw materials they could lay their hands on. Models considered sufficiently similar to the real thing were sent off to be used as crucial aids to the identification of airplanes in action. No one was paid, but Bob received several certificates for his contribution to the war effort

Bob became an adviser to the borough of

THE UNITED STATES NAVY
BUREAU OF AERONAUTICS
Washington, D. C.

HEREBY CONFERS UPON

Robert Cannard

the honorary rank of Cadet Aircraftsman in recognition of war-time service in making in accordance with specifications approved by the Bureau of Aeronautics of the United States Navy

SCALE MODEL AIRCRAFT

For use by the Government of the United States.

Given this sixteenth day of June in the year of Our Lord one thousand nine hundred and forty-two and of the Independence of the United States one hundred and sixty-six.

Superintendent

Admiral J. H. Towers, U. S. N.
Chief of Bureau of Aeronautics

Danville's victory garden program, giving lectures and providing advice to anyone who telephoned Vi with questions. As an air raid warden, armed with a stirrup pump, helmet, armband and nightstick, he tested the alarms, enforced the blackout, and made sure that a five-gallon stirrup pump was ready on every block. (He still has his nightstick.) He was also adept at collecting bucketfuls of smoothbore mini-ball bullets in the fields at Gettysburg, and he sold these to the lead-hungry war machine. It was said that the bullets used in at Gettysburg—made mostly at the John Brown Armory in Virginia—outweighed the soldiers, so there was a significant supply.

Bob's regular trips to pick up feed in Baltimore continued, but now he was required to join a convoy of trucks headed south, observing a strict speed limit of thirty-five miles an hour to save fuel. On one trip, a motorcycle cop intercepted the convoy, because they were going too fast. He had every driver stand at the side of the road by their truck and went angrily down the line telling each driver in no uncertain terms exactly what the rules were. Bob's respect for authority had him quaking in his boots; only fifteen years old at the time, he had no driver's license. Fortunately, the cop just glared at him and moved on down the line.

With all able-bodied men at war, boys were called on to fill in the gaps at home. Charlie Grimes was the regular postman in the area and asked Bob to help out at Christmas time during 1942 and 1943. Getting out of school more than compensated for the meager pay as far as Bob was concerned.

The post office was different then. There were contests to see who could figure out how to deliver a misadressed letter. My father once had a letter from England addressed to 'Sidney G. Cannard, USA.' A clerk in Philadelphia remembered the appropriate destination from many previous letters and sent it on to Danville. Could that happen today?

You wouldn't believe it today; people did anything they could to contribute to the war effort. It was quite amazing; there was a single focus, a single purpose. Everyone wore his or her 'E for effort' enamel pin proudly. If you didn't, why, you would be a social outcast. I have not witnessed a time since when the entire country was so committed to a single cause.

By May1944, Bob would be eligible for military service himself. Having grown used to determining his own way in life, and knowing that volunteers could choose which of the services they wanted to enter, he signed up for the United States Army Air Force and was sworn in at Indian Town Gap on December 2, 1943. After graduating high school the following year, Bob presented himself for basic training at Kessler Field, Biloxi, Mississippi, on June 15, 1944.

The training presented no challenges, but Bob was used to having money in his pocket, and pay was negligible. After GI insurance and laundry bills, there wasn't much left.

Always the opportunist, he struck up a friendship with a black maintenance worker and asked him if he could get watermelons. The man said sure he could, and agreed to bring them to the camp fence in the evening. The first night he came in a small car and threw a few melons over the fence. Bob caught them and paid the man twenty-five cents for each melon. He had no problem reselling them at twenty-five cents for one-quarter melon. Pretty soon a truck replaced the car, and sometimes Bob had to pay an additional "catcher" to unload the stack of watermelons quickly and unobtrusively.

Bob was never short of money from then on, but needing to get along with authority, he made sure he always had the tacit approval of officers. It was not unusual for one of them to follow an official order with "and save me a quarter Cannard."

We dropped a few as they came over the fence, but even with a price reduction I still made money on them, and so did the maintenance worker. I never asked where he got the melons.

I was called in one day and questioned by the CO. He said, 'I hear you are selling watermelons every night.' I replied that I was and told him of my efforts. He looked at me a while and then smiled and said, "A little unusual. Save me a quarter. Dismissed." He got a nice melon whenever the drill sergeant gave me the sign.

After basic training, Bob and his fellow conscripts were subjected to a battery of intelligence tests to determine appropriate deployments. By then the air force no longer needed aircrew, but with his IQ and training at Chanute Field, Illinois, Bob managed to get assigned to a cryptography unit in

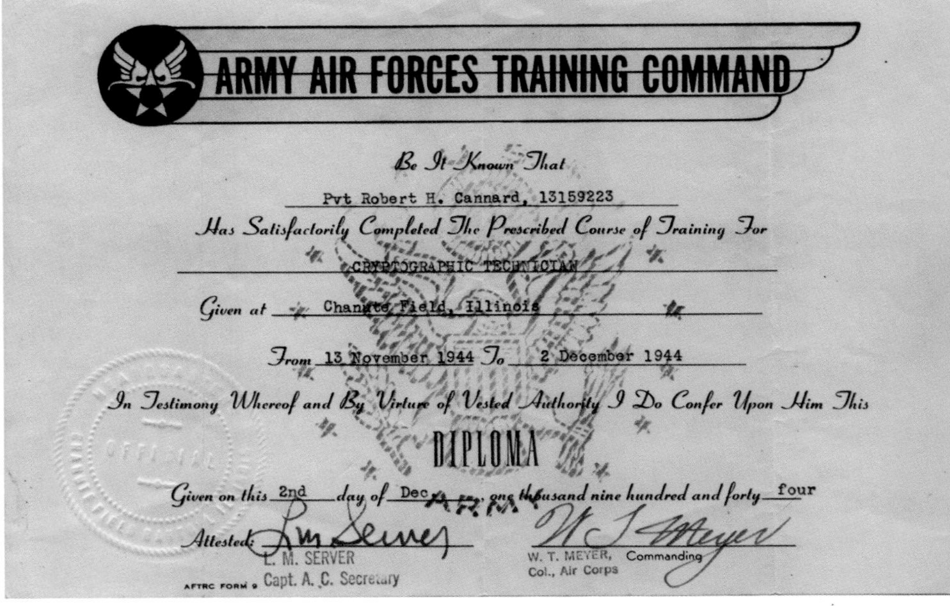

ARMY AIR FORCES TRAINING COMMAND

Be It Known That

Pvt Robert H. Cannard, 13159223

Has Satisfactorily Completed The Prescribed Course of Training For

CRYPTOGRAPHIC TECHNICIAN

Given at Chanute Field, Illinois

From 13 November 1944 To 2 December 1944

In Testimony Whereof and By Virtue of Vested Authority I Do Confer Upon Him This

DIPLOMA

Given on this 2nd day of Dec, one thousand nine hundred and forty four

Attested: L. M. SERVER, Capt. A. C. Secretary

W. T. MEYER, Col., Air Corps, Commanding

AFTRC FORM 9

the overseas CBI theater (China, Burma, India). He was duly dispatched to the embarkation camp at San Pedro, Southern California.

As a cryptographer, Bob needed security clearance and knew that there would be an official investigation into his background. He had nothing to worry about, and his father later confirmed that neither his high school nor the local police gave any black marks. In the back of Bob's mind was the knowledge that he had occasionally liberated one of his favorite stuffed green olives from the top of a jar on the shelves of Em Sherwood's store. But the secret was either safe or of no concern to the military and he gained his top-secret clearance before going to cryptographer school.

The recruits were warned that as cryptographers with top secret information in their heads, if enemy action came close enough to them to represent any danger of capture, they would be shot by their senior officers. They were then offered the opportunity to request reassignment if this issue was a concern. After being told that the only alternative that existed at that time was the infantry, everyone declined the offer.

The last ten days before shipping out of San Pedro, California, were spent playing poker and pinochle, swimming at the camp pool, and browsing local bookshops for reading matter that would cover the long journey to—well, they didn't know exactly where.

At a small store in San Pedro, Bob acquired a dictionary and three volumes by Herodotus on the history of the ancient Greek city-state of Sparta. Concerned that he "needed something lighter," the pretty middle-aged bookseller gave him a copy of the racy latest best-seller, *Forever Amber*.

This was a wise choice, because although nobody aboard the transport ship ever asked to borrow the dictionary or the volumes of Greek history, he rented out *Forever Amber* enough times to his shipmates to pay for all his book purchases several times over. It eventually fell apart in tatters, Herodotus was donated to the library in Karachi, then in India, and Bob came home with the dictionary.

Australia was the destination of the ship, and several hundred green servicemen settled in for the long and tedious trip across the Pacific. Playing cards was about the only form of entertainment that existed onboard, and shortly after embarking, Bob was approached by George Burke of Appomattox, Virginia, to become his partner for contract bridge. The only remarkable things about George Burke that Bob can remember was that he explained how you could take a crap sitting on the handle of a pitchfork, and he "had more hair on his body than most men have on their heads." The only remarkable things, that is, except play the game of bridge better than anyone on board the ship. George was the Virginia state bridge champion, and from that first day, pausing only for two daily meals, he and Bob played every day, all day, and rarely lost a rubber.

They played all the way across the Pacific to Melbourne, Australia, for the two weeks they were held over in Perth, and all the way over the Indian Ocean to Calcutta. By the time they disembarked, they had won just about all the spare cash that existed on the ship, which wasn't that much. As they parted company, Bob asked George why, of all the guys at the embarkation camp, he had picked him to be his bridge partner.

Bob was hoping he would say it was because he looked like an intelligent fellow, but George replied, "I watched you swimming at the camp in San Pedro, and you were the best there by a mile. I don't swim, and I knew you could save me if we got torpedoed. So I decided to stick closer to you than wallpaper the whole way here, and that's exactly what I did."

The ship experienced several scares during the voyage when the crew was called to quarters, but they did get through the Pacific safely—and George, in the end, didn't need to call on Bob's aquatic lifesaving skills.

After a short orientation at the US base in Calcutta, Bob was assigned to clerical duties in the well-protected code rooms occupied by the extremely bright PhDs responsible for decoding Japanese radio signals, as well as coding and decoding regular traffic. He was not particularly good at the work, and he really didn't like the idea of waiting for someone else to decide what he should do, so he began to spend time with one of the junior officers, just to see what might be available. The officer explained to Bob that the communication system used throughout the Far East theatre of war by the US and British forces depended on machines that encrypted wireless messages at one end and decoded them at the other. The machines were elaborate typewriters that converted clear typing into coded messages by changing each letter or numeral to an alternate, determined by the particular settings on ten rotors. When received, the message would revert to its clear version when put back through a similar typewriter having the same rotor settings as the sending device. The rotor settings were changed at pre-determined intervals, to make sure that even if the enemy was fortunate enough to crack them, the benefit could only last for a short time.

These settings were generated at random and contained in a coded sequence of letters and numbers. Each set of rotors had 125 different settings, so the code for each rotor comprised the same number of letters and numbers, in twenty-five groups of five. The total code was made up of ten lines of these groups, corresponding to the ten rotors on the "typewriters." Because a hard copy of the code could be intercepted in a volatile war situation, someone who could reliably memorize these sequences would travel around to all the Allied bases every few weeks and change the code machines. Holding out a typical page of code sequences, the officer said to Bob, "Why don't you give it a try?"

Thinking that the job sounded a whole lot more interesting than his clerical duties, Bob took the page of code

Continued on page 60

This portrait was taken in Karachi a few days before Christmas 1945

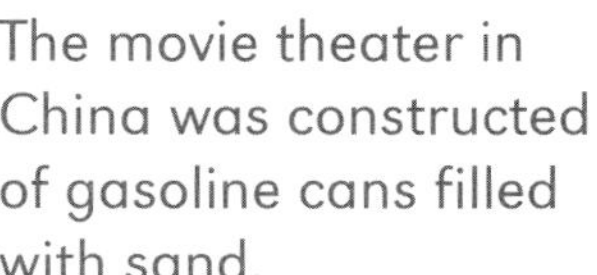

The movie theater in China was constructed of gasoline cans filled with sand.

The carved paper knife was given to Bob by Sikh friends. The lighter was made by local craftsman in a few hours from scraps of aluminum, complete with engraved insignia

Bob carved these intertwined hearts while serving in India, and sent them home to Edna

Continued from page 57

back to the code room that evening, pinned it on the underside of a table, then lay down under the table, staring hard at the rows and columns. (You might imagine that this was to focus Bob's attention, but it turns out that when he wasn't busy he slept under the table.)

> *Whether it was because I had grown accustomed to learning the Latin names of flora, I don't know, but in a very short time, the letters and numbers began to make understandable words in my mind, and the words began to make up sentences. In no time at all, I had the whole thing memorized, and the following morning went back to the code officer.*

The code officer took the page from Bob and asked if he'd like to try the first line. Bob repeated it flawlessly; then the second, and the third, and to the officer's utter amazement, recited the entire first five lines of code with absolutely no hesitation or mistakes. The amazement came from the fact that the existing code "runners" generally took a minimum of two weeks to learn what Bob had managed overnight.

Bob was soon embarking on his first "run," taking whatever military air transportation he could to complete the round trip of the bases in Cairo, Baghdad, Baluchistan, New Delhi, Agra, Bombay, Karachi, and "over the hump" (the 16,000-foot peaks separating India from Burma and China) to Kunming in China, stopping at each location however long it took to provide the new rotor setting and set up transportation for the next leg. Bob's preference was for the C47 transport plane. There were fewer of them, but they were worth waiting for on the run over the hump. The C47 had a lightweight stressed aluminum skin, which gave it a higher ceiling than the ubiquitous C46, and Bob preferred to take no chances.

And with only one exception, he never failed to give the correct codes at every base he visited on the numerous round trips he made. He forgot the code only once; it happened in Cairo after a night out. Suffering from a rare hangover, Bob's mind went a complete blank. He messaged his home base to tell them the bad news. "So you finally messed up, Cannard," was the laughing reply. They took it in stride and told Bob not to worry and head home. It transpired that the Allied communication system was never seriously compromised and this single unfortunate event only emphasises Bob's remarkable performance.

During the breaks between runs, Bob enjoyed the company of soldiers at the nearby British army base. It was a perfect relationship. They had gin and he had ice. They also had good canned beef, and there seemed to be a more relaxed atmosphere between officers and enlisted men. They even played golf in the desert. Bob also recalls that they more readily accepted his improvised scrambled egg breakfasts.

He had taken to swimming far out into the Indian Ocean and then trying to hitch a ride back to shore on the giant turtles headed for the beach. He later gathered turtle eggs from the sand, and occasionally a turtle. It could only be Bob Cannard with his array of skills that quickly mastered the art of killing and butchering turtles.

> *Turtle meat and scrambled turtle eggs—pretty good it was, too. There were a few that were squeamish about trying it, but if I smoked the meat most people couldn't distinguish it from turkey or chicken breast. The English had no fresh meat, and the Americans very little, so it was appreciated. I did send turtle shells back home to Danville, but they never made it.*

At the end of the war in 1945, Bob remained in active service as a cryptographic code clerk, but there was a reduced level of security. When he wasn't on duty, he took the opportunity to visit as many places as he could, becoming familiar with new forms of flora, as well as the birds and animals in the fine zoos at Bombay and Karachi, and "the miserable one in New Delhi." He became particularly friendly with groups of woodworkers in Karachi and Kashmir, but also took an interest in the methods and practices of all kinds of merchants, tradesmen, and farmers. Bob still uses the sharpening stone given to him by a family of Kashmiri Sikhs and is proud that merchants in Karachi gave him high marks for his natural ability to barter. "You are good at bargaining, Cannard sahib."

Traveling up the Ganges to the port city of Calcutta, Bob saw many bodies floating in the water, the result of a severe famine in India at the time. He later learned there were so many dead that British soldiers had been assigned to collect the bodies and take them to the burning ghats along the river. But some people simply died and tumbled into the sacred waters.

As Bob leaned over the ship's railing, he ate an orange and let the peel fall into the lazy current alongside the floating bodies. He remembers being struck by the thought that everything—corpses and orange peel—would eventually breakdown, and their tiniest constituent parts would re-emerge at some time in some other life form, maybe even in his own body.

But now it was time for Bob to re-emerge from war in some other form. The air force had been an interlude, and Bob had no intention of staying connected to the military by joining the reserves, even if it meant getting out of active service early. He was approached by the State Department to join the OSS (later the CIA) as part of a new Middle East team. But he didn't want a government job either, believing deep down that he still lacked a formal education. So, after shipping back to the States and suffering a few extra weeks duty and daily lectures, he was finally mustered out on June 16, 1946, in Indianapolis, Indiana. He took the Pennsylvania Railroad to Harrisburg,

DOMAIN of the GOLDEN DRAGON

INTERNATIONAL DATE LINE

Ruler of the 180th Meridian

To all Sailors, Soldiers, Marines, wherever ye may be and to all mermaids, flying dragons, spirits of the deep, devil chasers, and all other living creatures of the yellow seas, Greetings: Know ye that on this 28th day of May 1946, in latitude [illegible] longitude 180° there appeared within the limits of my august dwelling the

S S "Marine Panther"

Hearken Ye: The said vessel, officers and crew have been inspected and passed on by my august body and staff. And know ye: Ye that are chit signers, squaw men, opium smokers, ice men, and all-round landlubbers that Robert H. Cannard having been found sane and worthy to be numbered a dweller of the Far East has been gathered in my fold and duly initiated into the

Silent Mysteries of the Far East

Be it further understood: That by virtue of the power vested in me I do hereby command all moneylenders, wine sellers, cabaret owners, ______ managers and all my other subjects to show honor and respect to all his wishes whenever he may enter my realm. Disobey this command under penalty of my august displeasure.

Golden Dragon
Ruler of the 180th Meridian

Crossing the International Date Line on the way home.

and then a bus on to Danville and the family home. Bob had been informed some months before while in India that his father had died early in 1945, but the house was kept, mainly for Bob and his younger brother Ed, and only used occasionally by the dispersed family.

Bob recalls today that he had been looking forward to seeing his father again, because he had planned to give him a rare treat. While away in Asia he had figured out how to bake a pie in such a way that when the crust on the top was broken, out would fly a blackbird. Not exactly four and twenty, but nevertheless a worthy attempt at the pie in his father's favorite nursery rhyme. But with his father gone, the pie remained a theory, and a somewhat wistful memory.

The excitement of wartime service in foreign lands was over, his parents were gone, the world had changed, and Bob was at a loose end. He took a job on a turret lathe at the machine shop where his brother-in-law was supervisor, making parts for stone crushing and grinding equipment, and he picked up his delivery work at the weekends for the feed company. He learned what it was like to do repetitious work, and he learned that it wasn't for him. So that summer, he took off with his brothers George and Ed and drove north across Canada to Churchill on Hudson Bay, and then south and west by dirt road to Colorado and his grandfather's mining claims.

These were the claims established by his mother's father, Joseph Hiatt, when he explored the West with his brothers from 1858 to 1915. Joe and his brothers claimed to have walked the length of the Rocky Mountains, and the Pacific coastal mountains from San Diego to Seattle in search of coal deposits for their employer, a British mining company. Joe Hiatt had surveyed the west by foot, establishing legal claims for the mining company when he found coal, and legal claims for himself when he found traces of anything else, like gold, silver, or copper. This left him with considerable land holdings in San Diego, Seattle, and in the Denver area of Colorado. Some of the claims were productive, but Joe had closed them when he returned to Pennsylvania in grief after the death of his wife in childbirth. He and his sons re-opened the claims some years later after the boys had finished college, but the mines were closed permanently in 1912.

Members of the extended Hiatt family agreed to release their various titles so that Bob and his brothers could take over and work the claims, but they were content to demolish a few buildings and idly pan for gold. Bob still has a vial of gold flakes as proof of his adventure.

Continued on page 64

Potatos, bacon and
spare tires made up most of the load

Bob and Ed caught so many fish that the owners of the cabin salted away a full barrel.

An old timer directed them to this spot in the river, and reckoned that George looked exactly like his grandfather who had been there some sixty years before .

At the top of a steep switchback outside of Telluride, they had a flat tire. Out of spares by then, George said he'd take it back to be repaired. But taking one look down at the long winding road, he bowled the wheel right over the side and it bounced all the way to the bottom. "It's a wonder it didn't kill anyone, but it sure saved time"

Cont. from page 62

But during his summer in the mountains, Bob came to the realization that he was still "just a big dumb kid" and in serious need of an education. He had been left pretty much to his own devices since he was fourteen years old, and although he had done a lot of things and picked up a lot of useful and not so useful skills, he lacked the purpose to turn them into anything worthwhile. Bob had continued to correspond with Edna during his wartime service. They had agreed to marry over the Christmas of 1946, and became formally engaged the following spring.

So in the fall of 1947, Bob returned to Danville—to get married, go to school, and find his purpose.

Edna made the bow tie, and Bob insists that he can still get into his wedding suit almost sixty years on.

The GI Bill paid for college tuition for any service veteran. It was quite natural that Bob chose to take a degree course in horticulture at Penn State. Just seventy-five miles west of Danville, his sister Mary's husband was a professor of engineering there, and they took in any serviceman.

Although a large amount of new housing on the

campus had been made available to meet the big influx of students taking advantage of the GI Bill, Bob refused to be regimented. A week before classes started, he had still not found (or looked for) a home for Edna and himself. His sister Mary was becoming extremely concerned, because most of the available housing was already gone, but Bob had complete confidence in the probability of something turning up "once I put my mind to it."

So, with just a couple of days to go, he left Danville at 4:00 a.m. and drove to Penn State along rural roads. He was looking for a farm that looked like it could use a little help—ideally a good working farm with cows, pigs, and chickens but not too big and organized. It wasn't long before he found what he was looking for. At 5:45 a.m. he stopped the car beside a neat cluster of farm buildings and pushed his way through the door of a milking shed. When he found the middle-aged farmer at work hand milking one of several cows, he crouched down beside him in the straw.

The man continued working in silence, not even acknowledging Bob's presence. After a while, Bob broke the silence. "How would you like a day off?"

Without interrupting his rhythmic squeezing, the man replied, "Young man, I've never taken a day off in the thirty-three years I've worked this farm."

"Well now's your chance," said Bob, who went on to explain that he was looking for a place to live in return for doing farm chores. The two continued to chat while Bob helped with the milking. When they had finished, Bob accepted an invitation to breakfast with the farmer and his wife.

It turned out that the farmer's elderly mother, who lived in nearby Boalsburg, was in real need of help with her garden, furnace, and other heavy household chores. By 9:00 a.m. Bob was meeting with her and the farmer's brother, who was also a farmer, to arrange how to set up an apartment in her house. It was a Thursday. Over the weekend, they installed a stove, sink, and cabinets in a big upstairs room and erected a simple partition to separate the new kitchen from a bedroom area. By the following Tuesday, Bob and Edna moved into their new apartment and then paid a visit to his sister. Halfway through Mary's speech about the thousand of new mobile homes on the campus, already full of students ("What on earth was he going to do about a home for Edna?"), Bob interrupted with the good news about their new appartment. Mary was flabbergasted by his ability to pull a rabbit out of the hat.

A hallmark of Bob's life has been his innate ability to "make things happen" without any long term planning. He simply made up his mind, with a conviction borne of practical experience and luck—luck that has been a remarkably reliable companion throughout his life, and to which he gives full credit.

Bob took great care of his landlady, Mrs. Dry, and her garden, and regularly helped out her sons. Soon, one of them was able to take his wife on their very first vacation, which she later claimed to have been the best trip she had ever had. It was two days at the Jersey Cow Convention in Sayre, New York.

Jack Whiting, a dear friend of Bob's from this period in Pennsylvania, remembers that Bob similarly made up his mind that Jack and his wife should have a pet. They were not too sure about it, but one evening Bob turned up with twelve Springer Spaniel puppies and said he wouldn't take them away until at least one of them was picked out. They did pick one, and they have never been without the breed since. Jack remembers other classics from Bob's past: ["I suppose Bob told you about being a lion tamer's assistant?" I said I wasn't sure. The fact that I couldn't remember whether or not Bob *had* told me about being a lion tamer's assistant is in itself a tribute to the eclectic variety of his experiences. Later Bob insisted that he had. "Oh yes," he said confidently, "I told you all about it." Then he told me again.]

It was the trout opener of 1947. A good friend Ed Kolzaski and myself had spent the day fly-fishing on a northern tributary creek of the Susquehanna, hoping for a few brownies and brookies. But all we got were lots of suckers, and big ones, too. I mean two feet long! You've never seen suckers like them. Well, we didn't much feel like taking those ugly fish for ourselves—too many bones. But we remembered that Doc Keller, our art history teacher lived nearby, and he had a part-time business as a lion tamer. We figured that his big cats would enjoy the treat.

So we took a bag of fish the mile or so to his home in Orangeville. Classic Cape Cod house it was, I can see it today. Anyway, out comes Doc Keller, and we offered the fish for his lions and tigers. I felt sure that I had read of tigers catching fish.

"Oh no!" He says. "Red meat is all they eat. They won't touch fish." Then he called his wife, and she came out and walked toward us.

"But we will," says Doc Keller. And do you know, he took the fish and threw them straight at her, just a few feet away.

"Clean those for dinner," he ordered as she caught them, and I thought what a way to treat a woman. His wife too! Second wife I should think; she must have been half his age. Poor woman, she just took the fish inside without saying a word.

Then the Doc asked me if I cared for a job as his assistant in the lion taming business. He could use help getting ready for the summer shows on the boardwalk in Atlantic City. I asked him what I would be doing, and he said oh feeding, cleaning, clipping nails, that sort of thing. Twice a week it would be, after school, which for me usually ended in the college greenhouses only five miles away. He offered seventy-five cents an hour, which was ten cents over minimum wage.

Sounded simple to me at first, and I was always looking to make a little extra. So I agreed and started soon after. I got on well with Doc Keller, and the lions and tigers, as well.

Anyway, prior to the big show in Atlantic City there was to be a dress rehearsal at Selinsgrove, in Rolling Green

Park. One of my jobs was to hold two young lionesses on leashes at the side of the ring. It was just dressing for the show, but they were playful and had to be controlled. If not, they would try to join in the act with the older animals, and who knows what would have happened. I practiced a few times with the young lionesses at the Doc's place while he was putting the big cats through their paces. They were sixty or seventy pounds apiece, but I held them easily.

Well, people came to Rolling Green Park from all over. A couple of thousand I should think. They watched spellbound as the Doc cracked his whip, the tigers jumped from pylon to pylon, and the lions reared up ferociously. And all the while I held the leashed lionesses at the ringside wearing my lion tamer's assistant uniform.

Suddenly the audience was on its feet, shouting and applauding, and the Doc took a series of long slow sweeping bows, his face beaming at the wonderful noise. Then he looked at me and saw why the crowd was yelling. My pants had fallen down. The whole audience was pointing, laughing, and clapping as I stood completely unaware, looking foolishly serious as I proudly held back the lionesses with my shirt tails flapping and my pants around my ankles. You should have heard them!

I had been so intent on doing my job, I hadn't noticed. I guess the pants had been made for someone much bigger. Anyway, down they came, and I didn't feel a thing. Fortunately for me, it was one of the rare occasions I was wearing underwear. Well, the crowd loved it and kept up their applause for quite a time.

The crowd couldn't have been happier, but Doc Keller was pissed. He was incensed. Thought I had deliberately stolen the show. Not true of course, but that's what he thought. Really mad with me he was. I left him soon after and never did get to go to Atlantic City, but I couldn't stand his attitude.

During this period, Bob also helped his younger brother Ed collect specimens for a biological supply house in New York. Ed knew the species they were looking for, and Bob knew the trees and shrubs where they could be found. Soon he could identify twenty-five species. They found the three to four-inch long cecropia moth cocoons on wild cherry trees. "We could get twenty-five of them in fifteen minutes easy, and they paid Ed twenty-five cents each for them." They dug in tomato beds for sphinx moth chrysalises. Ed reared black widow spiders in aquaria in his apartment, but as Bob insisted, "You could always find plenty under the seat of an old outhouse."

The most lucrative things of course were the morels and truffles we collected for a city restaurant. Well, actually it was me that did the work. I knew what kind of trees and exposures produced each variety. In California, for instance, you will find chanterelles under some Douglas fir and live oaks on hillsides facing south. And they bring good money!

Bob started his horticultural studies at Penn State with the distinct advantage of knowing almost as much as his tutors in some areas, particularly those of a practical nature. When it came to identifying the five or six hundred species of trees and shrubs that grew in and around the campus and in the All American Test Garden, Bob's horticulture professor, Robert Mehl, sometimes relied on Bob to provide any genus, species, and common names he had temporarily forgotten. Professor Mehl and his wife had been married for a long time without children. He was so deliriously happy when his wife finally became pregnant and delivered a son, he named the boy Cladrastis after his favorite tree on the campus, *Cladrastis lutea*. At least it was marginally better than the tree's common name, "yellow root."

Bob developed a keen interest in pomology (the study of fruit growing) but was equally immersed in ornamental culture in the greenhouse and outdoor flora culture. As in many state colleges, much of the funding came from petrochemical industry endowments. This resulted in the strongly recommended use of insecticides, pesticides, herbicides, and fertilizer, but Bob remained convinced that with the right systems it was possible to maintain healthy growth with the limited application of chemical fertilizer and spraying only when insects became a problem. For the most part, he had found that manure and water were the mainstays of good horticulture.

Bob's views were very much at odds with the prevailing view, both then and now. He was taught that the typical growing calendar included the use of as many as twenty-two different sprays on fruiting trees and called for intense row culture for field vegetables with attendant heavy insecticide and herbicide use. However, his experience suggested that careful and judicious use of chemicals based only on local needs and the life cycle of the pest was more prudent. He was in complete opposition to providing the consumer with beautiful yet poisonous harvests—a notion that was unlikely to equip him for a future in industry or the academic institutions it subsidized.

As he did in elementary and high school, Bob tended to modify the curriculum to suit his needs. His enthusiasm, and willingness to take practical responsibility for many of the departments' functions, worked in his favor. He was never under much pressure to meet intellectual academic requirements at the expense of his personal need to be useful and productive. Bob wanted to gain an education, but it was inevitable that he would gravitate toward the practical rather than the intellectual. He worked in the root cellar, in the test garden where "tomorrow's vegetables" were being developed, and because of his great knowledge of bees, in the Entomology Department's bee lab. He knew when certain species of trees were ready for pollination, and would relocate the hives to appropriate groves, so that over time, he could produce some forty different flavors of honey. He excelled at grafting trees for research, and he vastly improved his skills with breeding and rearing poultry for meat and eggs. He considers himself to have been a good botany student, due to his mother's teachings and his own practical experience. He began to learn the genetic and biochemical details behind the processes that he had observed and manipulated instinctively, and the cellular level mechanics that validated his own experience.

Edna meanwhile worked as a design draftsman in the college's navy ordinance research labs, turning out perfect drawings for such things as remote control torpedoes and numerous other advanced defense projects.

Bob also worked at the Jimmy Stradling Greenhouse, preparing baskets and wreaths of flowers for churches and funeral caskets. It was there that he learned the art of dying flowers to meet custom color requirements. These skills stood him in good stead when he went to work for the local flower shop in State College. He was famously fast at making boxwood wreaths and developed quite a reputation for his corsages. He remembers making as many as five hundred for a weekend, which helped when it came to demanding and getting a pay raise from 65¢ an hour to $1!

But it was his expertise at dying corsages that gained him notoriety. He was challenged one day when a tall African American man came in with his girlfriend.

"I hear you can make a flower any color you like?"

"That's right," replied Bob confidently. "What color do you want?"

"Flesh color," said the man, holding out his girl's arm.

After a moment's hesitation, Bob had the man's girlfriend hold out her arm, and within minutes he had blended the dyes and matched her beautiful golden brown skin. "That's just right," said the appreciative customer and promptly purchased the most expensive white orchid (for $3.50) to have it dyed. Bob then sold him on the idea of a matching boutonniere, and reckons the overall effect was about the best he ever achieved. "We remained friendly for several years after that."

One day shortly before Christmas Bob spent an entire day delivering poinsettias in freezing temperatures. It was so cold he had to double wrap the plants before loading them on the van. As Bob was leaning into the van to get at the plants, he split the seam of his pants wide open, but without a safety pin, he had to carry on all day with them torn. At the end of the day, Edna and her mother were appalled that he could do such a thing—mostly because this was one of the days that he wasn't wearing underwear. The humor of the situation escaped his persnickety mother-in-law. She couldn't believe a son-in-law of hers could do such a thing and immediately rushed out to buy him some underwear.

Somehow, between the academic work, the flower shop, Mrs. Dry's garden, and his numerous horticultural projects at the college, Bob still found time to visit five or six widows who were great quilters. He would take them flowers and vegetables, and frequently put his young eyes to use by threading a whole bunch of quilting needles—at least enough to last them until his next visit.

So when Mrs. Dry died, Bob and Edna were able

to move to another similar apartment with one of the widows, Mrs. Gingrich, in return for taking care of her garden, barns, chickens and, of course, the furnace. Right next door to their new quarters was a German butcher, and Bob picked up more work from him, feeding, killing and cleaning his turkeys.

Across the road lived Pat O'Brian, a Speech Department teacher. Bob and Pat became hunting partners, although Pat was a poor shot. It's distinctly possible that Pat's hunting handicap was simply due to a certain lack of attention to detail. He told Bob a story about a trip he made to Harvard for a debating contest where he was invited to stay at the home of a faculty member. He hadn't been in the house long, however, when he managed to sit on the man's Chihuahua as it lay sleeping in a library chair, accidentally killing the poor creature. The host was so distressed he dispatched Pat to a nearby hotel.

Bob completed his studies, gathering far more information and practical experience than the course required, and graduated with a degree in Horticulture in February of 1951. The graduation address was given by Dwight D. Eisenhower, brother of Penn State's president at the time and destined to become president of the United States two years later.

Vi, Edna's mother, Edna and Bob with son Tim at his first Thanksgiving

His address was extremely boring as I recall, and my mind drifted off to thoughts of how lucky I had been to get all this education for free. It hadn't seemed like a great effort, and I felt that I needed to balance the books. I knew there had been a great depletion of the country's forests, and I decided there and then that I would plant trees and give them away for others to plant for the rest of my life. A million, I thought, would be the right number. Well, I believe I have managed about a third of that target to date. Although I have some time left, it doesn't look like I'll make it. Pity, I should have liked to have made good on my promise, but not bad, not bad at all.

Four months before Bob graduated from Penn State, Edna gave birth to their first son, Tim. The college asked Bob to stay on, but it was clear that academic life would not provide the income Bob needed to sustain his family, and he considered numerous offers from horticultural concerns around Pennsylvania. Always looking for more than just a salary, Bob took the time to find an opportunity that might quickly provide the kind of financial independence his own father had enjoyed from an early age. Both he and Edna also favored moving closer to their family homes, and when he was offered a job at Quality Nursery in

Allenwood, owned by Ira Frontz, that offered a base salary plus bonuses linked to sales, Bob jumped at the chance. He felt most at home when he was in rural, small town areas, especially those with that reserved and conservative Pennsylvania Dutch feel, and the bonus gave him all the incentive he needed.

The base yearly salary of $2,500 was a couple of hundred dollars less than the offer to teach at Penn State, but the bonus would be ten percent of increased sales. Sales the previous year had totalled only $7,000, but that was all wholesale business. The first thing Bob did was propagate half a million flower plants for quick retail sale.

He also knew that flowering trees like pink dogwood sold for five times what you could get for the white variety then being offered by the nursery, and he decided this was another way to build sales. He would also add Japanese maples to the nursery's line for similar reasons.

Grafting pink dogwood was a tricky business, but Bob knew the technique well, and he set about training the local farmhands who would be doing the work for sixty-five cents an hour. Despite their gnarled and knobby hands, they performed the delicate task with ease. In fact, they were so productive, Bob felt they were worth more and suggested a raise to one dollar an hour. The owner was fiercely opposed and argued that the employees would only spend the money on beer. He conceded when Bob pushed hard, insisting that they were entitled to the raise whether they spent it on beer or bread. Maybe this is a classic example of the Cannard personality; he's bent on getting own way, but sweetens the pill with a genuine desire for everyone to benefit from "his way."

At the nursery, Bob's inventiveness started to emerge in the form of caged birds, farm animals, and pony rides as a means to bring in business from families. Through a combination of such promotions, retail business boomed, adding to the increased wholesale revenues from higher-ticket items. Bob's efforts paid off. Sales in his first year topped out at $77,000 giving him a $7,000 bonus.

When Bob and Edna relocated to Allenwood with son Tim, they rented part of a duplex owned by an extremely eccentric veterinarian named Doctor McCarthy. Doc McCarthy lived in the other half of the house.

A strange fella was Doc McCarthy. Kept a camel hair coat hanging outside the front door to wear to work. Never cleaned it, and claimed its color meant you couldn't see the various kinds of animal shit that had accumulated on it over the years. You sure could smell it though. Doc McCarthy worked long hours and was always on the run. I helped him out on occasions. Do you know he never stopped at a stop sign in his life. Said he didn't have the time, although he did insist he listened for traffic as he approached an intersection. One time we were walking from the car to a cowshed, and he started urinating, without even breaking his stride. "Why Doc," I said. "I don't mind waiting while you stop to do that." "Certainly not," he said. "You don't get work done standing still, Bob." And do you know he walked on to the cowshed across the yard still urinating. Later on we discovered that he had a double life—kept another family, and not far away either. Maybe that's why he had to work so hard. My God, you wouldn't think he could stop long enough to enjoy it. His advice to a young man was if you wanted to be rich, make friends with people who would rather save money than spend it on a passing fancy. He was so miserly that he had a slice of lard for breakfast. Lard!

Just a couple of miles of country roads separated Bob and Edna's home from the nursery, and the daily drive took Bob to an intersection where he had to stop right opposite a small cottage with a large neatly tended garden usually occupied by its elderly owner. Every day, Bob would wave through his car's open window and shout from just fifteen feet away, "Good morning Mrs. Ulrich." And every day she would keep her eyes down and fail to acknowledge his greeting. It was a not unusual example of the reserved social atmosphere that prevailed in the region, but it was still a big surprise to Bob when several months later she replied out of the blue, "Why good morning Mr. Cannard," as if they'd known each other forever.

Bob had passed some kind of milestone. From then on, Mrs. Ulrich repeated the response every morning, and her entire family made it a point to "cultivate Bob's acquaintance." He became a regular in her home, and their relationship received a further boost when he contributed to the departure of a member of the community, a departure that grieved no one.

On the way to the original interview with Frontz at Quality Nursery, Bob had a flat tire just outside Allenwood and went straight to the local service station. It's owner, who also ran an attached restaurant, flat out refused to fix the tire, and only grudgingly allowed Bob to use the equipment to repair it himself. For the privilege, he charged five times the normal rate for fixing a tire. When Bob complained, the man replied that he only expected to deal with tourists once. Bob had no choice but to pay up if he wanted to make the interview. He did, vowing "to take care of the SOB if ever I get the chance."

That chance came almost a year later when the boss at Quality Nursery, Ira Frontz, took a long vacation. He signed a bunch of blank checks, bought a new car, and left for Texas where his son was stationed in the army. Bob was to take care of his cows, steer, and the chickens—whose eggs were supplied to local businesses, including the restaurant/service station owned by the man who had crossed Bob. This man had also upset a lot of other people when he refused to join the volunteer fire department, even though he was only two blocks from the station. In small town Allenwood, this was not acceptable behavior, but the population was too polite to discuss it openly. People reluctantly continued to patronize the restaurant, where, in return for coffee and a newspaper every day, Ira Frontz supplied the owner with fresh eggs.

With Ira in Texas, Bob decided to give him something a little extra, leaving a few nests to fill with eggs for a week or two in the warm weather until they were well and truly "ripe." He then handed those eggs over with a smile to the man who had entirely forgotten the episode with the flat tire. Bob asked

Bob is barely visible under a Pin Oak he planted for Bill Rumbaugh fifty years before.

a good friend Don Lynch, who was a regular for coffee at the restaurant, to let him know if anythingunusual happened the following morning, which just happened to be a Sunday and the busiest day of the week.

When the owner cracked the first of the new eggs on the grill, the stink was immediate and horrible. The owner quickly apologized to the patrons, scraped the grill clean, threw the offending eggs away, and cracked two more—with the same result. He tried two more—same again. By now the smell was so bad that people were leaving, holding their noses. It was too much for the owner. He cursed long and loud, slammed down his spatula and gave up on serving any more breakfasts.

That day marked the beginning of his end. Business declined and he finally closed up and left, never to be heard from again. Lynch had told everyone in town the story of the eggs. From then on, Bob was solidly accepted and befriended throughout the community, although everyone remained too polite to say quite why.

Some of the Nice Patterson landscaping

"That's the way small towns operate," Bob repeated, when he finished telling this story. "And it was worth it, if only for a slice of Mrs. Ulrich's pie on the way home from work at the end of a hard day."

In addition to retail sales, Bob was handling an increasing number of landscaping jobs through the nursery. Philco in Watsontown made cabinets for radios and the owner Bill Rumbaugh, who "thought he was mister big" had Bob put in three pin oaks outside his factory. A year later he called Bob to spray his elm trees at home against Dutch elm disease. It was supposed to be strictly a single heavy application against the elm bark beetle. But no matter how much Bob tried to talk him out of it, Rumbaugh insisted on having them sprayed every two weeks. So Bob obliged. He sprayed water, but to keep the client happy, he billed him $200 each time.

Bob also did a job for the local bank manager, Nice Patterson, landscaping around his house down by the river in Watsontown. Soon after he started the job, Bob found a small blueberry farm for sale, also close to the Susquehanna. It was $11,000, and Bob already had half of that in cash. So he applied for a bank loan for the balance. But Nice Patterson turned him down. That was a real shock to Bob. Ever since he was six or seven years old he had money in his pocket and had always managed to buy whatever he wanted. And of course he had absolute confidence in his own ability to generate income whenever he needed it. The blueberry farm would certainly help do that. But Nice didn't see it that way, which was unfortunate for him, because Bob immediately doubled or tripled the price of his plants and the Quality Nursery landscaping service.

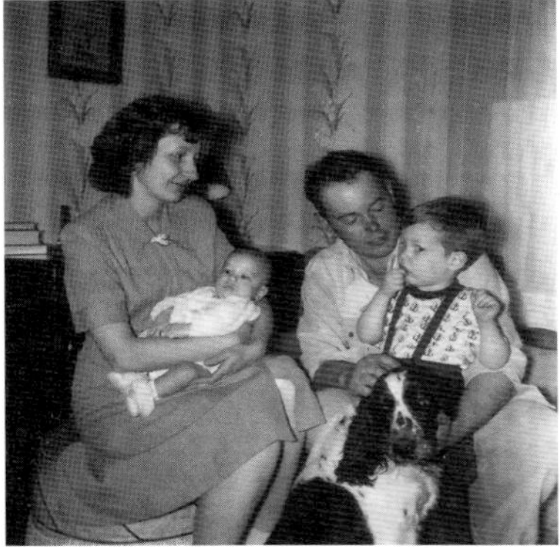
New son Bobby, Tim and "lady"

And would you believe that son of a bitch bragged about how much he was spending on landscaping? There's a good lesson there!

To promote the nursery, Bob involved himself with all manner of horticulture clubs, giving talks and demonstrations, judging and advising. He turned down a directorship with the American Rose Society because it would mean moving to Columbus, Ohio.

One day in the spring of 1953, not long after the birth of his and Edna's second son Bobby on Valentines Day, Bob noticed a man leaving the nursery obviously disgruntled about something. He caught up with the man before he could leave and asked him what the problem was. "I wanted trees that give seeds for the wild birds at my home and your boss says you have none."

This may have been the first time that an environmentally conscious customer had ever walked through the doors and Bob was not going to let him get away. "We have exactly what you're looking for," Bob said, and within half an hour had sold $5,000 worth of trees and shrubs selected entirely for their ability to provide for the local wildlife. Bob later asked Ira why he turned the man away and Ira replied "You told me those trees were trash."

Bob had indeed said that and should not have been surprised when Ira took him literally. The trees may have been no good for ordinary landscaping use, but they were perfect for what the man wanted. It was unreasonable to expect everyone to possess the same flexibility as he did, particularly when it came to sales—but of course Bob did.

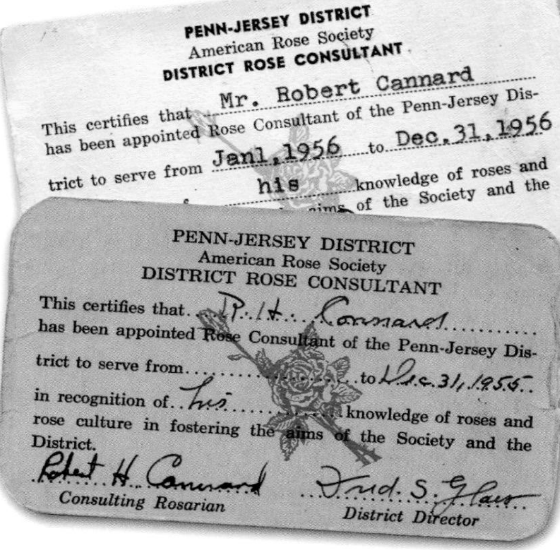
PENN-JERSEY DISTRICT
American Rose Society
DISTRICT ROSE CONSULTANT
This certifies that Mr. Robert Cannard
has been appointed Rose Consultant of the Penn-Jersey District to serve from Jan1,1956 to Dec.31,1956
... his knowledge of roses and ... aims of the Society and the

PENN-JERSEY DISTRICT
American Rose Society
DISTRICT ROSE CONSULTANT
This certifies that R. H. Cannard
has been appointed Rose Consultant of the Penn-Jersey District to serve from .... to Dec. 31, 1955
in recognition of his knowledge of roses and rose culture in fostering the aims of the Society and the District.
Robert H. Cannard
Consulting Rosarian
District Director

Bob went out to the man's summer home, located on twenty acres alongside Loyalsock Creek to plant the trees, getting to know Bill Waldeison well. It resulted in other landscaping jobs for members of Bill's family and, eventually, the offer of a job working for his textile mill.

The Williamsport Narrow Fabric Company produced rickrack, grosgrain, bias tape, upholstery supplies, and a wide range of braids and trimmings. Bob must have made a major impression on Bill, and it's not difficult to see why. At twenty-seven, he was overflowing with energy and confidence in his abilities. In a couple of years he had graduated college, inserted himself into a new community, and become well respected there. He'd turned a moribund nursery into a profitable and growing enterprise, making good money for himself in the process. And he had a new father's pride in a young family. You can depend on the fact that, most of all, he promoted his ability to be able "to get things done," regardless of the nature of the challenge. His early sense of intellectual inferiority, whether real or imagined, had pushed him to become a doer. He had made up for his perceived lack of intellectual acuity by being a practical wizard, and he reveled in it. At home with his siblings, at high school, in the army and at college, he had been able to modify the program to meet his needs, because he became the person who could be relied on to make the root beer, run the garden, manage the hives, get the orchard picked, or butcher the pig. Always appreciative of the good food provided by the women in his community, he had learned how to turn on the charm. And now, he had begun to figure out how to direct others to do the same, by providing enthusiastic direction, giving clear instructions, and rewarding for a job well done. At the heart of all his early business success was an acute understanding of the relationship between purchase price and sale price—and that what was in it for him was in the difference between the two. It's what he learned in Em Sherwood's store when he was just eight years old—you can't go broke making a profit!

Bob accepted the offer and took a job at the mill in Williamsport.

Bob's varied responsibilities included accompanying Bill on some of his sales trips. On one memorable business outing to Philadelphia, Bill insisted they go into a men's shoe store, where he asked to see a pair shoes that were in the window. Holding one of them, he took out a big leather-cutting knife with a curved blade and deftly sliced the sole in half to show Bob the cross section, remarking that it was pretty good construction. (He had started work in a shoe factory at the age of seven.)

> *The clerk's mouth fell open and he dammed near shit. Fortunately, Bill asked me what my size was. He purchased a pair for each of us and paid for the pair he had destroyed, but the clerk still looked dazed when we left.*

Bill Waldeisen's son, another Bob, recalls those times:

> *Bob Cannard came to work for my father, who was president of a narrow fabric textile mill in Williamsport, PA. I am not sure of the actual year but I believe it was in the late forties or early fifties—a long time back to remember many incidentals. He was always a cheerful and boisterous person, just as he is today, and there was much humor in our association.*

The company closed its cafeteria the first week in July, as the mill was closed for inventory. The office people and some of the mill people carried out this task, and at noon we would go over town to a restaurant. There was a Chinese place on the second floor of a building on one of the main streets of town that was a favorite of ours. This particular day was hot and Bob was sitting next to an open window. Somebody pointed out a fly swimming in his water glass and without hesitation Bob jumped up, grabbed the glass, and threw the water out the window. Scared the hell out of the rest of us, and we stampeded for the door. Fortunately no one on the street below was doused, although it would have been quite amusing if there had been.

Another time my brother was driving us over town, and Bob was in the front seat with him. These were the years when hand signals were still used, and for some reason a woman pulled alongside of us and wanted to make a left hand turn in front of us. Not really too bright. She stuck out her arm and pointed almost right at Bob, and again without hesitation, he reaches out and shakes her hand with a comment that made us all laugh.

This was Bob. His booming voice and laughter could be heard throughout the mill. He was a good friend and was missed by many when he left.

Bob should have known from his earlier experience at the machine shop just after the war that he was not right for the industrial environment. It was too stifling, repetitive, and gray. Soon he was yearning to back away from industry and work outdoors within his own community with the people he knew best. "The people at the mill were wonderful, but I consider it one of the most inappropriate jobs I've taken over the years."

All this time, Bob had a hankering for a farm and came close a couple of times. But Edna wasn't so sure. So following in his father's footsteps, he took the Prudential insurance tests. He passed the tests, and soon became one of the best insurance salesmen in the district—benefiting from his wide contacts, good standing, and confident tenacity.

By confident tenacity, that is to say he rarely took no for an answer. At the same time, Bob didn't believe in foisting insurance policies on people who couldn't afford them, even if most of the competition did. He developed closer ties to the people in his community, got an understanding of their personal and business lives' and sold them the insurance they could and should afford. And of course, he used the tried and true Cannard appreciation of good food to cement relationships. The husband of one of his regular customers once stopped him in the street and pointed out to his friend,

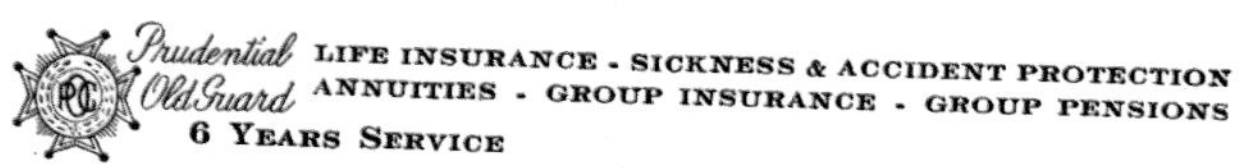

Prudential Old Guard LIFE INSURANCE - SICKNESS & ACCIDENT PROTECTION
ANNUITIES - GROUP INSURANCE - GROUP PENSIONS
6 YEARS SERVICE

ROBERT H. CANNARD
SPECIAL AGENT

THE PRUDENTIAL INSURANCE CO. OF AMERICA
428 MARKET STREET
WILLIAMSPORT, PA.

OFF. TEL.,
322-4658
RES., KE. 8-6891

"I always know when Cannard here is due to call, because my wife gets up at five a.m. and starts baking cakes and cookies."

When a team of competing insurance salesmen hit the area, it invariably resulted in Bob writing more policies. "They did most of the selling job, but the folks in my community wouldn't sign without knowing what I thought of the idea, and I never let them spend more than I knew they could afford."

Bob rarely needed to consult the tables. He memorized the rate books as soon as they came out, using the same techniques he had used for the Latin names of plants as a child and the secret codes during World War II. He made a comfortable living working just a few hours a day. His boss, George Hartman, paid him the ultimate compliment when he said, "Cannard, you're the only man I ever hired who was on the wrong side of this desk."

A funny thing happened in the process of being hired by Prudential. George Hartman, the district manager, visited our home in Allenwood. It was between Christmas and New Years in 1954. I had gone to the local livestock auction in Dewart, mainly just to see what was going on. While there, a crate of Muscovy ducks was put up for sale. There were five or six big ducks, and the bidding stuck at two dollars. I thought I had time to kill and clean those birds, so I bid three dollars, and got them. Well, lo and behold, it wasn't one crate I'd bought but five or six. So I went home with thirty or thirty-five big fat ducks. "Oh my god," said Edna, "we can freeze some and eat some, but you'll have to give a lot away.

It was bitter cold, and I was cleaning them on our enclosed back porch and kitchen. Ducks and feathers all over the place, what a mess. George Hartman chose that moment to call at our home as he did with all prospective agents. "I've never hired anyone while they were plucking ducks," he said, "but I suppose there's always a first time." Feathers and all, he told me I was hired.

When I went to see George before I left for California, he reminded me of the ducks, and that I had given him a big fat duck, cleaned and ready to cook, to take home. It was at that last interview when he paid me the ultimate compliment, telling me that I was the only man he ever hired

who he thought was on the wrong side of the desk. Before I left his office the last time, he also said, "I've never met a man like you before, Bob. You will be successful at anything you put your mind to. Good luck in California."

During his years in Allenwood, Bob's love of history began to pay off in the form of an eye for antiques. He collected and traded historic documents, books, coins, and furniture. He restored vintage autos. Being so well connected to his community, he always had his ear to the ground for a good deal, and he took advantage only when he knew absolutely that the item in question could be turned for a profit right away if need be.

Since moving to Allenwood and starting at Quality Nursery five years before, Bob had developed friendships with a rich array of eccentrics, and their names roll off his tongue in the stories he tells about them as if he is painting a picture. For years, Charlie "over-the-river" Rightmeyer rowed across the Susquehanna for trysts with a woman on the far bank. Handy Fegley, born in the 1870s, saw the wide river so jammed with logs that had broken loose from their holding pens upriver when the floods of 1889 hit that a man could have walked from bank to bank on their tops. Handy, his father, and Daddy Forseman, dragged those logs out, sawed off the brands, and built huge barns. After Daddy Forseman died, in a similar display of parsimony, Handy retrieved the ice that had been used to keep the body fresh in the coffin during the appropriate "viewing" period, and not wanting to waste it, threw it down the well to cool the drinking water. Handy came from Elvira, a homestead town in the middle of White Deer Valley that was emptied during World War II to store dynamite and then turned into a white-collar prison known as the "Country Club."

Then there was Mutt King who came from a fine line of poachers. Mutt's father, Ed King, was the strongest man Bob ever knew. At sixty years old he could hang by his fingers from a rafter with one hand—and not with his fingers hooked over the rafter but gripping the sides. Mutt's hand had been mangled when the dull-witted Ralph Farley started up the harvesting machinery while Mutt's hand was in there clearing the husks from the prongs. Ralph's own daddy blew himself up along with a big oak stump he was trying to remove by White Deer Creek. His widow called Bob when she found a milk can full of coins and Bull Durham sacks stuffed with bills hidden in the concrete floor of their home—ninety-four thousand dollars and change Bob counted, in coins and old "gold standard bills" all dated before 1929, and long taken out of circulation. The manager at the bank told Mrs. Farley that there would be a big penalty for converting old currency—and a service charge, too. "Nonsense," said Bob, and then called the Federal Reserve. They confirmed what Bob knew; the money could be exchanged at face value, and so Mrs. Farley and Ralph got the full $94,000. They offered Bob a bagful for himself, but he turned it down.

Mrs. Sigel of McKeesville and her deceased husband, Fritz, had restored an old manse after they returned from his native England where they had lived most of their life. She had a lovely home and garden and belonged to many garden clubs and rose societies. She gave Bob a gold coin holder inscribed "Fritz." Then there was the boy who lived down the road from Bob and Edna's next home, Willowgate, who had been introduced to tobacco at the age of four by his grandfather. He was allowed to chew an old cigar all day at kindergarten and when he went to town—to stop him getting wild from withdrawal.

All the time, the Cannard household had been steadily growing. Third son Edward came in 1954, and James in 1957, the year that Bob and Edna purchased "Willowgate" near Dewart. It was a beautiful house, built in 1778 or 9, standing on a rise overlooking woods and farmland, surrounded by lawns. It had outbuildings for workshops and birdcages, a big pond for the boys to swim in, plenty of land for a few animals, the inevitable vegetable gardens, orchard, and the ubiquitous Cannard poultry.

Idyllic you'd think, but apparently not so. Winters were long and hard. "The boys needed more opportunity." As tightly connected as Bob was with the solid Pennsylvania Dutch community, to him the local environment had begun to lack imagination, enterprise, and dynamism. He had the pioneer's itchy feet. He thought briefly about heading south, to the Shenandoah Valley, but the Civil Rights movement, while inevitable and totally justified in Bob's eyes, was going to bring unrest and conflict.

Willowgate

"And I wasn't going to subject my boys to a situation I didn't know how to confront myself."

One day, he took a call in the kitchen at Willowgate while Edna and the boys were sitting down to dinner. Edna asked what the call was about. "I've bought a dead elephant," said Bob, matter-of-factly. He'd paid a circus twenty-five dollars for it, and the call was to confirm that his friend at the abattoir was willing to skin it and remove most of the flesh in return for the hide. Bob reckoned the skeleton would make a great teaching tool and fun project for the boys. They would hang it from the trees, with the bones all wired together, just like he'd seen prehistoric fossil bones set up in museums. But first they had to remove the remaining flesh. So they wrapped great chunks of the elephant's body in chicken wire and put them out in the field so that the wild creatures could strip the bones without making off with them.

The project was never finished. Although Bob reserved two feet for umbrella stands that were later brought West, the bones remain hidden away in a forgotten barn somewhere near Willowgate. But the elephant was deeply prophetic.

The expression "seeing the elephant" had been adopted during the 1849 California gold rush to describe the feeling that consumed those who were intent on going west to find their fortunes. It represented an exotic sight, an unequalled experience, the adventure of a lifetime.

Well, Bob Cannard had seen the elephant, literally and metaphorically. It was only a matter of time, and in 1959 the entire Cannard family, including latest arrival Tom, left Pennsylvania in a station wagon to head west on their adventure of a lifetime.

Edna was not as wildly enthusiatic as Bob. She had already moved many times and was finally feeling settled and secure at Willowgate. It was a beautiful home, with everything she could ever want. Her parents lived nearby, and she had a network of close friends. Bob was something of a man of leisure, needing only to work one day a week to guarantee a comfortable living for her and the boys.

All that Edna held most dear was in this green and pleasant corner of Pennsylvania, and it was only by convincing herself if it didn't work out in California they would return, that she was able to give it a try.

All their friends said "you'll be back," and Edna hoped it might be true.

RANDOM RECOLLECTIONS

Bob Cannard has thousands of memories that spill out in random chronology, linked by the most tenuous of threads. Sometimes they are best left in haphazard order, rather than allocated to their appropriate place in the story. So here is a selection of such freewheeling notions.

. . . Of course, in those one-roomed schoolhouses the teacher had to maintain strict control, but they couldn't do the same in the outhouse. There were three seats for the girls on one side and three for the boys on the other. When it was full with kids—I must have been in the fourth or fifth grade—I would get a piece of weeping willow and reach through a hole at the end to tickle their asses. But willow wasn't at all scratchy . . . . . .

. . . Do you know that kids from the city would eat horse turds? And the kids from Panama visiting Danville; didn't know what they were, I suppose . . . In the Civil War the soldiers wiped their backsides with their shirttails! Can you believe it! And in the country it was corncobs or Sears catalogs—now they would be scratchy. And it wasn't unusual for kids to be sewn into their underwear for the winter . . .

. . . I went for walks in thin sweaters in the winter, to toughen myself up. And I opened the bedroom windows wide. My brother John hated it. He would shut the windows and I would open them again and by the morning there'd be snow on the beds—ha!

. . . My friend Art Young and I pushed a kid who was a polio victim in a wicker buggy to and from school every day: through the junkyard to the bridge over Blizzard Run. We'd stop and take a leak off the trestles and try to write our names in the snow banks below. Art was black, smart too—about as smart as me anyway. When Alice Small, a good Christian woman and English teacher at school refused to advance Art, I complained to my father. I told him we both had the same grades and it was because Art was black. I told Art's cousin Chip too. He only graduated because he was top of his class and they couldn't fail him.

. . . Vi told me that when she was a girl on the farm

milk was usually kept in crocks that were placed in the middle of a small spring – springs that were on most rural properties, and often covered with a small shed. The springs were a constant fifty-three degrees, which kept the milk even cooler in the crocks. They would put a couple of boards on top of the crocks, and then other food items could be kept cool. Vi said that if there was the slightest gap in the boards, rats would lower their tails down into the milk, then lift them up to lick off the milk. Did it all the time, she said. You could tell because the level of the milk in all the crocks was the same distance from their tops. . .

. . . It was Vi who told me about squirrels weighing the nuts too. Yes, they weigh nuts to see if they're good or not, then only open up the good ones. Hickory nuts I should say. Well in the sixth or seventh grade, I was intrigued by the idea of skinning and mounting a squirrel, and there was one shot next door. So my brother Tom—the chemist—made me up some arsenic paste to preserve the skin, that would you believe I rubbed on to the squirrel skin with my bare hands, my hands! I made a wire armature, with padding where it was needed, and remounted the skull. Then you cover it with horse hair, and sew the skin back on, tail to neck. Figured it out myself. I used marbles for eyes —peewees worked for squirrels —and painted on the toenails. Four of them I did. Squirrels I mean, and a chipmunk. But the first squirrel I did for Vi, with its front feet posed as if it was weighing nuts. Ha! She put it on top of the radio in the living room. I sold the others, but never made much of a profit. I tried birds, but they were not as good as the squirrels. Never did a rabbit—wanted to.

. . . My brother George was what you'd call bohemian: brilliant, but bohemian, registered democrat and a self-taught artist. He made pastoral candles in the basement to give to the church. Huge they were, and we had to cut a hole in the ceiling for him to pour the beeswax from the room above. When he had convalesced in Colorado after his bout with TB, he applied for a job as an engraver at the Denver Mint and would you believe he did a sample piece for them and got the job. Never done an engraving in his life but figured he could do it!

He was like me in that he could work out practical things in his head first to make doing them easier. He composed music in his head too, and held patents from when he worked for Wurlitzer on electric organs. He never worried about income because he knew he could always get by. He would stop someone on the street and ask if they'd like a portrait, or a painting of their house. He always had an easel and paints in his car, and a flat platform on the car roof to sit on for landscapes. He became an outstanding advocate for and champion of seniors in his later years.

George insulated all the walls of his cabin in Dumont, Colorado with books from floor to ceiling. Edna and I saw it on our trip west with the boys. George lost his sense of smell and that's why they believed he died in a residential hotel fire in Sunbury when he was sixty-three. Couldn't smell the smoke until it was too late. He did a painting for Edna and I of our home in Allenwood. Cost me a gallon of whiskey plus two pints to finish it off. . .

. . . Heating homes was a big problem during the Depression. We would jump up on a coal train when it stopped for a short time at a couple of places as it passed through Danville to the steel mills. We threw coal off until the train started up again, jumped down and filled our handcarts with what lay on the ground. I took mine over to trade some to Mr. White who made sausages and bologna. In the summer the place was full of flies and they were thick around the opening of the meat grinder. But the bologna was good if a bit spotty, and I went back with a ring of it and the rest of the coal to my hut, built against the side of a neighbor's barn, not far from home. It had good wood walls and a coal-fired pot-bellied stove, a small one. I was very proud of my hut, and the other kids thought it special to be invited in. I always had heat, and food. And I always had money in my pocket too. That was important to me. I not only worked for Em from an early age, but I knew enough to never buy anything that I couldn't sell for more. And I learned it was smart to know the value of things and how to improve that value. To be in control of a bartering situation. . .

. . . When Handy Fegley was a boy in White Deer Valley, there were lots of flies. So they had "fly brooms," slices of newspaper tacked to a stick, and the children waved them around to keep the flies on the move. . .

. . . I didn't mind putting in hard work to make something worthwhile. I had to get up before daybreak to collect maple sap from trees more than a mile away and

carry it home in five-gallon buckets. It took eleven gallons to make just a gallon of maple syrup. And dammit if my brother John wasn't drinking it up by the glassful before it was halfway boiled down. . . .

. . . I learned how to see value where other people didn't —in antiques and old documents, maps and books. But most of all in coins, coins sometimes of great value passing through all kinds of hands without anyone being aware. And more frequently coins with value just a little above face value. I guarantee you that if I purchased a hundred dollars worth of regular coins in circulation today, I could find enough of special interest to collectors to make more profit than the going interest rate for investment accounts. Knowledge is power. I have a collection today, but nowhere near as good as my son Tim's. He can identify the finest of differences in quality and adds great value to his collection all the time. He has the fifth best collection of silver dollars in existence . . .

. . . Tim could smell out certain people too, even after they'd left the house. He always knew when the area manager for the Prudential had called by. Nasty man. Dogs would always try to bite him, and female customers would invite me inside and tell him to stay on the porch. He was very careful about his personal grooming and resented that Tim could tell he had been in the house five hours earlier. . .

. . . I had great relationships with my Prudential clients, because they were part of my community. I used to call on a wealthy farmer by the name of Fogelman. Always took out insurance for his children and grandchildren. He told me that his father was a farmer before him, and at the end of one harvest noticed a lot of Canada geese in the field gleaning the corn. When they had finished feeding, they took off, leaving one with a broken wing that came round the farm buildings. The older Mr. Fogelman took it in and fed it while the wing healed, and it took to following him around as he did the farm chores. Quite a companion it became. Anyway, one morning the following spring, the goose followed Fogelman as he went out in the dark with a lantern to milk the cows before sun up, just as it had come to do every morning. But as they approached the cow shed, a flock of Canada geese flew high overhead, and the pet at his side looked up, startled, then raced off in their direction with wings flapping furiously and launched itself into the air. It all happened so fast it wasn't until the bird was climbing rapidly away that Mr. Fogelman realized it had swept up the lantern with the handle round it's neck and was

flying like a bright beacon into the dark of the morning sky, honking happily as it rejoined the flock. The following fall, towards the end of harvest time, the goose returned to the farm at the head of the flock. And this time, there were five young geese with lanterns around their necks, shining brightly in the twilight. . .

. . . Did I tell you about training for the Olympics? I swam in the Susquehannah River for hours alternating long periods of just keeping pace with the four knot current and occasional sprints a quarter mile upriver. A teacher by the name of Smith encouraged and trained me. He pushed me hard but the war put an end to the Olympic Games. It was in '38 for the '40 Olympics. Or was it in '42 for the '44 Olympics? Nevermind, it was one of the two . . .

. . . It was the summer of fifty four and I was driving along a dirt road by the side of the Susquehannah River. I saw a field full of ripe melons and a man working. "How are the melons?" I shouted. "Try one," he said, "best I've had in years." So I did, and he was right . "How would you like to sell 'em all?" I asked him, and he damn near fell over. "Well I guess for the right price . . ." I ended up buying the lot for $200, and it took a while to load just a portion of them—several hundred pounds—into my truck. I took them back to Williamsport Narrow Fabrics where I was working and told the boss that I had a lot more where these came from. "But we're in the braid business Bob, not melons."

"We'll give them to the workers," I said, "cheer 'em up." And we did. My boss Bill Waldeisen thought it was a great idea. . .

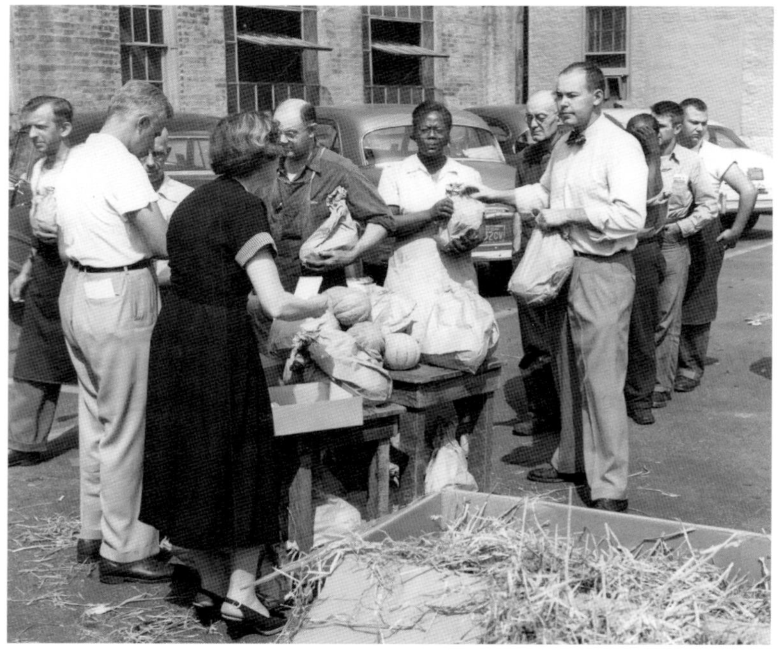

. . . In those days there were all kinds of fire and brimstone religious groups—Holy Rollers we called them—and one in Danville was named the Pillar Of Fire Church. They would get so worked up at their services that the congregation would go into a kind of mass hysteria I suppose you'd call it. Anyway, they would rave and rant and froth at the mouth and so on—quite a performance. Well one hot summer Sunday, I would have been about twelve or thirteen years of age, Joe Gerst comes to see me with a plan to have some fun with the folks at the Pillar of Fire. He'd rigged up a couple of hoses, one on each side of the church which was built toward the bottom of what we called Nanny Goat Hill. The windows were wide open to let in the bit of a breeze, and we waited until the congregation were all inside and took up our places at the hoses, Joe on the uphill side.

We waited a while and sure enough it wasn't long before the sermon and singing and testimonies had them all hot and bothered. Heads were nodding madly, eyes glazed over or closed altogether, and arms waving wildly in the air. They were wailing in an incomprehensible mumbo jumbo. Lost to the world they were, many of them rolling around on the floor in a kind of ecstacy.

And that's when Joe gave me the sign. We turned the hoses full on and sprayed the water in through the open windows. They were all well soaked before they began to come out of their trances, and the wailing turned to screams and shouts. I dropped my hose and ran as fast as I could down the hill. Joe ran round to the front of the church, and once the sodden people spilling out the door saw him, he set off up Nanny Goat Hill with the congregation in hot pursuit. But they were no match for Joe, he was the fastest runner in High School. He soon lost them in the bushes. I had run round the back of a mill at the bottom of the hill and in about ten minutes Joe joined me at our pre-arranged hiding place. We laughed and laughed so hard our sides were aching and the tears were running down our cheeks. What a day! . . .

Joe Gerst could run down a wild goat on Nanny Goat Hill, and did, to provide the meat for one of Bob's great feasts for neighborhood kids. He gave Bob deer ribs to make musical "bones." Joe joined the Merchant Marine at the outbreak of WWII. His ship was torpedoed and Joe was lost in the cold waters of the north Atlantic on his very first trip to Murmansk.

CHAPTER THREE

TRANSPLANTED. THE MOVE WEST

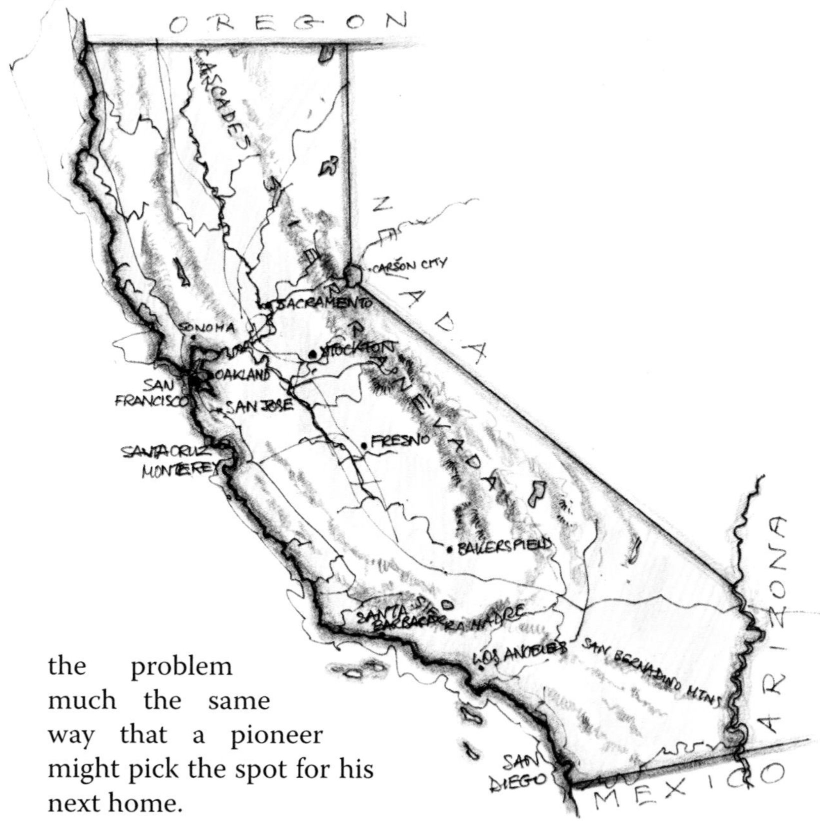

Choosing California as the destination for the Cannards was easy; deciding where in California took much longer. Bob knew that anywhere good for growing apples was good for humans too. The winter vernalization of 400 to 600 hours of cool temperatures that they required would mean defined seasons, and Bob needed that too. That kind of climate would allow him to raise the same plants he had grown up with in Danville, and he wanted a place where you could enjoy fresh fruit from May to November. But his list of other requirements was as long as your arm: daylight hours, temperature ranges, frost free days, winter sun, rainfall, humidity, fog free, elevation, scenery, industry, agriculture, horticulture, transport, water availability, towns, schools, colleges, politics, history. All of these factors needed to be taken into account. He approached the problem much the same way that a pioneer might pick the spot for his next home.

He wrote to every chamber of commerce in California. He sent away for published information on every city and county, studied maps and surveys, and everything the USDA had on crops and conditions. By the end of 1958, he had short-listed nine areas of particular interest—from Eureka in the north to San Diego, 700 miles to the south. Now all he had to do was visit each location. His outstanding performance for Prudential meant that he was able to maintain all his accounts and hit his personal targets working only a couple of days a week, so taking time off was not a problem.

At the start of 1959, Bob's sister-in-law Irene was moving to California to take a position in the hematology department at Stanford University. This was a good opportunity to kill two birds with one stone, and Bob decided he would take some time out and drive her cross-country to Stanford. To cut down on unproductive time, he decided to make the trip non-stop, and apart from three short periods when Edna's sister drove, they completed the three thousand-mile journey in just three days, arriving in Southern California two days before Irene was due at Stanford. It gave them time to briefly check out Santa Barbara, San Bernardino, and Pasadena. They called on Edna's cousin, a very successful Santa Monica real estate developer, who suggested that it wouldn't be too long before he was ready to retire and leave the company in someone else's hands. There wasn't much chance that this would be of real interest to Bob, because he despised the type of huge subdivisions that were springing up—all featuring the same model home. But it was good to know that work of some kind was available, although the thought of not finding exactly what he wanted was inconceivable to Bob.

They drove north through the Central Valley, stopping only long enough to confirm that the featureless expanse was not for Bob, even if he could have taken the broiling summer heat. When he and Edna visited UC Davis, near Sacramento, a couple of years later, to follow up on a job offer at the college, it was Edna who said, "It would boil my eyeballs."

There was the possibility of a job in the botany department at Stanford, and Bob did talk to a few people there after dropping off his sister-in-law. But that possibility remained in the background, and his intent to find a rural setting remained the priority.

He went to the Santa Clara Valley and liked it a lot. But the rate at which green fields were being incorporated into San Jose was certain to mean that the area would be built over and built up far too soon. So he headed north to San Francisco, over the Golden Gate bridge and on to the bucolic valleys in the North Bay—Santa Rosa, Sonoma, Napa, and on up all the way to Eureka. But it was those North Bay valleys with their ranches, farms, and the beginnings of a wine industry that caught his attention. It must have helped that Petaluma, at the southern end of Sonoma County, had been the egg and chicken capital of the United States, and that the renowned horticulturist Luther Burbank had chosen Santa Rosa as the place for his work. And then to the west was Sebastopol, home to vast apple orchards.

So with a preference for this area already forming, he picked up every scrap of published information he could find and headed back to Pennsylvania.

He agreed with Edna that they would close up "Willowgate" and move to Santa Rosa for a year. It would be their headquarters for further research, being halfway between Bob's favorites of Sebastopol and St. Helena. At the end of the school year in 1959, they packed the boys, some clothes, and essential papers into the station wagon and drove west into the sunset, following a similar path to that taken by the Donner

Party, but with less dramatic results.

As you can tell from Bob's notes on the following pages, the trip was far less challenging in a station wagon than a covered wagon—and a whole lot faster. The family was soon in a rented house in Santa Rosa, and the boys enrolled in school.

For the next year, as soon as the boys were out of school on a Friday afternoon, the family jumped in the wagon and headed off to spend the weekend crisscrossing the counties of northern California, examining every city, town, and village in the quest to narrow down the long list of potential locations for their future home. They minutely explored every back road and street, examined every school and community. Bob was determined to leave no stone unturned, and while his energy for the search seemed boundless, the weekends became miserable for the boys. "Do we have to go away this weekend father?" was the complaint every Friday as they were ordered into the station wagon. But there was no let up.

The long and exhaustive investigation continued through the winter, and by the end of the school year, Bob and Edna had narrowed the probable list down to Sonoma Valley and St. Helena, a spa town at the north end of Napa Valley, and only twenty miles east of Santa Rosa. Work opportunity was not a major consideration for Bob, because he had absolute confidence in his own ability to make money wherever he found himself. Early on, he did visit the area offices of Prudential Insurance in the Napa and Sonoma county seats. The management did not impress him. "I knew right away that I could do better than any of 'em," he declares.

And to prove the point, he asked to take the state license test immediately. They protested that it would take time to learn the local rules and regulations. "Just give me a sample contract and I'll be back," Bob said. Sure enough he took the contracts home, read them through, and soon aced the tests. But he took an instant dislike to the pompous manager of the Napa branch and decided to work out of the Santa Rosa office.

The area staff manager was Ed Sellman. He and his wife Elsie have been life-long family friends with Bob and Edna, and remain the only positive links that Bob has with the Prudential in California.

Just a few hours a week it took. I knew exactly how to dig out the prospects, meet people, establish my credentials, look at their needs and sell them the appropriate policies. It was a boom time, and I knew how conservative rancher types think. They understood the need to plan for the future. Conservative—conserve for the times ahead. They knew the uncertainty of the weather, the need to be ready for lean years. You save summer food for the winter, and you save

Continued on page92

Sunday
Crossed into Nevada in the morning and arrived at Reno about three in the afternoon. Edna and I decided not to get a divorce while we were here. Seemed to be a lot of activity for a Sunday. Headed west and into California about six p.m. and into Sacramento by about eight o'clock. Stayed in a very nice motel and had a first taste of sleeping in California. The family had a good swim in the pool.

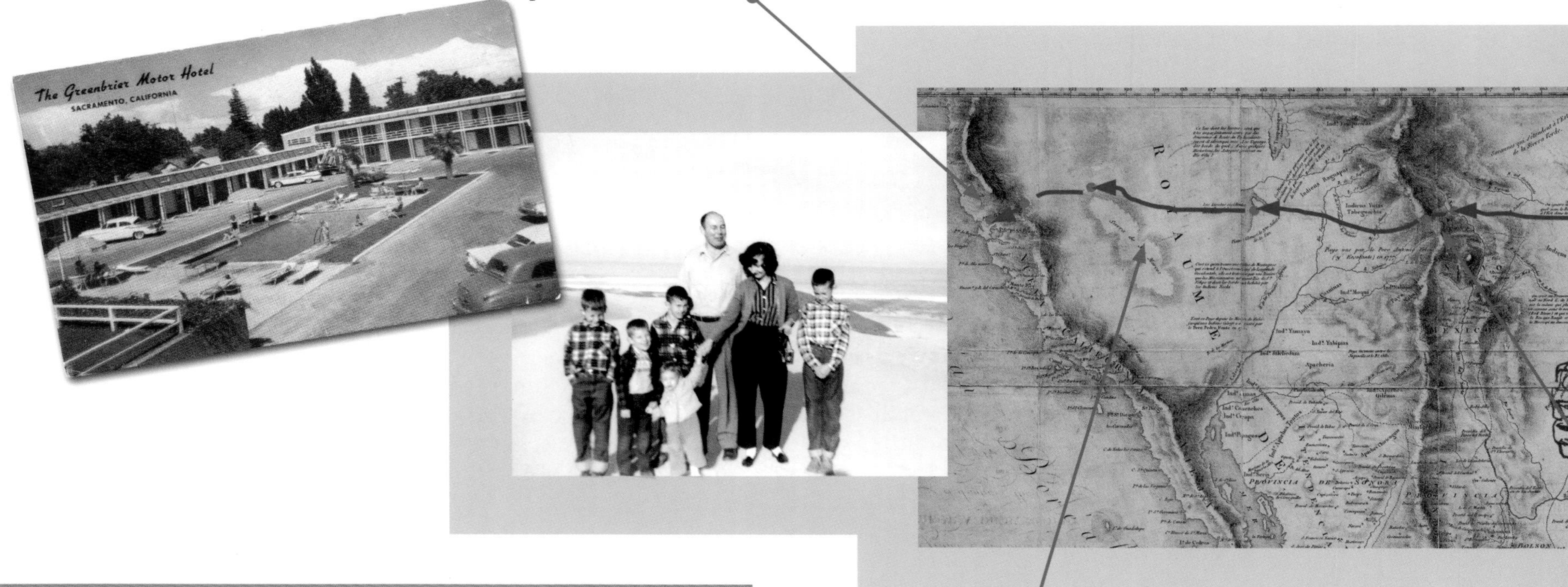

Saturday
Continued through Colorado and Utah into Salt Lake City by suppertime. Not too nice a place - I don't know how Brigham kept all his wives happy here. Crossed the salt flats west of Salt Lake and saw where they hold the big speed races. Kept lots of ice in cups to cool the boys

"I should say we had a very easy crossing. Nobody sick. Tom slept most of the way and got plenty of attention from the boys. Car and trailer worked well. No flats or any trouble at all. The boys behaved well, and Edna seemed to enjoy the trip. Father just plugs along taking one day after the next."

[In fact, Edna says to this day that this first trip across the country was the best week she had with the family in her life.]

Thursday

Got a late start and didn't get to Hannibal, Missouri until after lunch. Terribly strong warm winds. Very good roads though and arrived St, Joseph, Missouri about suppertime. Crossed into Kansas and just kept ahead of a violent hailstorm. Nice rolling country. Stopped at Marysville, start of the Pony Express and let the boys try out one of the saddles at the museum.

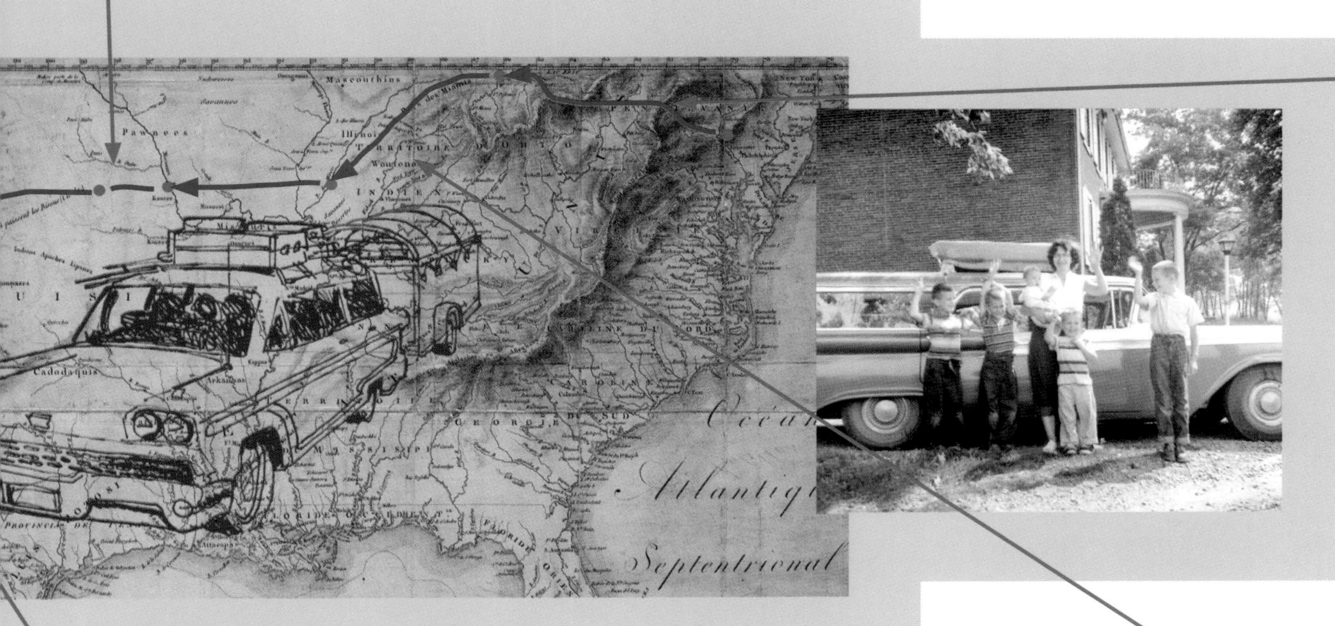

Tuesday

Went to Harrisburg on Route 15, got on the turnpike and headed west. Had a little rain just before Pittsburgh. Spent the night just west of Toledo, Ohio

Friday

Traveled through Kansas and Colorado. Spent the afternoon at George's cabin in Dumont, Colorado, looking over the trash. Everything in terrible shape. Didn't load much in the car to take with us. Showed the boys the property where my mother was born in Idaho Springs, and the location of grandfather's gold and silver claims. Mother and I felt a little squeamish going over the Continental Divide at Berthaud Pass, but still nobody got carsick yet. Spent the night at a national park just west of the pass.

Wednesday

Started early and and headed south through Ohio to get on Route 36 west of Indianapolis. Everbody traveling well. Nobody gotten sick in their stomach yet. Traveled to Springfield, Illinois on Route 66, arrived about six-thirty and toured the Lincoln Shrines. Bought two dishes from the home of Lincoln's neighbor. Same pattern that Abe had in his house. Stopped at a motel just west of Springfield

Continued from page 89

funds in the good times for when it's not so easy. That's the road to independence and the way to take responsibility for your own actions.

Living in a rented house in Santa Rosa curtailed Bob's horticultural ventures, so he raised canaries instead. When it came time to return to Pennsylvania in June of 1960 to sell the farm and tie up affairs for the permanent move west, their cage full of birds went inside the station wagon along with the five boys. It was cramped and uncomfortable, but they made the most of it. They camped or stayed in motels, visiting all the places of interest along the way. In Jackson Hole, Wyoming, the canaries got loose. "They didn't go far and I managed to catch them, all but one. I had strapped a bird net on either side of the roof rack—just in case."

It took a year to cut the ties with Pennsylvania, and after yet another cross country drive with boys, birds and belongings (the dog was air freighted), the Cannard family arrived back in Santa Rosa in August of 1961, having finally decided the area was close to ideal. The same realtor that had rented them a home on the previous visit soon found them a place to buy on Grace Drive. An ex-official of the state of Montana by the name of John Kiel owned the house. Nearly ninety years old, Mr. Kiel was deeply nostalgic for Big Sky Country and had decided to return to Montana to die.

The sale went through quickly and three weeks later the boys were in school and the family had moved in to their new home. But it wouldn't be home for as long as they thought. As Bob was trimming hedges in front of the house over the Thanksgiving weekend, he heard his name called and turned to find Mr. Kiel standing at the gate, demanding to buy the house back as soon as possible. "It's too damn cold to die in Montana," he complained. Mrs. Kiel insisted that they live in the same house, and so Kiel was willing to be very generous if Bob agreed to part with the house so soon after moving in. While the realtors looked for a new place for Bob and the family, Kiel and his wife would be at the Occidental Hotel near the center of town.

Nothing quite right had turned up until one weekend early the following February, when Bob went on one of his regular trips to the Pagani winery in Kenwood, eight miles south of Santa Rosa in Sonoma Valley, "The Valley of the Moon." One of only four wineries then in the valley, Pagani would fill customer's containers direct from barrels for around a dollar a gallon. "Interesting man Julius Pagani, always laughing. Used to meet with his friends every day and they would all speak Italian. Julius didn't say much, but he would laugh and laugh —in Italian I suppose."

Bob made his purchase and returned to the car. Close by, on the west side of the highway opposite what is now Swede's Feed, there was a small nursery fronted by a little store. On an impulse Bob went in to find the elderly owners huddled next to a kerosene heater.

Bob introduced himself, then on an impulse said confidently, "I understand this place is for sale."

"Why how did you know?" replied the little old lady.

"In fact it is, but we haven't told anyone yet."

By the end of the day, they had shaken hands on the deal and two weeks after that, Bob and Edna were the proud owners of the Kenwood Nursery. They had also made a windfall of $5,000 on the sale of the Grace Drive house back to the Kiels.

When the Cannards took over the nursery, all it had going for it was a great location and the license to operate. It desperately needed revitalizing. The place was full of toxic chemicals, and the first thing Bob did was get rid of drums of parathion, the poisonous orchard spray that resulted in ill-health among local fruit farmers, and possibly the death of one—Palmer Peterson. All the stock, including potted camellias that had been around since 1947, was put on sale right away, and Bob set about building up new stocks of plants and shrubs, starting his own seedlings and grafts and buying in what he couldn't grow.

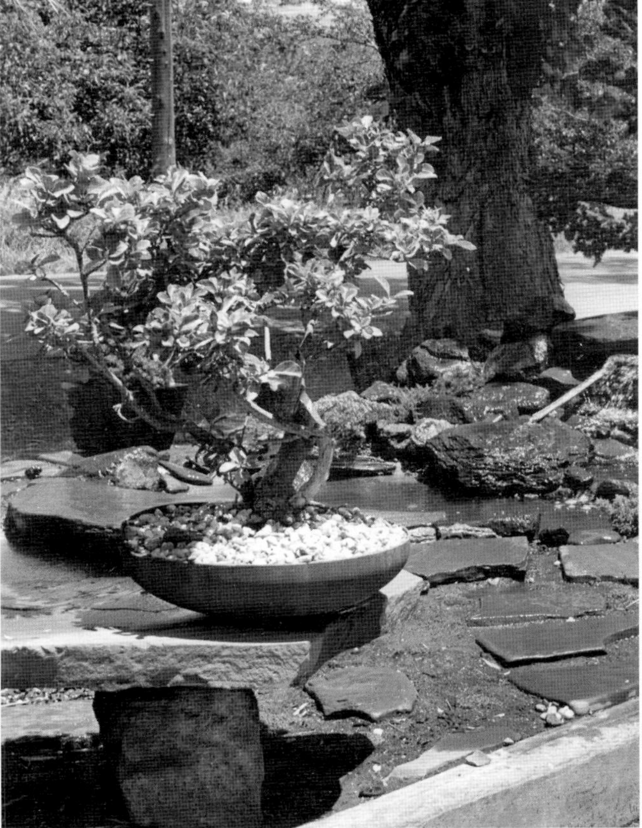

The very first customer purchased a can of tree seal for $1.15, putting down a dollar bill, a dime and a nickel. Bob picked up the nickel immediately and as soon as the customer had left, he quickly took it to Edna and showed her what was a buffalo nickel—in almost uncirculated condition. "I sold it to a fella from Humboldt for $20!"

A fanatic for researching the market, it was Bob's practice to visit competing nurseries all over the county and beyond, to make sure he was up on whatever was new or fashionable, and to figure out what it would take to do better himself. On these visits, he was intrigued that bonsai trees were frequently on display but rarely for sale. But he was interested more in the fact that these little trees commanded big prices.

Reading everything he could on the subject, he came to the conclusion that the reason for scarcity was that nursery owners believed only experts with long experience could master what was a subtle combination of art and science developed by the Chinese before 1300 A.D. and then taken to Japan. Bob would not be intimidated by any of this. After some preliminary experimentation, he and son Bobby would be turning out bonsais by the dozen with sales to match—all at an impressive $12-$15, for two dollars worth of tree.

He found just the right shallow pots in San Francisco and contracted with wholesalers from the Anderson area in northern California, and north of Flagstaff, Arizona, to collect native trees that had been stunted by rugged location and harsh climate. "Nothing higher than your knee," Bob told them. When they turned up with truckloads of trees, most of which were up to his shoulders, he still managed to select a lot that he reckoned would be ideal for manipulating into bonsais. Despite their small size, they already looked "old" because they were—around thirty -five years for every inch of the relatively thick trunks. Exposing the roots a little, and adding moss to the soil surface to imitate grass, added to the illusion. Small pots would restrict winter root growth and severely limit subsequent vegetative growth.

The illusion of even greater age was fairly easily achieved by looking at nature. We all recognize an old tree when we look across the fields at a particular specimen, but why does it look old? It has a large trunk. It has a flat top, whereas a young tree is pointed by its upward growth. The few big branches are spreading wide and being pulled down by gravity. Some of the roots and rocks at the base are exposed, having been washed clean by water running down the trunk over the years. The bark is cracked and gnarled with age and maybe there has been storm damage. Whatever it is, we just know it looks old. Create the same illusion in a small potted plant and it will look similarly old —a bonsai. First the Chinese and then the Japanese learned the techniques that would bring the look of the mountains to their gardens, in miniature.

Inspired by the sight of fully-grown trees silhouetted on the ridges along Sonoma Valley, Bob and son Bobby learned, with practice, to prune so as to form foliage "clouds" that floated around the trunk and branches that had been wired to imitate the contortions of an old, old tree. They became so good at it that they could "make" a bunch of bonsai from their own grafted stock or stunted natives on a Sunday morning and sell some of them the same afternoon.

But many of Bob's best bonsais would take more like a couple of years to create, and people would come from all over in the hope of finding a prize-winning example of the art, for which they were happy to part with upwards of $250.

In seven years, Bob sold as many as 70,000 bonsai. Large trees would go for thousands, and over the years, Bob supplied as many as 200 of these to landscape contractors who installed them in a number of Las Vegas hotels and malls. He still has a few of the larger ones today. Besides the bonsai, Bob estimates the number of trees and shrubs he sold during eight years at the nursery added to the tree population of the Sonoma Valley by half a million.

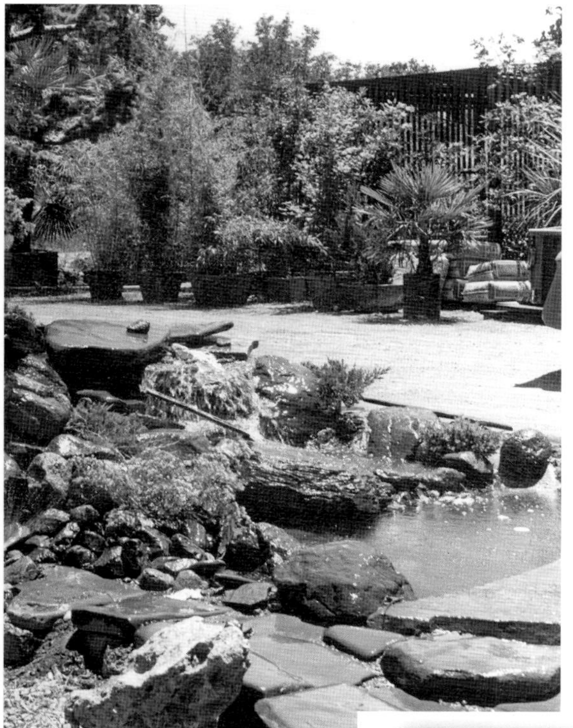

He went on to demonstrate the same creativity when it came to pricing the regular stock of shrubs and trees. Buying from wholesalers or growers meant that he was restricted by what was available on the one hand and subject to prices driven by high demand on the other.

I asked growers what discounts they would give me for trees purchased a year in advance, and they said 15 to 20 percent. Well, it was obvious this was a lot more than the prevailing annual interest rate for borrowing money. So I went to Bank of America, got myself a one-year loan, then ordered and paid for the trees I wanted. When they were delivered a year later, they sold quickly because I was able to undercut the competition by 15% and sometimes a lot more—and still make my margin. I believe I was the first person in the country to do this kind of cost plus marketing, and it set a trend that is now commonplace.

When it came to the success of the nursery, it also didn't hurt that Bob

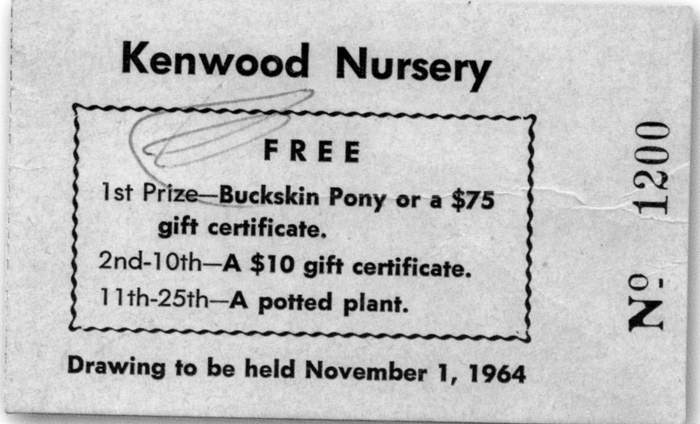

Kenwood Nursery

FREE

1st Prize—**Buckskin Pony or a $75 gift certificate.**

2nd-10th—**A $10 gift certificate.**

11th-25th—**A potted plant.**

Drawing to be held November 1, 1964

№ 1200

had a ready supply of cheap, if not free, labor by way of Edna and the boys. It's certainly what enabled Bob to devote so much time to the Sonoma Valley Chamber of Commerce and other valley organizations and public works during this period. Although young Bobby had the particular aptitude for manipulating plant material that Bob had inherited from his mother, all of the sons had an area in the nursery that they were responsible for. When they returned home from school, their first priority was to water their area. (And woes betide them if they didn't.)

Huge customer traffic could be generated in the spring at the nursery with "color spots"—annuals in four-inch pots that gardeners who wanted instant color could use to fill their beds. At first Bob grew these himself, but later could get them at such great prices from MV Nurseries in Richmond that he could offer them for fifty cents each or three for a dollar. He also made a visit to the Kenwood Nursery a pleasant experience for families far and near with hundreds of caged birds, pony rides, and a variety of promotional schemes.

The number of people that came to the nursery to make purchases without ever getting out of their vehicles was always a source of amusement to Bob. They included Sabina McTaggart, Sally Stanford, and the San Francisco businessman who had a weekend place up the valley. He arrived one Friday in a Cadillac convertible and parked out front but stayed in the car, waving a bare arm for Bob to join him. When Bob got to the side of the car it was obvious why the visitor wanted to stay in the car by the side of the busy highway; he wasn't just shirtless, he was nude.

The man needed three bales of peat put on a tab and delivered the next day. That was fine with Bob, and at 8 a.m. the next day set out up the valley with the peat. When he arrived at the property, not only was Bob's customer wandering around nude, so was the man's wife, son, and daughter, which made it tough for Bob to know which way to look. And while unloading the peat bales, he noticed something even more curious—the man had his testicles in a Bull Durham tobacco sack, with the drawstring tied in a bow to keep everything in place.

"Where shall I put the peat?" asked Bob. But there must have been another question apparent on his face, because the man said quietly to Bob, "I don't want to get them sunburned," and then pointed to the garage.

Sally Stanford, ex-mayor of Sausalito and the most famous of the Bay Area's madams, was a regular client of the Kenwood Nursery, and one of the nursery's customers who made her purchases without getting out of her car. Her white German shepherd, also named Stanford, usually accompanied her. If Edna was working at the nursery, Sally would just drive away. She lived on a Kenwood estate with perhaps the best views in California. It comprised three or four houses, some occupied by those of her "girls" who had opted for retirement rather than the offer to be set up in their own businesses.

Bob recalls Sally as short and by then none too pretty, but she was a good customer and as tough as they come. ("I liked her the first time I met her!") During a police raid on her house in San Francisco's upper crust Pacific Heights district, she had jumped out of a second story window, broken a leg

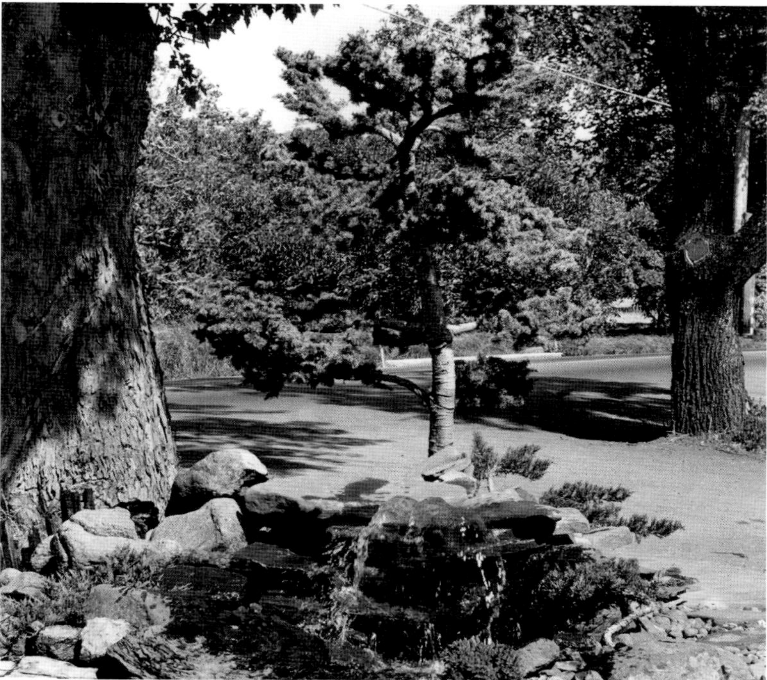

and still managed to make a getaway in a taxi.

Sally, born Mabel Busby on a farm in Oregon, had apparently adopted the name Stanford because she liked the college's football team. By Bob's account it was because many of her more notable clients were famous alumni.

It was Bob's habit to make deliveries to Sally in the early morning, taking advantage of coffee and pastries in the kitchen with "the girls." Sally would generally greet him with a cheery "Is that bastard freeloading here again?"

As a qualified appraiser, Bob had once helped Sally out with her insurance claim when a tree had fallen on one of the houses. Having received the settlement, she told Bob to bill her for the appraisal. When he refused, Sally insisted that he take an electric golf cart as payment. (Why a golf cart remains a mystery, but it is still in use at son Bobby's farm on Sobre Vista.) Later she also insisted that he take a Brunswick pool table that had come out of her bar and restaurant in Sausalito, the Valhalla.

"Those drunken sons of bitches keep on tearing the felt with their heels when they sleep on it. I've already had it recovered twice, but never again, so take it Bob." Bob asked if he could put the table in the Kenwood Firehouse. Sally said yes, and it is still in use there today.

She was less than beautiful, but other than that, I have nothing negative to say about Sally—she was always good to me. Honest as the day is long, and she paid with an interesting check featuring a girl behind a parasol.

Then there was old Professor Cowan. What a character! He used to come and sit by the fire in the nursery every Thursday, Friday, Saturday, and Sunday afternoon. Over ninety he was, born in 1872. Lived in Kenwood, but he still taught music in San Francisco—in the same studio that he had started seventy-five years before. The Professor was a music prodigy—guest conducted the San Francisco Symphony when he was only twelve years old! Twelve years old! His old family home on Treat Street was a mansion on a lake in what's now the Mission district in San Francisco. They lived opposite the Spreckels mansion on the other side of the lake. The Professor and one of the Spreckels boys were the first to fly in a hot air balloon over San Francisco. Crashed it, I think. Anyway, his father was a cousin of Queen Victoria who had been sent to San Francisco in 1851. He complained to the queen in a letter that there were no suitable women in the city, so she arranged to have an eligible girl from the right kind of family in Ottawa sent round the Horn on the sailing clipper Flying Cloud in 1856. I have her steamer trunk to this day. The Professor had shooting galleries in the city, as well as his music. His family had summer property in Kenwood, so he had always been a regular visitor. Professor Cowan said he'd often had to beat Jack London with his walking cane in Glen Ellen where Jack lived. Drunk I should imagine. London often was. He'd pick fights, but only with smaller men. Local people hated him. Made a lot of money but was always broke. Didn't pay his bills with local trades people like the blacksmith. Anyway he must have been in the habit of making off-color remarks to the ladies when he was drunk because he'd done it to one of the Professor's three sisters more than once when they were out walking. So he took his cane to London to teach him a lesson. Do you know the Professor could hypnotize a chicken with that cane? I saw him do it many times. He'd hold the chicken, stroke it with the end of his cane, and its head would flop over in a trance, just like that. Sitting by the fire, at the nursery. Bobby loved to see him do that. It was Bobby who got the chair for the Professor after he'd complained that we didn't have a decent one to sit on. Expert shot, Professor Cowan. Learned in the San Francisco shooting galleries in the 1880s. Kindred souls he and I. He owned four or five homes in Kenwood, and twenty pianos. Twenty! Gave me his entire collection of sheet music collected from 1880 to 1935. I gave it to the Dan Ruggles music collection at the Community Center.

Bob also bought some items from Professor Cowan as the latter became less interested in his various collections with advancing years. Among them were Tiffany lamps that he was willing to part with. Bob was so convinced of his ability to quickly make money on such fine pieces that he occasionally gave Professor Cowan a check on a Friday night for an amount he didn't have in his account with the firm belief that he could sell the lamp over the weekend and have the money in his account on Monday morning before the check was presented for payment. Knowing the value of the lamps made it a risk free deal to Bob, but it drove his wife Edna frantic, and she was extremely upset. But Bob made the calls on Saturday morning, more often than not to Corinthian Studios in Los Gatos, and made the sale, getting sometimes double what he had paid.

Bob arrived in California committed to donating time and energy to whichever community he found himself in. As soon as the family settled in Kenwood, he set about making social connections, joining the Kenwood Improvement Club and becoming a member of the volunteer Kenwood Fire Department. To provide the fire department with funds, Bob joined other Kenwood stalwarts to form the Kenwood Fireman's Association,

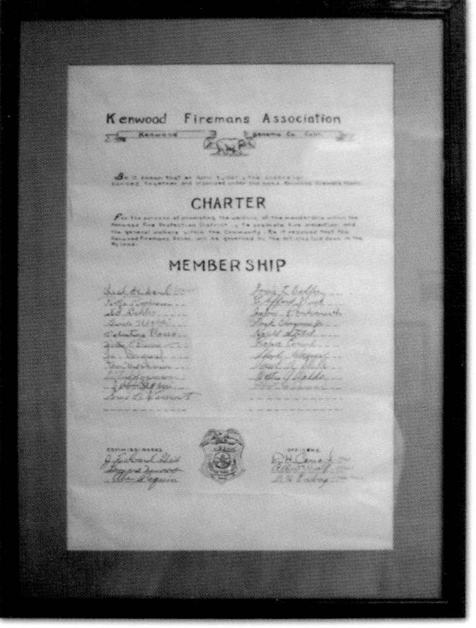
Kenwood Firemans Association

CHARTER

MEMBERSHIP

and it wasn't long before he was organizing fundraisers and publicity stunts.

On one occasion it was decided that the association would set up an emergency blood bank. The county's mobile blood bank had a minimum for turning out, but on the basis that the sixteen or so members could drum up two or three donors each, the twenty-pint minimum could be met. Unfortunately, on the afternoon that the mobile unit turned up and parked in the fire department's yard off Highway 12, the vast majority of the potential donors were turned down for one reason or another—age, high blood pressure, or former diseases—leaving them well short of twenty pints.

The blood bank's attending director, a tough old nurse, took a very dim view of the turnout.

"Young man," she said to Bob, "if you don't get more folks down here, I'll drain you dry, because I'm not leaving here without twenty pints of fresh blood."

"No problem," says Bob, who grabbed an appropriately red flag and began waving down every car that passed by on Highway 12 from Santa Rosa during the evening commute, such as it was in those days.

"We have set up an emergency blood bank, and I need your blood," he demanded, as soon as the startled drivers wound down their windows. Given his relentless powers of persuasion, a total of sixty pints was gathered by 6:30 p.m. in a uniquely Cannard form of highway robbery. The tough old nurse was astounded at what Bob was able to achieve, "I've never seen anything like it in my life, Mr. Cannard."

BOB'S BUFFALO BEANS

"Nothing was easy for the pioneer making the trip across the country in a covered wagon. Cooking and feeding the family was a very difficult chore. All food by necessity was prepared as one-pot meals in a large iron kettle. The kitchen equipment may have also included a frying pan and a coffeepot. That is all.

Dried beans, rice or corn was put on to soak in the morning before starting out so as to lessen the cooking time a night. Herbs and fruit or berries were added to the kettle during the day as well as any game that could be killed. Buffalo, antelope, jack rabbits, birds, bear or any other game was added to the pot, and the resulting mixture cooked.

I make buffalo beans with beef. The only seasonings are salt, pepper, sage and summer savory, and like the pioneers, I add a hand full of dried apples. It would usually be eaten with some kind of fried bread along with coffee. The leftovers were eaten for breakfast. Cooking for the family was one more of the great demands put on the pioneer mother."

CHAPTER FOUR

HOME RULE & PILLOW FIGHTS

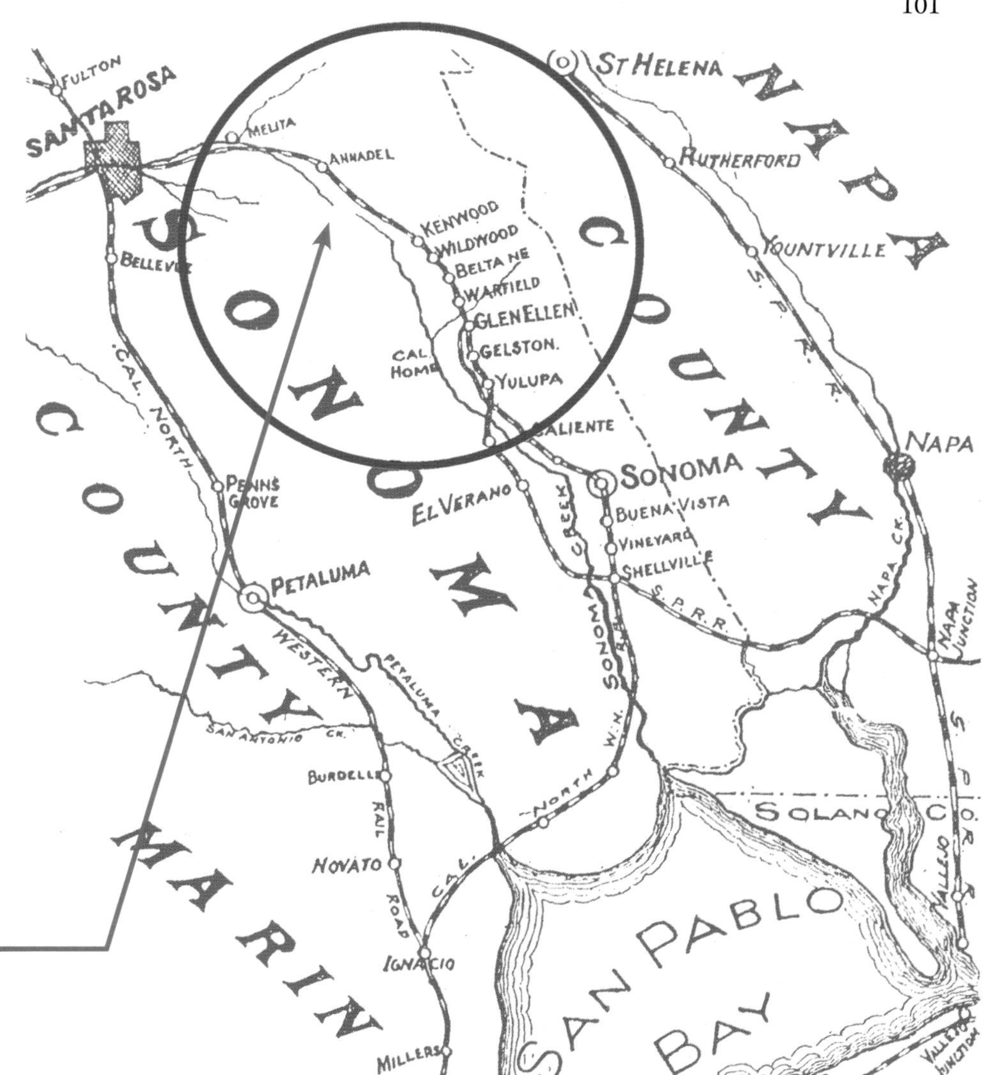

Developments to the north, in Oakmont, soon had Bob Cannard take up his first political fight. It was a fight against the encroachment of the city of Santa Rosa southwards down the valley toward the idyllic country village of Kenwood—the place that Bob had spent so much time and energy to find. He was not against development per se, but felt that it should be controlled and designed by existing residents rather than have it foisted on them by tax hungry local government or developers insensitive to the aesthetics of country people.

And if what had already begun in Oakmont, just a few miles to the north was anything to go by, that's exactly what was about to happen to Kenwood. In 1962, a huge tract of land had been purchased near Oakmont from the Hill Steamship

Company. It had been Annadel farms, and soon there were grandiose plans that included housing for 10,000 people, a golf club, supermarkets and a lake.

With the creation of the Sonoma Aqueduct in the early sixties, which replaced an antiquated and fragmented water supply system and brought water down the valley from the north, the way was clear for Santa Rosa to claim a "contiguous connection" to Oakmont, four miles to its south, and annex it for its tax base. There were advantages to the residents of Oakmont by way of sewer and other services, but it would also be the thin end of a development wedge that would allow cities to sprawl out in every direction with no regard to the protection of green space and coordinated planning for the future "shape" of the county.

Bob was president of the Kenwood Improvement Club at the time. At his urging, the club soon sent a written request to the Santa Rosa City Council entitled "SLOW DOWN! WHATS YOUR HURRY?" In it, they drew attention to the fact that the annexation plans were hardly in line with the recently adopted General Plan's vow to create concentrated growth rather than create inefficient sprawl. Further, they noted that Oakmont would increase the size of the city of Santa Rosa by 20 percent in one fell swoop, with no study as to how it would affect services and no cost benefit study. And despite the fact that the developers said they would encourage families to buy if retirees did not take up all the housing, there were no plans for schools, parks, or play areas. True to form, the city did not respond to these critical issues.

Construction began on new homes in 1964, and the following year, despite opposition, Santa Rosa, under Mayor Jack Ryerson, voted to annex Oakmont's 400 acres.

Bob's connections in the county and the city were telling him that greedy eyes were also on the prize of Kenwood, along with twelve other pending annexations. The Oakmont annexation had already bitten off 400 acres of assessed valuation belonging to the Kenwood Fire District, increasing the latter's fire taxes. "Contiguous connection" was well established through the aqueduct that the residents of Sonoma Valley were paying for, and Mayor Ryerson had declared his interest in taking Santa Rosa all the way south to El Verano Avenue on the outskirts of Sonoma, claiming the area and people could be better served by Santa Rosa.

While the fight over valley annexations was brewing, there was also a bill under discussion in the state capitol in Sacramento that would remove the arcane provision in the law that was producing these balloon annexations. The "contiguous connection" provision, under which new areas could be annexed and rezoned residential by cities looking to rapidly grow their tax base—with the ready compliance of the landowners and developers—was producing rampant sprawl across California. The state government was taking action precisely because the kind of grubby duplicity evident in Santa Rosa was taking place across the state. It had already happened in Los Angeles and San Jose. The population were provided the sop of a General Plan pretending responsibility and promising concentrated growth, but it would be promptly thrown out of the window when profitable prizes like Oakmont, well outside what might be called a sphere of interest, arose.

It wasn't known if this new bill would pass in time to protect Kenwood from becoming an extension of Santa Rosa and losing its right to have a hand in local zoning. If Kenwood fell, what would protect the rest of the valley from falling under Santa Rosa's governance? The problem was exacerbated by large landowners who considered it their right to cash out for development if their ranching enterprises failed to produce adequate profit. In fact, many saw selling for development as their retirement plan. At that time, wine-making in the valley was in its infancy, and there were no corporate wineries seeking to buy vineyard land, which would have offered alternatives.

So with Bob in the chair, the Kenwood Home-Rule Committee decided it must fight back vigorously. At a public meeting, the committee decided to hire an outside consultant to assess the implications of Kenwood incorporating itself. They then filed notice with the county that this study was under way, and that dependent on the outcome of the feasibility study, Kenwood would request an election to determine whether or not to incorporate. The committee's action effectively provided a ninety-day period during which no annexation action could be taken, and the members then started collecting signatures for the election petition.

The study by William Zion, a professional planning consultant, indicated that an incorporated Kenwood could provide the same services to residents as those claimed by Santa Rosa, with only a minimal increase in taxes. The committee submitted 356 signatures to the County with a petition for an election, claiming that the signatories "owned" around half of the assessed valuation of Kenwood, and then began to prepare for a campaign. A hearing was scheduled by the County supervisors to consider the proposal. It was paid for by Bob Cannard.

At this stage—and it is not clear exactly what the motives were and whether or not it was just another delaying tactic—residents of Glen Ellen, just south of Kenwood began to claim that they would oppose Kenwood's plans if slices of Glen Ellen were included in the incorporation plans. Bob vowed that he would try to keep them in line, but insisted that they were not critical to his group's plans to draw a defensive barrier to the north. Incorporation would have protected Glen

RAR:jp 8/c 1/2/64

THE WITHIN INSTRUMENT IS A CORRECT COPY OF THE ORIGINAL ON FILE IN THIS OFFICE.

ATTEST: JAN - 7 1964
EUGENE D. WILLIAMS
County Clerk & ex-officio Clerk of the Board of Supervisors of the State of California, in and for the County of Sonoma.
By ________ Deputy

Cannard

RESOLUTION NO. 8126-1

Dated: January 6, 1964

RESOLUTION OF THE BOARD OF SUPERVISORS, COUNTY OF SONOMA, FIXING THE AMOUNT FOR PROPONENTS' DEPOSIT PURSUANT TO GOVERNMENT CODE 34308 IN THE MATTER OF THE INCORPORATION OF KENWOOD AND SETTING A TIME FOR DEPOSIT THEREOF.

WHEREAS, a petition for the incorporation of Kenwood

OFFICIAL RECEIPT 26323
COUNTY OF SONOMA
SANTA ROSA, CALIFORNIA

DATE Sept. 19 1963
RECEIVED FROM Home Rule Committee
ADDRESS R. H. Cannard, Charman
~~THE SUM OF~~ Received at 4:26 p.m. Notice of intention
~~FOR~~ for proposed incorporation of K.

Ellen as well as Kenwood.

At the same time, some Kenwood residents, through their leader and local real estate developer Roy Halston, expressed opposition to an incorporation vote. They claimed that they, not the pro-vote group, had a majority of the assessed valuation and could block an election. Nobody would force them to do anything. Sonoma County Assessor R.J. McMullen weighed in and declared that the anti-incorporation group did have the signatures of people representing 64.16 percent of the land value within the proposed city.

Bob asserted that the issue was not dead. He vowed to fight on, and threatened to sue. A "Right to Vote Committee" was formed, and Bob was quickly made chairman. He claimed that many of the anti-vote people had been coerced with false information and wanted their names removed from the nay list. "Harriet's Notebook," a program on Santa Rosa radio station KHUM planned a showdown debate between Bob and Roy Halston, chairman of the Committee Against Incorporation. The whole situation seemed to be spinning out of control with the newspapers trying to keep pace with developments. But by Bob's account, incorporation plans were not really "serious." Instead, all sides had a very much under-the-table private agreement to keep the controversy going long enough to stymie annexation by the rapacious Jack Ryerson and his Santa Rosa City Council until the new regulations coming down from Sacramento could render the question moot.

And that's exactly what happened. LAFCO (the Local Agency Formation Commission) was empowered in the summer of 1964 to oversee city and other special district boundary changes throughout California, effectively removing the threat from the city of Santa Rosa to Sonoma Valley.

The over-blown rhetoric, threats, front-page newspaper coverage, public meetings, and blizzard of flyers abruptly ceased. There was no longer any need to proceed with incorporation plans, and quiet descended on the valley. But forty years later, when development corporations arrived in Sonoma Valley with their plans to build luxury spas, the residents of Kenwood again found themselves at a distinct disadvantage. They had no bargaining base and their vote was "lost" in a county district that included thousands of people in Rincon Valley with little or no consciousness or care for happenings down the valley. Kenwood folks can only turn to their county supervisor, who will in turn claim to be only one of the five votes that control the future of growth.

Forty years before, Bob's relentless activity on behalf of the Kenwood Improvement Club and the Right to Vote Committee had drawn fire from all sides. But to get the attention of a system geared to processing the plans of monied developers, citizens need a very thick skin and little fear of the personal and public criticism they will certainly have to suffer. Bob is such a citizen, and to his credit, he has never relinquished his point of view in favor of social status or "club membership," unlike so many others that have avoided taking a stance on critical issues.

Five years after the Kenwood incorporation issue, Los Guillicos, eleven miles from Santa Rosa, was annexed to that city by vote of LAFCO, largely because of a weasel clause built into the nearby Oakmont annexation years before. Jack Ryerson was the only pro-annexation voice at the public hearing, having recused himself from the actual vote as was required by law, but ensuring a like-minded replacement in the form of the mayor of Petaluma, would vote for him

Ig Vella, the valley's supervisor, a LAFCO member and exactly the person that should be voting on the issue, decided for some reason to recuse himself as well. He was not required to but did so supposedly at the request of Ryerson.

A pro-annexation supervisor whose own district included Santa Rosa replaced Vella on the board for the vote.

Both Barry Hill, a bold and vocal supporter of Kenwood incorporation, and of course Bob Cannard, spoke against the aspirations of "Hungry Jack," but their voices were in vain. At that time LAFCO appears to have become yet another opportunity for political horse-trading; it is hard to imagine any other reason that would justify Ig Vella seeming to shoot himself in the foot.

The incident serves as another reminder that "elected representative" is frequently an oxymoron, and that the rest of us should be grateful for the few people who stick their necks out and try against the odds to hold such people's toes to the fire.

Life in Kenwood wasn't all politics. It was a small community that had fun and celebrated just about everything on the calendar. A lot of the events were organized by the Kenwood Improvement Club, which Bob had joined as soon as he became a resident in the community. The club had been formed as a local women's organization in the 1940s, and the members had managed to negotiate the purchase of the old Southern Pacific Railroad Depot as their clubhouse. While Bob was club president, there was also a junior improvement club for the younger set, but some of its members had vandalized the clubhouse. "Put 'em to work, but give 'em some fun," said Bob, who collared the miscreants. In return for refurbishing the walls and floors of the clubhouse, the adult club members made sure that the kids got dances and "feeds"—and maybe the older teenagers got to drink a little beer.

It was an example of how everyone pulled together to create a community answer to a problem. That's what it was like in those days. I remember when two young men came to see me, Joe and Gary Bengerel it was. They said their boss Tom Rooney, who ran the San Francisco Boat Show, had been to England, the Midlands I believe, and seen some public pillow fights. Apparently it was a lot of fun and very

popular, and they thought it would be a great idea to try them in Kenwood on the Fourth of July. Well, I thought that it was a splendid idea. The fire chief, Ed Geib, had the department dig a hole in the creek that runs through the Kenwood plaza and provided the pipe to lay across it, and someone wrote up the rules. I got some prizes together and in 1966 or 1967, we had the first World Champion Pillow Fights in Kenwood on the Fourth of July. Since then of course, it's become a huge event, and people come from all over to see the fun. It's a major fundraiser for the Kenwood Fireman's Association.

The traditional celebrations for the Fourth were held in Kenwood Park, the only coherent center of the community. There was food, starting with ham and eggs for breakfast and continuing throughout the day. There were bands and sideshows and raffles and bike races and footraces and beer drinking contests, the latter won one year by a Hells Angel. That year about twenty-five of them had ridden into the adjacent Kenwood plaza, their aggressive posturing making the locals anxious.

"I'll talk to them," Bob said in his confident, take-charge way, and walked over to the gang. Opening with "How nice for you to join us for the Fourth," he explained to them that they were welcome to stay but that the locals felt threatened. He suggested they take off their scary leather jackets and leave them with their Harleys—so they would blend in with the families and everyone would be happy. He even offered to guard the bikes and the jackets, though it's hard to imagine anyone foolish enough to try to steal them. Bob also suggested they might like to try the beer drinking contest. The bikers agreed. Off came their jackets, and the festivities restarted. By the end of the day, all were friends, albeit drunken friends. One of the Hells Angels won the beer-drinking contest by only just outlasting the local favorite, a Danish merchant seaman, who finally fell to the ground. His wife was a teetotaler, and she refused to even try and wake him. Bob threw a blanket over him as the night wore on, and his loud snores were only muffled when the Hells Angels disappeared into the darkness on their roaring Harleys. There hadn't been a single complaint from local people all day. "What a day!" recalls Bob.

Three years later I was in Sonoma for the Vintage Festival and another big group of bikers rode into town. Chief Cartwright told me he'd run 'em out of town. I told him, you can't do that there are too many, let me talk to them. Well, I thought there'd be a pitched battle if he tried to confront them. So against his orders, I went over to these Hells Angels and said nice to see you. Would you believe that one of them was in the Kenwood group three years before. He remembered me and the beer-drinking contest. I told him the police chief was afraid they'd disrupt the festival, and they agreed to take off their jackets like before. I told them the chief would take care of the jackets. Boy was he pissed, but I saved his ass.

BOBBING FOR APPLES

ONCE AROUND THE OUTSIDE, TWICE AROUND THE MIDDLE.
THAT'S THE WAY YOU STIR AN APPLE BUTTER KETTLE

"Not too many of us stir a fifty-gallon kettle of apple butter anymore, but we can still enjoy that good old-time flavor right from our modern kitchens. The secret is in the apples. The apples were once grown exclusively for the flavor they gave to the various recipes they were in.

I have no argument with the beautiful, big and perfect apples that we have on the stands everyday, but there are numerous growers around the country that are producing the old time varieties that can be used for special purposes.

American apples are truly our gift to the world. Not that apples were not grown in both northern and southern Europe when the colonists first came to Virginia in 1607. But the great variety and combination of flavors came with the crossing of these old European varieties with native American species. These hybrids were then carried west as seeds and planted extensively throughout the Atlantic seaboard and east and west of the Allegheny Mountains, often by John Chapman (Johnny Appleseed) and hundreds of others and families moving west. Seeds were easy to carry and the combined genetics of the European and American natives produced the incredible quality of American apples. The superior ones were soon sorted out at the local then regional fair. By 1850 there were more than 250 named varieties known from these seeds. Many of these were found best for a specific apple recipe. The colonial housewife did the rest. Here are just a few samples of specific recipes using known varieties for a reason."

APPLE BUTTER

Using a combination of Winesap and Northwest Greenwings you can make sweet, spicey apple butter without the additives of either sugar or spice. Boil juice from Winesap apples down from four gallons to one. It will begin to get a little syrupy and have a sugar content of about 50 percent. Add peeled slices (snits) of Northwest Greenwings (2 quarts) and boil until as thick as desired. You may want to add a few more snits. Your friends will absolutely say that you have added both sugar and spice to this apple butter. It will taste better than anything you get out of a jar—unless it is made the same way.

CIDER

For drinking fresh from the food processor, there is nothing to compare with the color, fragrance and flavor of Winter Banana apples. A light pink aromatic juice that is nectar for the angels. Method: Prepare as your processor directs using washed quartered Winter Banana apples. Seeds and cores are fine if the processor says OK. The skin gives the beautiful pink color and adds to the fragrance.

APPLE PIE

No apple makes a better pie than Northern Spy. Some people on the West Coast might argue for Gravenstein but they never ate a pie from Northern Spy using a cup of boiled down Winesap juice for part of the sugar. With cheddar cheese, ice cream or cream there is nothing to compare.

CHAPTER FIVE

SOWING SEEDS & SAVING THE CHAMBER

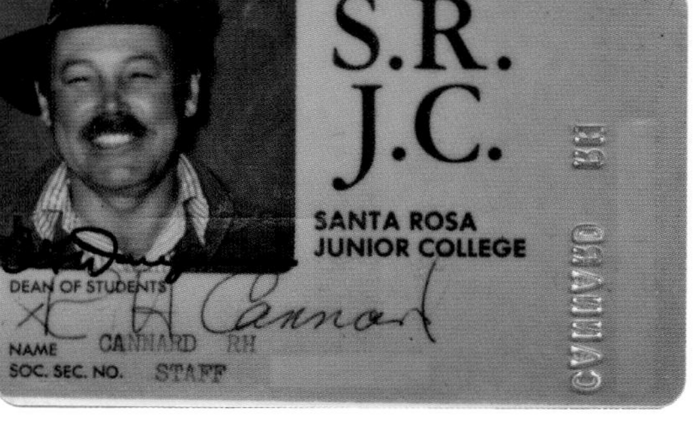

When Bob and Edna first arrived in California, UC Davis offered him a job in the horticulture department, but having spent so much time to find his ideal spot, Bob was not too keen on Davis' Central Valley location. Edna got him off the hook when she decided after a trip to the campus in the early summer that it would "boil her eyeballs" if she lived there.

But Bob's name stayed on the recruitment records. In January 1966, he got a call from Jack Healy, dean of the Evening College at the Santa Rosa Junior College asking if he could take over an evening botany class in the spring when its existing teacher left due to worsening health. Bob thought that would be something new and interesting. He took over the class, and at the end of the first semester had in mind some changes that he figured would benefit the county.

He asked Jack why it was that there was no agriculture department in a county with a predominantly agricultural economy. Pretty soon, they had a few more vocational education classes and a year later Bob was pushing for an agriculture department. Both Jack Healy and the dean of vocational education Charlie Beldon were in favor, but it was Beldon's view that the conservative board of trustees would never approve it. Not in the least bit deterred, Bob went to see his friend, cattle rancher Barry Hill, who in turn went to see every powerful rancher in the county and impressed on each of them the importance of having a trained labor force, encouraging them to call each of the college's trustees with the message. By the time Charlie Beldon took the proposal for an agriculture department to the college trustees, all had received a recent phone call from at least one influential rancher, Angelo Sangiacamo included. The proposal was approved without question.

The first teacher hired taught animal husbandry. With Bob's network of friends in the agri-business there was never a problem with enrollment, and all the classes flourished. With the wine industry beginning to show signs of major expansion, Rich Thomas was hired to teach viticulture. It was not unusual for Bob to have sixty, seventy, or even eighty people enrolled in a horticulture class, which supported the fledgling classes in other agriculture subjects. The staff grew and finally, in 1974, Beldon persuaded Bob to become a full-time instructor. Bob eventually moved on from the college in 1982, but the department has continued with all the classes that Bob originated. He is rightfully proud of the department, and the hundreds of students who passed through his hands, but recalls hiring a few duds, and remains critical of academic "softness."

In the early years there were no rooms for many of my classes. We met under a roof in the maintenance yard until new classrooms were built. Why, the landscape drawing class I taught met in an old Quonset hut where the library is today. The roof leaked. I can remember water dripping onto the students' drawings, but they got on with it. It's all to do with the teacher. Today they wouldn't stand for it. But if you plan for a nice environment, you're not planning for results, and that's what really counts.

It is more than probable that Bob never endeared himself to the academic faculty with his forthright opinions and practical bent. He may have been the only teacher who supported Proposition 13. But his reputation as being a fine teacher remains alive with the students that now run many of the county's agricultural and horticultural enterprises. Some of his students put on the first horticulture show that was the forerunner of the very popular "Day Under the Oaks" event. His streamside walks that introduced students to the natural world with an encyclopedic knowledge of every plant encountered are legendary.

In 1982, graduating students in Bob's horticulture class at Santa Rosa Junior College decided to honor their teacher by dedicating a tree to him in Golden Gate Park's Strybing Arboretum. They made the necessary arrangements with the park's management, and one afternoon in May 1982 made their way to the designated spot armed with a young dwarf conifer, grafted by Bob in the junior college nursery. Under his supervision, the students duly planted the tree and added the commemorative plaque. Bob had asked Brady T. Brady, a previous graduate of his class and now a good friend, to speak at the dedication.

Brady is not the kind of person given to somber words and grave pronouncements, preferring the quick thrust of a humorous barb to make his point. So he spoke a few words about Bob's fine achievements and then turned to what Bob was really like.

> *Apart from his wonderful horticultural knowledge, Bob Cannard is a master of timing, and I'll give you an example. A few years ago we were in this very park, following Bob on one of his famous guided tree tours, listening as he expounded on many rare plants with a whole lot of sentences starting, "Now not many people are aware of this, but..." Anyway, one of the female students was as talkative and as self-opinionated as Bob, but although she tried hard, she wasn't able to get a word in edgeways until noon when we took a break and sat under the trees with our sack lunches. With Bob silent, she took the floor and launched off into one of her own speeches. Suddenly, this really big bird dropping fell down out of the tree right on her forehead and splashed down her front. She stopped in mid-sentence with her mouth open in horror. Without a moment's hesitation, Cannard commented with a broad grin, "They sing for some people."*

Brady's telling of the story got an even bigger laugh at the dedication than Bob's comment had when he first made it.

Brady confesses that it was this humorous side that most endeared him to Bob. That, and the fact that even as a lecturer he was more than happy to give the car-less Brady a ride to school from Glen Ellen. It was during these trips that the two got to know each other and Brady became captivated by Bob's sheer joy in living and his ability to laugh at himself.

He remembers that Bob was never afraid of saying exactly what he believed to his students, regardless of the consequences. Bob became really annoyed with the Army Corps of Engineers who were then busy concreting streambeds and turning them into trapezoidal ditches to speed rainwater away, instead of allowing it to percolate down and recharge the groundwater. So he recommended to the students that they throw seeds into the ditches in the hope that they would germinate in cracks and grow weeds that would break up the concrete and eventually return the stream it to its natural state.

Some of the students and more conservative members of the faculty took exception to this subversion of authority, but it only served to strengthen Brady's opinion of Bob. Thirty years later and with the benefit of hindsight, the City of Santa Rosa is now spending a small fortune on doing exactly what Bob suggested. They are breaking up the culverts, creating nature walks along the restored streams, and even interpreting the importance of the mini ecosystem to passers by on colorful signs.

Brady makes it a point to explain that he was invigorated by Cannard's commitment to the practical application of his teaching. He was a realist, and Brady recalls that, typical of the late sixties, classes had their fair share of Birkenstocked and long-haired folks returning to the soil with the intention of making peace with everything. Bob was concerned at their naivety and warned, "Don't be so benign that you end up doing nothing."

At the same time, Bob was extremely protective of his students, and insisted to the conservative faculty that they should not dismiss students just for their unconventional habits. A shoeless, long-haired and wildly unkempt student —the now famous botanist/environmentalist Jessie Longacre —may well have been pushed out simply because of his lack of personal hygiene (he stank) had it not been for Bob's intervention and Dean Healy's support. Brady admits that there were people in the faculty that may have found Bob's style inappropriate to academia, and it's true that another of Bob's off the cuff remarks did have repercussions.

He stated to one class that in his opinion, "a tree is more important to the environment than I am." An innocent remark, you'd think, but one mature student considered it blasphemous ("You were made in the image of God!") and complained to the faculty. Bob stood by his remark and didn't see why it should be considered at odds with anyone's religious convictions. Why should he compromise what he believed or "knew" from his own experience or observation—just to make someone feel better about their own beliefs. She complained to Dean Healy but nothing ever came of it. Healy was too smart to get into that.

Bob was a strange mixture of traditional conservative and free thinker. A radical environmentalist with a firm eye on the business opportunity. For him horticulture was a means to economic independence as well as ecological understanding. He knew he could always make a living, and somehow that gave him the confidence to be uncompromising. He didn't need 'the establishment,' and so was always in the wonderful position of never having anything to lose.

"I think you'll find I'm right" is his favorite phrase.

Brady went on to write some political tracts for Bob when he ran for supervisor of Sonoma County. He's one of the few people who could distill concise ideas from Bob's wordy rhetoric without necessarily agreeing with him.

Brady remembers another of Bob's controversial off the cuff remarks to a large audience.

"Put your new houses in the hills, this valley is prime agricultural land."

Brady's response—"Wonderful! Heresy to some environmentalists, but gives you a different perspective right? Makes you think about priorities."

Brady T. Brady and Bob have remained firm friends.

As a testament to his own unconventional habits, Bob happily submitted to one of his female student's unusual requests that she innoculate herself with as many antibodies as possible by licking his tongue every time she entered the classroom.

And to his great and enduring credit, he provided not only the knowledge to allow students to 'grow', but the ideas and encouragement to turn that knowledge and ability into income and commercial success. He urged viniculture students to learn how to sell wine, not just grow the grapes. And when a couple of girl students from Healdsburg came to see him shortly after seven a.m. one spring with the plea "we must have a job," he gave them the solution in the class that started an hour later. It was Rent-A-Duck. The idea was to catch a few of the unwanted ducks in Santa Rosa's parks, and hire them out to people whose gardens were overrun with slugs and snails. For a mere $10 a duck could clear a garden in two weeks and not harm the plants. The eggs would be a bonus. Bob showed the girls how to catch the ducks, and with ads in the local newspaper they soon had a thriving business.

And to a couple of Vietnam vets from Guerneville, he suggested a plan to sweep roofs and clean gutters for a nominal amount, then sift through the sweepings for viable redwood seeds to clean and sell for a big bonus. The seeds from single trees—like those next to houses—would be viable, whereas those in groups are not.

As Bob repeatedly said to his students "Horticulture is personal agriculture." The thought certainly stuck with a lot of the hundreds of students that passed through Bob's classes. Here are the recollections of some who became close friends as well as committed students.

PAUL PELS
Sebastopol, California
Arborist with the City of San Francisco.

Whenever my thoughts flash to my dear friend Bob Cannard, it seems like a newsreel of our thirty-plus year friendship is just ready to be seen. For some strange reason, many of my shared experiences of him are seared into my memory.

It all started innocently enough in 1974 in an evening gardening class at Santa Rosa Junior College. What amazed me about him then, and has ever since, was his ability to pass on his practical knowledge of horticulture at first, then his other invaluable life experiences in such a compassionate and understandable way. I have also been impressed, as I have gotten older, by his ability to dispense his thoughts, knowledge, and wisdom in a positive way—all with that great smile and glint in his eye.

All of this might sound either like I have been paid for it, or it's like a huge pile of compost. It's not. It's so vivid in my memory, it's as if it happened yesterday

I can think back to a class in which he spoke so highly of the Northern Spy apple, a prized eastern cultivar. I can remember many of the plant identification walks, where the class would follow him like the pied piper, most more than half his age younger, trying to keep up with him. He would give information about the plants being studied as well as general landscape tips—whether they be what he might have done on big estates back in the eastern part of the U.S., or how it might improve the appearance of the junior college campus.

There was another time when during a plant identification class that we keyed out one of the trees on campus and it turned out that Bob had been giving us the wrong name of the tree. I'm sure to this day that it was all part of the exercise on the value of being able to use a taxonomic key for the budding horticulture students. On another plant walk, when we were encouraged to take samples in order to help us remember the plants, he advised us not to take any samples from a particular tree because of its small size. which brings me to another of his great qualities, his love of trees. This love is infectious and he has never hesitated to pass on his passion to the countless students that he taught or mentored. This is probably Bob's most important career legacy.

Eventually it was time for me to move on to a four-year college, in my case Fresno State University. But the mentoring didn't end when I went away. Many times I would come back to visit Bob on breaks from college, in need of encouragement. He seemed to know this and was always willing to pitch in with his special brand of advice and optimism.

During the course of my working career, I had the opportunity to teach at SRJC in the evening program. I felt that for the ten years that I taught that I had come full circle and was also able to give of some of my knowledge and experience to budding horticulture students or interested members of the community. During one of my classes, I'm happy to say the tree that was once too small to take samples from is now over thirty feet tall, and during one of my classes I was able to tell a group of my students the story of the tree too small to take samples from.

In closing, I would like to say how blessed my life has been with the friendship of Bob and Edna Cannard. I would like to submit this poem by one of our favorite authors of horticulture books, Liberty Hyde Bailey. The title is "Daybreak." It reminds me of Bob because he loves to awaken early and because of his special brand of optimism, which has helped me and others throughout our lives.

Paul Pels January 2005

DAYBREAK

Have you risen at the day break
When the world is cool and free
And the dawn comes up triumphant
Like the freshness of the sea?

Have you felt the nature kinship
As you go in fields alone
When the first new light is breaking
And the world is all your own?

Have you heard the first bird calling
From the passing of the night
When the dew is on the grass-land
And the corn-tops feel the light?

Have you walked through fog-filled hollows
By dim pathways soft and damp
Ere the pasture-lying cattle
On their fields had broken camp?

Have you known the youthful laughter
Of the brook upon its bed
While the shadows of the darkness
On its scented pools are spread?

Have you seen the wild things feeding
In the sun-break and the shade
Living each his mode and habit
When there's none to make afraid?

Have you smelt the tonic fragrance
When the morning airs distil
And you spread your chest and breathe it
Till it sends your nerves athrill?

So the dawn is rousing
Rousing bird and bee,
Thro' the ages calling
Calling you and me;

Yet we still are sleeping
Sleeping with our ills,
While the world is waking
Waking on the hills;

Spending hours at midnights
Making mimic day,
Longing for amusement
Burning life away;

For we yet are children
Playing with our toys,
Grasping at the fire-lights
Humored by the noise.

But I think I see the future
In the distance where it lies
Like a vision of the morning
Stretching out beneath the skies;

Nor mankind will know its mission
Nor its doubts will be withdrawn
Nor the race will be perfected
Till it rises with the dawn.

From *Wind and Weather,* by L.H. Bailey

LAURA WESTON
Washington State

I met Bob as an Ornamental Horticulture instructor while I was a student at the Santa Rosa Junior College in the 70's. The more I got to know and love him, the more I felt I became the daughter he never had. And after all those sons I can sure see why. As a single student, I loved being a part of their family and I would house sit and take care of the younger boys quite often while I was there in the area.

One of the things I remember about Bob is his never ending generosity. He would always be bringing people plants and gifts from the greenhouses or food from his garden.

He loved where he lived. He loved Sonoma—he loved his Valley of the Moon. In fact he had quite a thing about the moon. Whenever there was a full moon he would get everyone out of bed at night and go watch the moon rise. When Edna got tired of going, Bob would take me if I was staying over there, and we would pile into his truck and go over to the airport to watch the moon rise. In fact, when I was living with another family in Petaluma, I remember waking up to a serenade outside my bedroom window and guess who that was? He was out there singing and I'll bet there was a full moon that morning!

The values that Bob and his family had were those that I held dear. They were the values of family togetherness, living off the land and creating a home that felt welcoming to all. Now when I look at the life we are living here with my family, we are living those values. Not that I was trying to match Edna with all those boys! (We have 4 boys) But the lifestyle of traditional stay at home values was an inspiration. Just having someone home all the time to "keep the homefires burning" was a big priority for the Cannards. Edna was my inspiration. I loved their family traditions, like having a special pork dinner on New Years Day. But the one I loved the most was when the sons bought a new car. Edna was always the first passenger in that new vehicle. The Cannard boys were excellent wood workers and gardeners and cooks, and our first son was lucky enough to be rocked in the cradle that Bob had made for his boys!

Bob was always so unassuming—so much so that when my friends and I would come over to their house to visit, it didn't matter what Bob was doing, we were always welcomed. Even when he was taking his bath, we'd all file into the bathroom for a little chat next to the tub! My girlfriends still remind me of that crazy professor of mine!

Has he shown you his Civil War chest? He is a history buff extraordinaire.

I learned so much from Bob—he taught me about life, and his family was an example of the traditional American values that I was searching for. I am so thankful they included me in their family when I was searching for that kind of support. It gave me the confidence to find my own special partner and raise our four boys on this beautiful piece of property we have here in the Pacific Northwest. We have goats, chickens, ducks, geese, turkeys, and many other assorted household pets. Our garden grows bigger every year and the pleasures of providing our own food stem from the education I received from Bob, in and out of the classroom.

Let me know how the book goes and if you need anymore stories. I'm sure there are more!

Thanks for listening

Laura

The stories that students tell about Bob are no different in their display of admiration and pride and affection than his stories about them. He wanted every one of them to suceed, and was brimming with unselfish pride when they did.

"One time we had a tall rough fella turn up for a horticulture class, and I don't believe he had any more than an eigth grade education, maybe no more than a seventh. But I saw something in the man. Sincere, hardworking and honest he was. He'd been a lumber worker up north by the coast but the mills were closing and he'd come down to Santa Rosa and got himself a job working as a laborer for the highways. He wanted to move up to landscaping and came to take an evening course with me for three winters because he wanted to learn more about horticuture. Well he worked hard, got on the highway landscaping crew. And he knew all about small engines. Whenever we had a question in the class, why I would get him to answer it. Big raw-boned devil he was, couldn't string more than three words together. He would shamble up to the front and draw a picture on the blackboard and somehow explain perfectly how to fix a carburetor or whatever. He turned up in a work shirt and dusty old pants and boots, but I got him to teach a class on small engine repair, and do you know he got so many enrollments we had to make it two. We'll I heard about the new Silverado Country Club over in the Napa Valley and they needed a foreman for the landscaping crew on the golf course, so I told him about it, and would you believe he went over there and got the job. I met his boss, the engineering foreman, and he told me that . . . . I can't think of his name. Richard? Dick? Yes, that's it, Dick . . . . he told me that Dick was the best worker he'd ever had. Ran his crew well and got in there and worked with them. Didn't stand around on his shovel giving instruction. What an achievement! But that wasn't the best of it. After six or seven months there was someone from Alaska playing golf at the Silverado—offered him a job up there. Seven months of work a year, and then five months paid leave in the Bay Area. What d'ye think of that!

I told Jack Healy. The man was getting twice Jack's salary. Twice! And Jack was the Dean of Evening College! That didn't bother Jack a bit. It was just what he wanted. He wanted the students to have a good experience and move on up with the help of the classes we provided. You did a good job there Cannard, he said. But I knew that man would have made something of himself even if he'd never met me. What a story!"

Recently, Bob was walking through a farmer's market in Hawaii during one of his regular winter vacations. Someone selling all manner of chocolate products asked if he was from Sonoma.

"Yes I am."

"Well I was one of your students many years ago, and I remember you told us to pick something that no one else was doing. I picked chocolate, and here I am in Hawaii with all my family involved in making products that come from our cocoa plantation." It was a very pleasant surprise, and Bob returned later with Edna to meet his old student.

Bob will tell you that he tried to tailor his teaching to the individual requirements of his students, and fill their heads with ideas for the practical application of their newly acquired botanical and horticultural knowledge. Judging by the stories related here, it was a great success.

Maybe his methods were an indirect and unconscious way of meeting the personal commitment made at his own graduation, to populate the country with trees in part payment for the education given to him through the GI Bill. More likely, it was the manifestation of the belief planted in him by his mother, that understanding of the ways of the natural world give the possessor a unique connection to it, and hence a special position in it.

That he wanted to share this with students was to their great advantage.

This is just one of the many gifts and letters of gratitude that Bob has received over the years from students who have established themselves in a wide and rich variety of botanical and horticultural fields.

In the late summer of 1966, Sonoma resident Helen Hernandez called at the nursery in Kenwood and dramatically changed the course of Bob's career. She simply asked if Bob would like to join the Sonoma Valley Chamber of Commerce, for a mere $15 a year. For the life of him, Bob couldn't imagine what the Chamber could do to the benefit of his or anybody else's business for just $15 a year, but he joined and was determined to find out. It soon became apparent that not only had the Chamber become moribund and listless, it was also bankrupt, and in danger of being forced to withdraw its sponsorship of the Vintage Festival, already a twenty-year Sonoma fixture representing the agricultural plenty of the valley and unique charm of Sonoma.

Bob began attending the Chamber's board meetings and was soon elected to represent the north valley on the board of directors. Bob found the Chamber not only devoid of ideas. For whatever reasons it seemed to him that it had also become no more than yet another social club incapable of managing its limited financial responsibilities, instead of a force to promote business development. And try as he might he could not get a clear financial statement from any of the officers. It seemed that local business people were more interested in backslapping and complacent self-congratulation than developing a real plan to put Sonoma on the map. Printing a simple brochure had turned into a confused money losing venture, as had the Vintage Festival. Ten percent of the members were in arrears with their dues, the manager had resigned, and the president, Luis Vela, was recommending that the Vintage Festival be dropped altogether, or given to some other entity to take care of. The Chamber had managed to turn the $5,000 in assets of the Vintage Festival Association into a $7,000 debt since it had taken over responsibility for the festival some twelve years before, when the association's energy had been depleted. The Chamber's own debts were believed to be around $7,000, but turned out to be in excess of $13,000.

Yet the city was growing, the infant wine industry—there were then four wineries with about 500 total acres in vines—had huge potential, and Sonoma's historic heritage should have offered a basis for the development of a strong tourist trade. So why was it that people perfectly capable of running their individual businesses were failing so miserably to run one jointly? It appeared outrageous to the constantly enterprising Bob Cannard that when the value of an area depended on the vibrancy of its business climate, so many civic leaders were comfortable with letting the Chamber and the biggest showcase for local industry drift quietly away. He told them so at meetings, and in his usual style, suggested all kinds of inventive solutions.

He didn't, however, make known his view that the problem lay in Sonoma's pervasive and complacently provincial attitude that arbitrated against the development of a strong civic structure, including the Chamber of Commerce. As an example, although there were some who thought a paid professional manager might help the Chamber, there were many others who reckoned that "a few questions from visitors could be handled by a retired person." Still more thought the Chamber needed to sell itself and explain what it did for the valley, failing perhaps to realize that it wasn't doing anything, hence its demise. In fact, about the only beneficiary of the Chamber's activities was the local newspaper, taking the lion's share of the annual advertising budget generated to promote money-losing events.

Bob must have made some sort of impact on the board and membership, because despite his arguing vigorously against it for around twenty minutes, they voted to make him the president for 1967 at an early November 1966 meeting. On reflection, Bob thinks he must have been nuts to take on this responsibility without knowing the full extent of the insolvency. He had asked for a financial statement, but it was not forthcoming for another six months.

Soon after, the Chamber's interim manager, Bill Wetzel, suffered a stroke, and Bob required that the directors and member volunteers support the efforts of the only full-time staffer, clerk Sharon Howlett. It was agreed that the long-term goal would be to hire a full-time professional manager, and members were encouraged to donate towards a separate fund for this purpose. Although the full extent of indebtedness was still not known, Bob had discovered drawers full of unpaid bills and realized that it would take a huge personal effort to turn the Chamber around.

He was horrified by the sense of stagnation and was amazed that the board was happy to sweep the problems under the rug. He found the board sluggish and backward and was constantly urging them to get their collective act together in the interests of Sonoma's commercial future. Bob saw that Sonoma was overly protectionist, with its businesses jealously guarding their monopolies, and its trade associations and clubs giving glossy veneer to a commercial atmosphere that discouraged competition.

He would have nothing of that, and it took an outsider to do what should have been self-evident to the existing board.

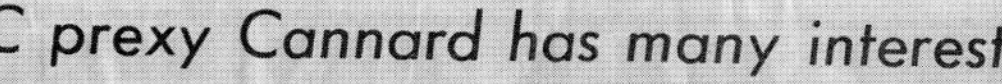

CC prexy Cannard has many interests

B JERRY PARKER

Bob Cannard, the new presi-dnt of the Sonoma Valley Camber of Commerce, is a mn of diverse interests and an aiding love for this area. This readth of view and intense eling about the valley being chosen spot should work well r the interests of all whom annard will represent.

Owner of the Kenwood Nur-ery, Cannard has lived here r 4-1/2 years. He spent wo years prior to that travel-g around the state to find e best place to live. This as after he came here from ennsylvania.

EVENTUALLY he narrowed is choices down to seven, five nd then two sites. It was toss-up between the Sara-oga-Palo Alto area and So-oma Valley.

What was Cannard's prime eason for picking this area?

The nurseryman was born in Danville Pa., 40 years ago. He graduated from Pennsy-lvania State College, where he majored in landscape horticul-ture.

He went to work after college as foreman for a Pennsylvania nursery which specialized in moving large trees. "There's not a tree in Sonoma Plaza I couldn't move", he declared during his interview.

It wasn't long before he open-ed a nursery of his own, as he's had now for 17 years.

As a nurseryman, Cannard has specialized for years in the culture of bonsai plants. These miniature masterspieces he makes for many Bay Area nur-series as well as the general public.

THE ART of bonsai, Cannard said, originated in China, but has reached its zenith of its development apparently, in Ja-

can be made to duplicate in miniature each detail of its full-size counterpart.

Cannard's bonsai plants, which include grafted beeches, maples, cedars and rare coni-fers, sell for anything from $3.50 to $1,500.

The roster of Cannard's out-side interest is unusually lengthy and interesting. But just to list some of them you would have to mention collector of rare historical documents, rare bird breeder, coin col-lector, and antique car con-noisseur.

Not all of these activities occupy Cannard at this time. But perhaps the dominant one is his search for rare docu-ments. Among his pri are a copy of th minating the C was relaye Genera

2.

The Kenwood nursery o realizes he has taken on job as president of the Chamber of Commerce. Chamber's faltering opera were further compli recently with the unfort stroke suffered by manage Wetsel.

Various directors are putting in a few hours eac to help secretary Sh Howlett cope with the inqui

Cannard has several im diate objectives in the Cham First, he wants to explain t community just where Chamber stands, financ and otherwise. At the same

At his urging, regular meetings were changed from a once a month 7:30 a.m. breakfast, to soup at noon every week—and attendance improved. (The newspaper headline read "King Robert says let them eat soup.") Membership drives were started based on more realistic fees—$1 a week or $50 for the year.

Two thousand private citizens responded to the request to support the Chamber with three dollars per year associate memberships. Fundraising became a priority. Debts were prioritized, and each week the directors approved payment as corresponding funds were generated.

The image of the Sonoma Valley Chamber of Commerce was changed from one of purely advertising to one of service to the community. The office was kept open on weekends, and people could call twenty-four hours a day for help. As a side benefit, at least two suicides were probably prevented as a result of this service. People knew they could get help in any emergency.

Soon after joining the board of directors of the Chamber of Commerce, it became apparent to me that there were financial problems. There was little or no discussion of what the true picture was or how we were operating. There was no balance sheet and almost no treasurer's report, even though I asked questions regarding our financial status, I was told the paid manager took care of the details.

At one early meeting, the discussion turned to a debt the Chamber owed to the Index-Tribune for about $2,200. It was decided to take out a loan with the Bank of America to pay this bill. I asked how we were going to pay it back and was assured that it was a normal part of the operation and would be paid out of income. This did not satisfy me, but being new to the board, I said nothing further.

After I was elected president and started digging into the true financial status, I was convinced that the Chamber was in deep trouble. Jerry Jolly, another newcomer to the board, had been elected treasurer and started to unravel the mess. He quickly identified six or seven thousand dollars of current bills that were unpaid. In auditing the previous Vintage Festival accounts, he found another seven thousand dollars of unpaid bills.

At this time, our clerk came to me and said there were several drawers full of old bills that were unpaid, and she didn't think that the rent had been paid for eighteen months. After exhaustive work, Jerry Jolly found that the Chamber of Commerce was more than $20,000 in debt. It was bankrupt. Our assets were less than $1,000.

When the board of directors was confronted with those figures, they immediately seized on the idea of dropping the Vintage Festival. Only Lee Tunkis and I opposed this move. I appealed to the board that I be allowed to hold a public meeting to see if it could be saved by an independent public group. This did happen.

In concentrating on the Chamber debts, it became obvious to me that the Index-Tribune had been receiving payment of its outstanding advertising and printing bills, when others creditors were not paid at all. Bob Lynch was a member of the Chamber's board of directors, and I did not feel his organization should be getting preferential treatment, especially when it came via a questionable loan that Bob himself had voted for at a time when the Chamber was flat broke. I went to see him and laid the cards on the table. In return for the special payment arrangement, I demanded his ongoing help in advertising the Chamber's plight to regain the confidence of the people and business community of the valley.

The rest is history. From that day until I left the Chamber of Commerce, whatever I requested of the Index-Tribune became a front-page story. I suspect that it didn't hurt that Lynch had a guilty conscience either.

Bob secured financial support from the county and city, and by March of 1967, an austerity campaign had paid off so that debts were significantly down.

Bob was convinced that despite problems, the Vintage Festival must continue if Sonoma and the wine industry were to be put on the map. Stringent financial controls would be needed, as well as other changes. There was a widely held view that what had started as a spontaneous and charming local event featuring good food, dance, music, pageants, and enthusiastically decorated retail stores, had deteriorated into an over commercialized, tinselly, and shallow imitation.

With the Chamber voting not to sponsor the Festival, Bob proposed a public meeting to determine the future of the festival, to be held May 1, 1967, at the Veteran's Memorial building. It was opened by Bob, who provided an outline of the Festival's history and problems, and an enthusiastic recommendation that it should be reborn with a new public board of directors and with the Chamber guaranteeing no burden of debt. And that's pretty much what happened, with Henry Maysonnave chosen as president of the new festival board.

The Vintage Festival remains today the highlight of Sonoma's event calendar, and it was saved because of Bob's tireless urging. And through his efforts the Chamber was on the way to recovery with the first of its new fund raising promotions—a drawing for a new Chevy Camaro—which took place on the Fourth of July, 1967, and netted $3,000 for the Chamber. This was the start of an energetic and inventive campaign which continued to promote the interests of the Chamber while at the same time bring in much needed funds.

It was an uphill struggle, with only Lee Tunkis sharing Bob's vision and commitment to the Vintage Festival and Chamber, and the Chamber's debts close to $20,000. Bob's efforts took a huge amount of time away from his Kenwood nursery business, but Bob's sons stepped in to cover for him, as did Edna, and they somehow made it work. It remained Bob's firm opinion that if businesses were to thrive in Sonoma and the valley, the Chamber of Commerce was integral to the promotion of its products and services. He would find that others were not so committed to helping the whole as a means to helping themselves, but he did not let this stand in his way. He would put Sonoma on the map by whatever means were necessary, including embarrassing the Chamber's board with its own mismanaged accumulation of debts.

These debts came down as Bob's efforts increased. August Pinelli and Herb Batto were owed large amounts, the latter for eighteen months of rent arrears. "Neither expected to be paid, but I said if we can pay the others, we'll pay you. And we did. They became my biggest supporters. August Pinelli also became Sonoma's first Alcalde, and he was a natural."

It became apparent to Bob, though, that it would always be an uphill struggle to maintain the membership and fundraising activity at the level needed to provide sufficient resources to make a difference. As an energetic but unpaid volunteer with his own business to run, he remained hopeful but was tired of the constant stream of telephone questions that came from the staff to the nursery every day. The solution was clear.

At the Chamber's regular meeting at noon on Monday, September 18, Bob handed the meeting over to the vice president and excused himself, leaving the following letter:

Dear fellow board members:

Please consider this an application for manager of the Sonoma Valley Chamber of Commerce. As I look at the work and the problems facing the Chamber, I am convinced that we need the services of a full-time Chamber manager.

The conditions under which I will accept this position are these:

1. That no salary will be paid to me until all Chamber bills are paid and we have a $4,000 bank balance.

2. That we continue the austerity program.

3. That you commit yourselves to help develop a program and present it to the community.

4. That you make the decision today.

You know me and my qualifications. If you need any specific information, please feel free to call me at home. Thank you.

The local newspaper described the board members as "stunned." But to their credit they wasted no time in appointing

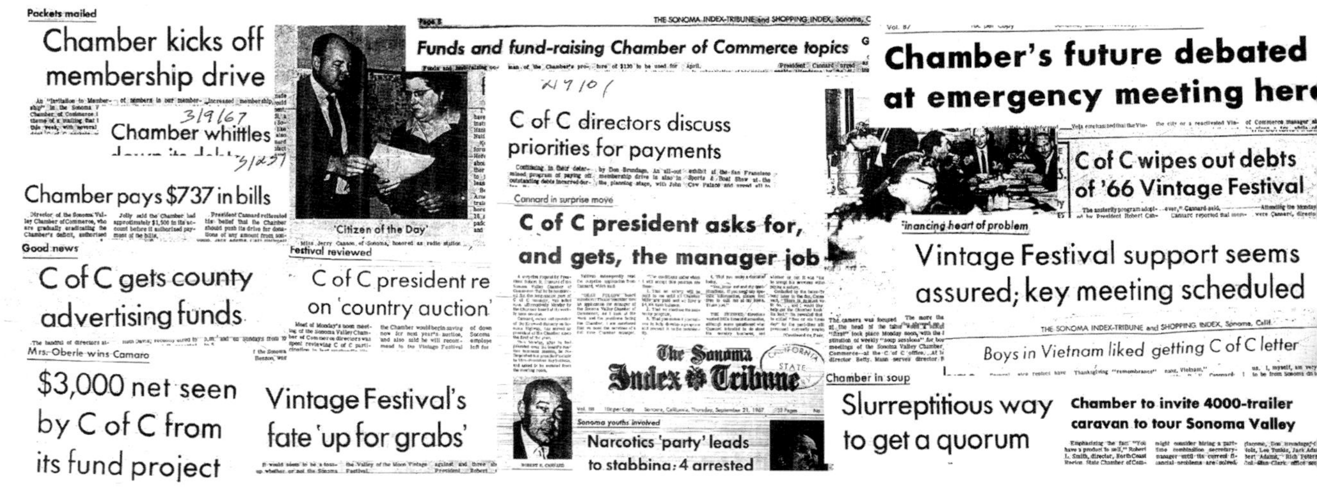
Packets mailed
Chamber kicks off membership drive
Chamber whittles
Chamber pays $737 in bills
Good news
C of C gets county advertising funds
Mrs. Oberle wins Camaro
$3,000 net seen by C of C from its fund project
'Citizen of the Day'
Festival reviewed
C of C president re on 'country auction'
Vintage Festival's fate 'up for grabs'
THE SONOMA INDEX-TRIBUNE and SHOPPING INDEX, Sonoma, C
Funds and fund-raising Chamber of Commerce topics
C of C directors discuss priorities for payments
Cannard in surprise move
C of C president asks for, and gets, the manager job
The Sonoma Index-Tribune
Sonoma youths involved
Narcotics 'party' leads to stabbing; 4 arrested
Chamber's future debated at emergency meeting here
C of C wipes out debts of '66 Vintage Festival
Financing heart of problem
Vintage Festival support seems assured; key meeting scheduled
THE SONOMA INDEX-TRIBUNE and SHOPPING INDEX, Sonoma, Calif.
Boys in Vietnam liked getting C of C letter
Chamber in soup
Slurreptitious way to get a quorum
Chamber to invite 4000-trailer caravan to tour Sonoma Valley

Bob and agreeing to meet his conditions. They paused only to comment on the fact that it seemed unreasonable to expect Bob to work for nothing, but nevertheless appointed him right away.

It's hard to know whether Bob had simply reached a crossroads and reacted quickly and instinctively to a new idea as usual, or whether he had been planning the gesture knowing that it would dramatically focus the attention of the board and probably force a decision. Either way it would clarify his own position, and contrary to their usual uncertainty, provoke a definite commitment from the board.

Within a month, Bob had the directors agree to a new charter, emphasizing the Chamber's role in fostering a dynamic business environment, welcoming newcomers, protecting open space as it related to the agricultural community, and building tourism.

Within nine months of Bob becoming manager, the Chamber was $6,000 in the black. It could finally afford to pay him a salary —$900 a month plus expenses.

Bob's huge personal efforts in the preceding year had been matched week by week with publicity for the Chamber in the pages of the *Index-Tribune*. Ironically, a year after confronting him over his part in the questionable Chamber loan, Bob Cannard was presenting Bob Lynch with a certificate 'For outstanding community service in helping to rebuild and revitalize the Sonoma Valley Chamber of Commerce.' But Bob asserts that this was only because the editor had kept his half of the bargain. The award ceremony did nothing to alleviate the bitterness between the two men, the results of which would repeatedly manifest themselves in the pages of the newspaper for another thirty-five years.

Over the next few years, Bob led the Chamber in a relentless program of business promotion. There is no question that had the Chamber (and the Vintage Festival) gone under, which it most certainly would have without his personal efforts, Sonoma's business and residential growth would have been

Index-Tribune

Sonoma, California, Thursday, August 1, 1968

In Sonoma Plaza

Ox Roast, Chess Festival Sunday

Contribute ransom please

Here's to A&W

'Citizen of Day' award to CC manager Bob Cannard

City water bond issue gets support of Chamber

To go with the ox roast 3/13/69

'Look like General Vallejo' hirsute contest suggested to C of C board

Getting the bird

Anti-shoplifting clinic Tuesday

C of C action

Cannard voted salary--plus a brand new title

Model for hair growers

General Vallejo contest rules

Bull-etin on ox roast

Y'all come! 6/5/69 FRONT

Ox Roast, sideburns and music on Sunday

'congress'

stry, Highway 12 of C priorities

Chamber's valley map fund within $200 of $3,000 goal

Advance sale saving 5/16/68

Tickets to big 4-ring circus June 8-9 being sold by Chamber of Commerce

seriously slowed and the valley's preeminent position in the wine industry taken many more years to establish.

The Chamber went on to play a vital role in zoning changes, protecting agriculture, building police services, supporting county business development programs, Highway 12 upgrading, and valley incorporation studies. At Bob's instigation, it even found time to contact servicemen in Vietnam, and made sure they knew their efforts were appreciated.

Bob tried to make the process of business development fun, too. There was the giant pumpkin festival, an auto giveaway, new maps of the town, the anti-shoplifting clinic, and the great General Vallejo look alike contest, to name but a few.

© the *Sonoma Index-Tribune*

I remember thinking "what can I do in the summer?" A circus seemed an obvious choice and I'd enjoyed them so much as a child. So I wrote to a number and one agreed to come. Arrangements were made for the management to get rooms at the Sonoma Mission Inn, and the circus tents were put up in Maxwell Park. It's a natural amphitheater—there used to be a rodeo every year. And my son Bobby got to ride an elephant the two miles from the Sonoma Mission Inn to Sonoma Plaza as publicity. Wonderful!

Helen Hernandez was always willing to go along with Bob's Chamber publicity plans. As Pilgrims, Helen and Bob do not seem overjoyed by the Thanksgiving bounty

© the *Sonoma Index-Tribune*

And now, thirty-five years later, the issues in Sonoma are to an extent the result of the growth and vitality engendered by efforts like those of Bob and the Chamber. Over-development, astronomic real estate prices, excessive traffic, infill problems, water shortages, and of course, a central plaza dominated by tourists and real estate offices.

Whenever Bob complains about any of these subjects, his wife Edna is quick to point out that he is as much to blame for them as anyone.

Bob held the position of Chamber manager until January 1972. One of the most noticeable legacies from his tenure is Sonoma's annual Ox Roast, still going strong since 1967, and one the first events Bob organized to draw attention to the newly revitalized Chamber. He not only set up and promoted the event but roasted the ox as well. It was a skill he had picked up in Pennsylvania many years before.

The first Ox Roast in front of City Hall. The Cannard tradition is still going strong almost forty years later

In 1932, a member of the Democratic National Committee, Frank De Long, held an ox roast in a staunchly Republican area—Washingtonville I think it was—for Roosevelt. My oldest brother George went. He came back impressed by the democratic cause but less so by the roast ox, and he showed me an inedible charred piece to prove it.

Four years later he went again, and exactly the same thing happened, but this time he returned with a raw piece of meat that we were at least able to cook.

You see, a long time ago in England, drovers roamed the countryside with small herds of cows, for sale to farmers or cooks. They came to the United States and did the same here. And wherever they stopped, in Lancaster say, they would attract the farmers from miles around by roasting a steer as advertising for their product.

In 1948, the young republicans

decided to hold an ox roast at Belfonte, and as a member, I volunteered to do the roasting. Knowing that we would drive the public away unless it was cooked right, I figured that too much flame and not enough heat had been the problem, so I built an oven around the steer and above the flame. It worked out fine and I've been doing it ever since. What a lot of people don't understand is that in the time it takes to get the outside temperature of a good sized steer up to the right level, the inside could become dangerously high in poisoning bacteria. So I learned to stuff the beast with bread soaked in wine, and pour wine on the outside too. Then when you hoist the animal over half a cord of blazing firewood, the wine is flash heated to steam, which sterilizes the inside of the animal.

In Sonoma, the editor of the local newspaper said you'll never cook a steer above ground Bob. I guess I showed him he was wrong. I started that one on the plaza at 10 p.m. the night before, and by morning, the wonderful cooking smells attracted the attention of all the folks attending early mass at St. Francis. I believe many of them returned at 11 o'clock to swell the numbers when the beef went on sale, and it was all gone by noon. We even sold the bones!

In an effort to involve more of the local public, I decided to hold a party the night before the ox roast, after I'd started the fire to cook the ox. It was a great time with wine, french bread, and small steaks cooked over the open fire. Many of the same people came every year and stayed until well after midnight.

Jerry Parker and Dick O'Neil were regulars. One year they both drank too much wine and Dick said he was going over to the photo shop to sleep. A little later Jerry said he would go join Dick and started off. When he got near the duck pond, he walked into a tree and fell down. I could hear him swear. He got up, made a right turn, and walked right into the duck pond. I had a terrible time getting him out and over to Dick O'Neil's to sleep.

One year we advertised the party in the San Francisco paper, saying people could sleep in the Plaza. We got a big response and quite a few from San Francisco slept over. Within a few months, the chief of police had all the bamboo and brush cut from the Plaza. He said that too many people were fornicating in the Plaza, and he wanted to be able to shine the spotlights from the police car into the Plaza."

As Bob circulated among the diners during the first event in 1967, a couple from Fresno stopped Bob and insisted that it was the finest beef they had tasted since enjoying a similar ox roast years before in their original home town of Belfonte, Pennsylvania.

A year later in June 1968, at the annual banquet of the Chamber of Commerce, Ig Vella, one of Sonoma County's recently re-elected supervisors, paid tribute to the turnaround in the fortunes of the Chamber by saying "The phoenix has risen from the ashes." In part, it seems, they were the ashes from the ox roast.

Despite the generous comments, Bob was having serious doubts about his support for Ig. In 1964, he had been impressed by the Sonoma cheesemaker and thrown his considerable support behind Ig's first run for county supervisor, canvassing all his network of contacts in the Kenwood area. But the events surrounding Santa Rosa's annexation aims suggested to Bob that Ig was not aggressively promoting the interests of the valley, and was tending to fall in with what he called the suede shoe fat cats in downtown Santa Rosa. If Ig had political aspirations beyond the county, it was of growing concern to Bob. He could foresee some unique aspects of Sonoma Valley being lost by the imposition of highways and water supply systems that were being developed by a board of supervisors insensitive to the marked difference between the character of the valley and the rest of the county, and seemingly more interested in supporting the interests of Santa Rosa developers and the compliant mayor Ryerson. Nevertheless he supported Ig's successful 1968 re-election campaign, discouraging any opposition.

By 1969, Bob was working full time for the Chamber of Commerce and teaching more classes at the junior college than a full-time teacher. He belonged to some twenty clubs and societies and was out almost every night of the week speaking at one or another of the then 120 social and business organizations in the valley. Somehow he found time for three years to write for *Sunset* magazine in San Mateo as a consultant. There was nothing going on in the valley that he wasn't involved in. Edna and son Bobby were the mainstays of the nursery, but all members of the family worked to keep it going during the week, with Bob doing the buying and promoting at the weekend. At the time, it was probably the most successful nursery in the county.

About the only time he and Edna got to talk was when they were in bed, and it was there in August of 1969 that Edna announced in no uncertain terms that Bob had to cut down. He had too many things going on and needed to slow down. When he asked what the answer was, Edna told him he should stop teaching, sell the nursery, or give up the Chamber. Bob replied that he would do any of the three; she could make the choice.

Within a week Edna had sold the nursery to a lawyer who lived in Kenwood for a price that Bob of course insists that he could have bettered by at least $10,000, but a good price nevertheless. It was on the condition that the family could stay at the nursery for six months, which they did, moving to the house on Third Street East in Sonoma where Bob and Edna still live, in February 1970.

CHAPTER SIX

POLITICS AND RUFFLED FEATHERS

A week before Thanksgiving in 1971, the local newspaper reported that a Henry Mayo development project, "Villa Vallejo," featuring 125 houses, some of them three story, was planned for twelve acres of green space to the northwest of Sonoma Plaza adjacent to the historic Vallejo home "Lachryma Montis." It would go before the local planning commission in December. By any measure, this was a huge development that would dramatically affect the character of Sonoma.

The announcement in the paper came only days after Bob had presented ideas for expansive green areas, recreational areas and bike paths in and around Sonoma to the newly formed Ecology Club. It seemed to Bob that this new project would begin to erode the green space he and others were determined to protect for the future, and he was appalled that the *Index-Tribune* was offering no opposing point of view, even though it clearly existed on the street.

At the commission meeting, the California State Department of Parks and Recreation asked for four acres of the proposed project to be reserved for them to create a twenty-acre green buffer zone around the historic Vallejo home. They were anxious to link the house with the planned Depot Park and other historic buildings closer to the plaza. But they were unable to commit because state funding was not yet available. They even offered to buy all the land and cede some back to the city for its own park, together with another parcel of land further to the east that they owned.

Despite the objections of a majority of the public speakers, and the support declared for the state park plan, the commission voted in favor of the project the following February. It was the commissioners' view that Sonoma should concentrate population at its center, and they complained that the state operated far too slowly for them to take the offer seriously.

The First Congregational Church, sitting right next to the proposed development, filed an appeal, claiming that the state parks department would have funds to buy the land in July. The appeal was rejected 3-1 by Sonoma's city council at a packed meeting, despite presentations from the church, a lot of concerned citizens, conservation groups, and state parks representatives. Councilmember Henry Riboni voted in support of the appeal, and Nancy Parmelee abstained, but Chet Sharek, Mayor John Lobsinger, and Dr. Switzer all voted against the appeal and for the development.

In the remarkably insensitive words of Switzer, people who wanted open space could "take a hike."

The action of the council in general and the words of Switzer in particular enraged local residents. Although it was commonplace—and still is—for elected representatives in Sonoma to side with developers even against overwhelming citizen objections, this decision was particularly offensive to a large number of people, including Bob. He had recently filed to run for county supervisor against Ig Vella, whom he accused of adopting a similar attitude to the Sonoma Council in ignoring the wishes of local people in favor of the developers in Santa Rosa. Not only did Bob believe that green space was vital to the well being of people, he did not want to see the legacy of the city's founder General Vallejo—in the shape of his heritage home and its surrounding expanse of green fields—treated with such disdain by what he saw as a money grubbing bunch of insiders.

A group of objectors, with Bob as one of its more vocal cheerleaders, decided to fiercely fight the plans which were following the usual pattern of being rubber stamped by a majority of the council members in league with city bureaucrats. The council majority and city staff were more amenable to the financial objectives of the minority "establishment" than to the wishes of the majority of the general population. There was a degree of confidence expressed by those city insiders who seemed to sneer at the objectors, and this only served to make them more determined.

They decided to get the decision overturned with a three-point plan. First, start a petition to have the issue placed on a ballot to be decided by Sonoma voters; second, get new people elected to the Sonoma Council so they could reverse the vote, and finally, make contact with Sacramento legislators so that the alternative to development could be provided with state purchase of the land. The core group who would work incredibly hard to these ends were Marge Eliason (whose home was used for meetings), Virginia Merkel, Eula Long, and Hilton Taylor, along with Bob. Many of these people were members of the informal Ecology Club.

At their request, attorney and former councilman Paul Jess built the case for a referendum, arguing that the council action was in effect legislative, while the city attorney, John Klein predictably argued that it was an administrative decision, and therefore not subject to a referendum. Either way, the committed group set about obtaining the necessary signatures—10 percent of the registered voters.

Bob promised that he would beat the bushes for new city council candidates. The election was only four weeks away and two current council members, Lobsinger and Sharek, both supporting the development plan, were standing for re-election unopposed. There was no time to get new names on the printed ballots, but it was quite legal for someone to declare themselves a write-in candidate and have voters insert their name on the ballot.

After an intense search, Bob came up with local favorite Dan Ruggles, a forty-one year Sonoma resident and local merchant who had served on the council before, and Thomas Pitts, a retired lawyer who had moved to Sonoma's Moon Valley Mobile Home Park two years previously. The small group began a vigorous campaign for both men.

High school students and other helpers flooded the city with literature in support of Ruggles and Pitts in a door to door drive, and posters went up at the mobile home parks. Bob worked tirelessly himself to directly speak to as many citizens as he possibly could in the two weeks prior to the election. Dan Ruggles' mother made it a point to contact every older female voter in Sonoma, urging her to vote for her popular son.

Neither Pitts nor Ruggles received the endorsement of the *Index-Tribune,* which to the surprise of nobody, declared itself solidly behind the incumbents. At the time, the owner of the newspaper, Bob Lynch, and his partners, were planning their own development for another lot adjacent to the Villa Vallejo parcel, and would not be anxious to see officials elected who might derail their proposals.

Paul Jess reminded the voters in a letter to the *Index-Tribune* that, with the requisite number of referendum signatures delivered to City Hall, the issue of the "Villa Vallejo" development would only go to a vote later in the year if the new City Council decided not to rescind the council's previous decision. So it was pretty clear to the electorate that a vote for Ruggles and Pitts was a vote to stop the desecration of Sonoma's beautiful and unique open space.

Knowing that write-in candidates were at a disadvantage because voters had to precisely and correctly insert their names on the ballot, supporters organized stations near the Community Center polling booths, giving voters all the instructions they needed (and even pencils to do it with when it was discovered that there were none at the booths.) They also provided rides to the Community Center for anyone who needed one, and spent the day encouraging all eligible voters to turn out and make their wishes known.

The efforts were well rewarded, when in the largest voter turnout ever, Ruggles and Pitts were elected with big majorities. Almost 100 percent of the Moon Valley Mobile Home Park residents voted for them, a fact which must have truly irritated Bob Lynch, owner of the *Index-Tribune*, who had in previous editorials characterized mobile home occupants as paying less than their fair share of city taxes with the implication that they were really second class citizens.

The new council members took office mid-April, and one of the first items on the agenda was the future of Villa Vallejo. But by this time, the developer had recognized the weight of public opinion and agreed to postpone his plans until the state had been given time to see if it could raise the money to purchase the land. Private attorney Paul Jess and city attorney Klein continued to be at odds over the validity of a referendum, but this was rendered moot by the new council's agreement to similarly put off their decision until the State's position was definitely known.

Bob had little doubt on that point. He had gained the assurance of Randolph Collier, candidate for First District State Senator, that if he helped get him elected, Collier would return the favor by ensuring that the money to purchase the land around the Vallejo house would be put in the budget. At the same time, Collier had urged that Bob not oppose the Lynch's development plans.

And sure enough, the director of California's parks and recreation department, William Penn Mott, wrote to the council in July confirming that Governor Reagan had approved the 1972/73 state budget, which included $350,000 to acquire additional land at the Sonoma State Historic Park.

At no time in the extensive coverage of these events did the *Index-Tribune* ever mention Bob's name, and very few of the other campaigners. All those houses that came within a hairsbreadth of being built, with the full support and participation of the city, council, and newspaper, would have made a gigantic difference to the aesthetic, recreational, and cultural assets of the City of Sonoma. Make no mistake, stopping that cynical development was huge. If you have ever used the bike path from Depot Park across to the Vallejo home and crossed that wide expanse of grassy fields replete with wildflowers, or if you've sat with thousands of others and marveled at the fireworks on the Fourth of July just a couple of blocks from the city's center, spare a thought for the folks who made it all possible. If Bob, Marge, Virginia, Eula, Hilton, Ruggles and Pitts hadn't said, "No, you're not going to get away with it this time," then all the institutions—civic and commercial, government and media—would have failed the people of Sonoma.

The value of Sonoma's assets today, whether in property or commerce, depend on its appeal to visitors and would-be residents. Thanks to the likes of Bob Cannard, many of the historic and environmental factors that create that appeal are still in place.

It is worth noting that the development co-owned by the newspaper's editor, featuring fifty houses that occupy the southeast corner of the same field, managed to get through unscathed.

Other than the personal satisfaction that a major portion of Sonoma's green space had been protected, Bob gained nothing from the campaign and its achievements. To the contrary, being spread so thin may have cost him his own election bid for county supervisor.

While the 1972 Sonoma City Council election was taking place, the valley was voting for its county supervisor. This time Bob was running against Ig Vella, the famed Sonoma cheesemaker and incumbent for the preceding eight years, along with a third candidate from Rincon Valley to the north.

Bob had developed suspicions about Ig over the Los Guillicos development to the north of the valley during Ig's first term, and only reluctantly supported him in the 1968 elections. In 1969, Ig, as president of the Board of Supervisors shepherded through and personally voted for a plan to redraw the county supervisorial districts. Four of the five, including his own, would now each contain a wedge of Santa Rosa. The population distribution in the county would have allowed for two south county districts, two Santa Rosa districts, and one district covering the north county and coast—thus giving a fair spread of supervisorial interests. But now, four out of five supervisors would be beholden to the interests of Santa Rosa, and hence its development plans would dominate the county, as they do to this day. The rural voters in Sonoma Valley are outnumbered in the First District by the urban voters in Santa Rosa. Bob considered this an outright betrayal of the valley's special interests, and believed that Ig had broken his word on the subject. The same year, Ig had switched from being Republican to Democrat. Bob was convinced this was all part of Ig's wider political aspirations—maybe even governor of California—and perhaps explained why he would go along with the "downtown crowd" and their re-apportioning plans.

And in Bob's view Ig had failed to respond to a worsening water situation. Through drainage of swampy areas, putting flood water runoff into culverts and concrete ditches, and digging too many wells, the water table in Sonoma Valley had dropped to such a degree that most of the natural springs were gone and streams had dried up. The new aqueduct bringing water from the north was never quite able to keep up with demand from new homes.

Demands on the aqueduct were made worse by the

development of Oakmont, which had its greatest effect at the south end of the valley. It came to a head when political chicanery allowed at least one large landowner up the valley to siphon off a huge volume of drinking water to irrigate recreation land (actually polo fields and a golf course) in the middle of summer when Boyes Hot Springs a few miles south was, ironically, out of water. The pumping occurred in the middle of the night, Bob charged, but this was bitterly denied and the people so accused threatened a lawsuit. It was quickly dropped when Barry Hill and Bob mentioned the fact they had photographs of the meter readings taken over time. The pumping stopped—even if the official denials didn't. The debate over water heated up in the papers with Bob vociferously alleging that not only was Oakmont pumping more than they should, they were paying less for it. Oakmont had never shared in the cost of building the aqueduct in the first place, and maybe they needed to catch up with that too.

The denials this time came from every direction, but the explanation from the water district's representative—who got very hot under the collar—was so convoluted that it lacked credibility. They basically said it didn't happen when patently, it had. The *Index-Tribune* played a classically Sonoma establishment role. It criticized Bob for not being "nice" and implied that he didn't understand the experts. It briefly reported his complaints, and then gave extensive coverage to the officials' rebuttal.

The situation was never resolved, and it did nothing to stop the widening rift between Cannard and the *Index-Tribune*. There is absolutely no doubt that residential development and an utter lack of official interest in water conservation created the problem. But the water authorities, whether county supervisors or local boards, were never going to do anything about it as long as they could get more water from somewhere else. (This attitude towards water management continues today. Water from a long ways away is stored in huge tanks above the city of Sonoma for peak summer usage, yet nothing is done to conserve the valley's own aquifers. To make matters worse, the efficiency of the system that collects rainwater and speeds it away has been improved, guaranteeing that aquifers will not recharge. The problem is exacerbated because decisions about water are made by the county supervisors, who also act as the board of directors of the county water authority).

There are of course two issues, the supply of water to faucets, and the health of the valley's ecology in relation to water. Only one of them is addressed by the water authorities, that are simply concerned with supplying water to homes and businesses. They do not consider it their role to get involved with the water health of the valley. They exist simply to deliver water; if one source becomes unreliable they adjust to other sources to make up the shortfall. It doesn't matter to them if the water table drops, the rivers run dry or wells fail. It doesn't matter to them if the entire ecology of the valley changes like it has in San Jose, where the water table has dropped to 2,500 feet and the entire eastern side of the hills is denuded of trees. But it matters to Bob Cannard.

As a horticulturalist, environmentalist and

conservative, Bob was so concerned about the water situation that he developed a broad plan to reverse the drop in the water table and make the valley less dependent on outside sources.

He proposed a series of locks on Sonoma Creek that would create four lakes at strategic points in the valley. Each of the lakes would not only conserve water and replenish the aquifers, they would become a recreational resource, a tourist benefit, and a means to enhance the value of many properties adjacent to the proposed lakes. Some of the less desirable homes in Boyes Hot Springs could become lakeside cottages.

Although the proposal generated a great deal of interest among valley residents and particularly those with failing wells, the official response was predictably tepid. And probably because the idea came from a Cannard, the local newspaper editorialized against it. But then, the newspaper has never gotten behind anything that might adversely affect the rate of development in the area. It is an unfortunate by-product of rural conservatism that elected representatives and the establishment in Sonoma Valley have invariably failed to seize any opportunity to be progressive, because it usually requires, god forbid, proactive planning. Preferring the safe route of the status quo, they generally say no on the basis that at least you can't be proved wrong if you do nothing. To quote a recent member of the Sonoma City Council on the issue of constraining the boundaries of the City as a preventative measure against sprawl—"We shouldn't do anything now because in forty years from now people might want to do something different."

One person who did respond to Bob's ideas was Bud Castner. Bud was extremely influential with state and county officials and was largely responsible for setting up the Valley of the Moon Water District, wielding power behind the scenes. He was a longtime director of the Golden Gate Bridge Authority, and wealthy from insurance and savings and loan businesses. Bud asked to see Bob when Wes Hill, the manager of the valley water district retired in the early seventies. He asked Bob if he'd like the job, and when Bob replied that he wasn't a water engineer, Bud replied, "but you know water, Cannard."

It was an attractive idea, and there was the $17,000 salary. But there was also the fact that his bosses would be the county supervisors, and that included Ig Vella. Bob declined.

"Bud had a problem with the Index-Tribune too. He strongly objected to the way he was portrayed on some issue or other, talked it over with Bob Lynch who disagreed of course, but offered to eliminate Castner's name entirely from the paper. That arrangement suited Bud just fine, and probably accounts for the fact that he respected me."

Bob's proposal for revolutionizing the valley's water policy was not pursued, and the valley still suffers from failing wells and a falling water table. New municipal wells, and a few huge business wells installed since 2000 speed the downward spiral.

While agencies and municipalities promote drought tolerant plants and xeriscape gardens, and give away low-flow hose nozzles, and the Ecology Center rips out invasive alien species, nothing is done about the underlying problem—a fundamental change in the valley's ecology caused by the plummeting water table. And it continues to gall Bob Cannard that conservative people cannot find the energy to conserve their most precious resource.

His published documents on water issues over the last thirty years infer as much about his environmental convictions, understanding of history, sense of place, and his sense of responsibility to that place, as they do about the politics of water and the people who have shaped policy. And they speak reams about his confrontive style.

Bob wrote the following in August of 1972 shortly after many valley residents lost water service during an especially hot spell. Bob submitted it for publication to the *Sonoma Index-Tribune* but also copied and distributed it throughout the valley. He had no concerns about calling it like he saw it.

> *Sonoma Valley's water problem is a complex one, made only more so because it is directed and controlled in Santa Rosa by people who want to serve their own interests. First District Supervisor Ignacio Vella has helped this to happen against the interests of his own constituents here in Sonoma Valley. Although he was conveniently absent this year during the vote, he voted 'Aye' last year on the same contract that cost valley residents both money and water. It is just one more example of Mr. Vella's lack of interest or concern for the people of Sonoma Valley.*
>
> *It seems inconceivable to me that the newspaper (Index-Tribune) could run several major articles on the water problem in Sonoma Valley and ignore the basic reason for the rate increase and why many people were out of water during the recent heat spell.*
>
> *Take the lack of available water to begin with. Both the Valley of the Moon Water District and the City of Sonoma buy their water as prime buyers from the Sonoma County Water Agency. The county water agency controls all of the contracts for water to our two local entities and everyone else who buys wholesale water. It is run by the county supervisors.*
>
> *During the recent water shortage, the Oakmont golf course continued to irrigate and pumped more than 500,000 gallons onto the course while homes in the Springs area were without water. Oakmont's water came out of the aqueduct that the people in Sonoma Valley bought and are paying for. The county water agency (supervisors) sells water from the aqueduct to Oakmont. If this were not bad enough, during this hot summer, the supervisors have entered into another agreement with wealthy Santa Rosans to supply water to their new polo field that will also come out of the aqueduct and be largely paid for by people in the valley. The recent water shortage in the Springs area was due to gross mismanagement by the water agency (supervisors).*
>
> *Now, consider the increased cost to the people of Sonoma Valley. The water agency (supervisors) sells by contract to Oakmont and the polo field, water at less than a third the cost that Sonoma Valley pays—$21.00 per acre foot to Oakmont*

and Polo Field; $75.00 per acre foot to Sonoma. The water agency (supervisors) claimed that the recent 5 percent rate increase was for increases to the distribution system. That is a blatant lie. The 5 percent increase was charged to subsidize the Santa Rosa developers and their special interest friends like the owners of Oakmont. The people of Sonoma Valley have already bought distribution facilities sufficient to carry us through the year 2000.

If anyone cares for specific public, but suppressed, facts or meter readings on how much water Oakmont used, I will be glad to supply them. Interestingly, Oakmont uses about one-third the amount of water the City of Sonoma does and yet is charged only one-third the rate. In fact, Oakmont rates went down 30 percent last year while those for city residents went up. In addition, while all agricultural meters were turned off for two weeks during the recent shortage, the Oakmont golf course continued to pump water even during the most critical times.

Even as a newspaperman, I don't suppose Mr. Lynch is interested in these facts because each one reflects unfavorably on Mr. Vella. In the newspaper's effort to protect and elect Mr. Vella, it has done this valley a decided disservice in not presenting a complete picture as to why water costs more and some people did not have any in their homes.

Water concerns in Sonoma Valley never went away. The arid West's now classic issues of seasonally limited supply, growth and the competing demands of cities and agriculture dogged the valley—and continue to do so today. Bob repeatedly pushed for a more proactive approach to water management that included all of the various interests throughout the valley and one that would make the valley more self-sufficient when it came to supply. Holding up San Jose's example as a road to be avoided at all costs, he has appealed repeatedly over the years for better utilization of the winter rains and run off—for storing the excess in times of plenty, slowing the flow to allow for recharge and other secondary benefits, and never overdrawing the area's capital—the groundwater.

In January 1998 Bob wrote to the *Index-Tribune*, pushing plans outlined for the valley years before.

In 1940, the hills in eastern Santa Clara County were green with trees. Today they are bare. In 1940 the water table was about the same as ours, twelve to thirty feet. Today the water table in Santa Clara County averages 3,500 feet below the surface. Water has been pumped for domestic and industrial use. Agriculture and the trees can not get the water by natural percolation in the soil. The trees die and agriculture disappears.

In the mid-1950s the Army Corps of Engineers did a water survey in Sonoma Valley and identified seven dam locations that would provide water for a century. I supported this regional system over the Warm Springs Dam project for many reasons.

First and foremost was the replenishment of the ground water. The streams are the arteries of the water table. In the winter the streams feed the water table and in the summer the water table feeds the streams. When we lower the water table, the streams don't run in the summer. Groundwater must be preserved for agriculture and for people who do not live on public water systems. The rest of us must use publicly stored water.

The second reason was regional recreation. How many Sonoma families can go to Lake Sonoma forty-five miles away on a summer evening for swimming, boating or fishing? The number one site selected by the Army Corps was a dam on the headwaters of Aqua Caliente Creek, right in the center of our most populous area.

Another very important reason to build the regional system was the control of floodwater at Schellville. Until we hold some of this water back, during heavy rains, we will be flooded every year.

We are fortunate to have plenty of water in Sonoma Valley. We just have to be smart enough to use it properly

This article was never published, and the following May the board of the Valley of the Moon Water District voted to eliminate storage tanks from the district's capital improvement plan, and Bob blasted them for what he considered a dishonest abandonment of their charter. Their decision so offended Bob's understanding of the issues, that he questioned their competency. He did reassure the board: "However, even though you are dead wrong, it is not too late to change."

As with so many things, Bob's ideas for valley water were steeped in his understanding of history and the practical demonstrations of common sense. He collected information on the water supply from reports, old newspaper articles, and historical and anecdotal accounts. Bob had no interest in proving the "facts" to satisfy the nay-sayers; he was looking for a plan of action. Others' hesitancy to act on such an important issue that impacted so many exasperated him.

Climatologists, water company engineers, hydrologists, and others can talk until they are blue in the face but cannot dispute the fact that our groundwater has been seriously depleted.

It was exactly the same story with roads and traffic. Sonoma suffered because it offered through traffic no way of avoiding city streets, yet the valley has wanted to preserve the rural quality of its existence by keeping highways at bay. The dilemma has produced inactivity, and Sonoma has become a hostage to fortune.

In the late fifties and early sixties, when highways were "in fashion," all the big lots in the county where overpasses, interchanges, ramps, and bridges might be built, were snapped up by Santa Rosa developers who rushed construction plans ahead. It's why the highway bridge over the Napa River was built six years before it was linked to anything. It's why there's a spur off the Highway 101 freeway in Santa Rosa that heads toward Sonoma and then stops suddenly. Fortunately the excess of greedy developers was curtailed by the activities of groups like the "Highway 12 Committee." Mel Lawson was a member for fifteen years, with Bob and Barry Hill as the most active members, and from the early sixties stood guard at the north end of the valley. They organized letter-writing campaigns, lobbied supervisors, presented their case to the state government in Sacramento and petitioned ranch owners. The committee's tireless efforts stopped the freeway heading down the valley, and prevented the appearance of huge advertising and road signage that would have destroyed the rural charm of the valley. There are no new advertising signs along Highway 12 that were not there in 1969 when the road was designated a scenic corridor—another accomplishment of the Highway 12 Committee.

In 1970, Bob wrote this amusing piece about roads and traffic. He has resurrected it whenever the issue has resurfaced.

The Dragon That Eats Towns

Once upon a time a small dragon came to the Valley of the Moon. His name was Highway 12. At first, he was a very small dragon and the people liked him because he made it possible to drive between those small historic California towns of Napa, Sonoma, and Santa Rosa and all of the little villages in between. It was a beautiful drive and everyone loved the dragon.

Then, when lots of people moved to California from elsewhere the dragon began to grow. No one gave much thought as to why the dragon was brought here in the first place—to make it easy for people to get from one place to another. There were far better routes to move people, but the dragon just kept on growing. The dragon grew and grew and pretty soon he had eaten up all of the little villages from Schellville-Vineburg to Kenwood-Melita. In fact, some of them are gone forever.

The scar that this great dragon has left on the Valley of the Moon will take a long time to heal but it can be done. The sooner we start the better. The only answer and the only hope of saving this valley and restoring the identity of the villages is to move the dragon to a route where he will be happier and eat less people. That route has been planned for many years. When the dragon is moved it will help everyone.

The City Council of Sonoma can force the owner of the dragon to take him to a happier home. But it will take the support of a lot of people in Sonoma to make this happen. City government will never on its own take the leadership. The dragon scares them and only the people of Sonoma can make it happen. Now is a good time to start.

When the dragon moves, all of the small towns along the route can get back to being themselves. The plaza in Sonoma can return to being the center of town and all the good things that go with that change. The commercial strip that has choked the dragon for years will gradually disappear with zoning and land use direction.

The dragon will be happy in his new home where he will be able to grow as the needs change over the years. Our fifty years of living with the dragon will then be remembered as a time when the people here learned to appreciate what they have and everyone will live happily ever after.

At the time the traffic pressure was building again, and Bob was anxious to head off the congestion that would certainly develop down the road. He found from his researches that over 90 percent of valley residents, all of its schools except for the high school, and all four wineries that existed then were within a quarter mile of the old railroad track. But the rail service had become a victim of the GM/Standard Oil push to remove all but buses from the Bay Area transport system. Nevertheless, the infrastructure remained in place. Bob hired a transportation consultant who calculated that a limited rail service could handle the school traffic, and the tourist traffic to the wineries too, provided that parking lots were built at the south end of the route at Schellville. It could be done with a two-tier fare system that would have cost children nothing and eliminated the school bus system. For five cents a day anyone could ride the tram. It would charge twenty-five cents a day on the weekends when the tourist traffic was high. Any new wineries would have developed along the tracks. What's more, only one property would have to be purchased. Finally the plan was put to the county officials and the public, with estimates of a significant reduction in traffic.

But the plan died. It was not supported by Supervisor Vella or the *Index-Tribune* editorials—despite reporter Jerry Parker writing a very positive article.

When Supervisor Ig Vella failed to oppose more annexation of valley areas into Santa Rosa (Pythian Road and Lawndale), and championed the Santa Rosa-based county supervisor redistricting, it pushed Bob over the edge and he decided to run against him. Many think that when he had resigned earlier in 1972 from the Chamber of Commerce, it was with the intention of running for supervisor, although Bob denied it at the time. It was an ambitious move, considering Ig's strong position as an eight-year incumbent, his high profile as a member of one of Sonoma's bedrock families, and the standing of The Vella Cheese Company.

There were the other candidates too. Paul Tunkis of Sonoma, and Dave Eby, a fireman from Rincon Valley, a populous area of Santa Rosa that had now been included in the electoral district with redistricting.

Naturally, Bob received no support from the local paper, which was solidly behind Ig. Between his involvement in the council write-in campaign, lecturing at the junior college, writing for *Sunset,* and his commitment to transportation and water issues, it was an extremely busy period leading up to the election. Bob was stretched thin, but he was obviously incensed by what he saw as Ig's sell-out of the valley, and he made no bones that he was running to expose the fact. He publicly claimed that Ig was not responsive to valley people and failed to represent the valley's special interests. He argued that Ig was falling in with the Santa Rosa crowd, going along with what they wanted for the county, and becoming so polished at "politics" that what he said and what he did were not always the same. It was pretty vitriolic stuff, and Ig threatened to give as good as he got if the mud-slinging didn't let up.

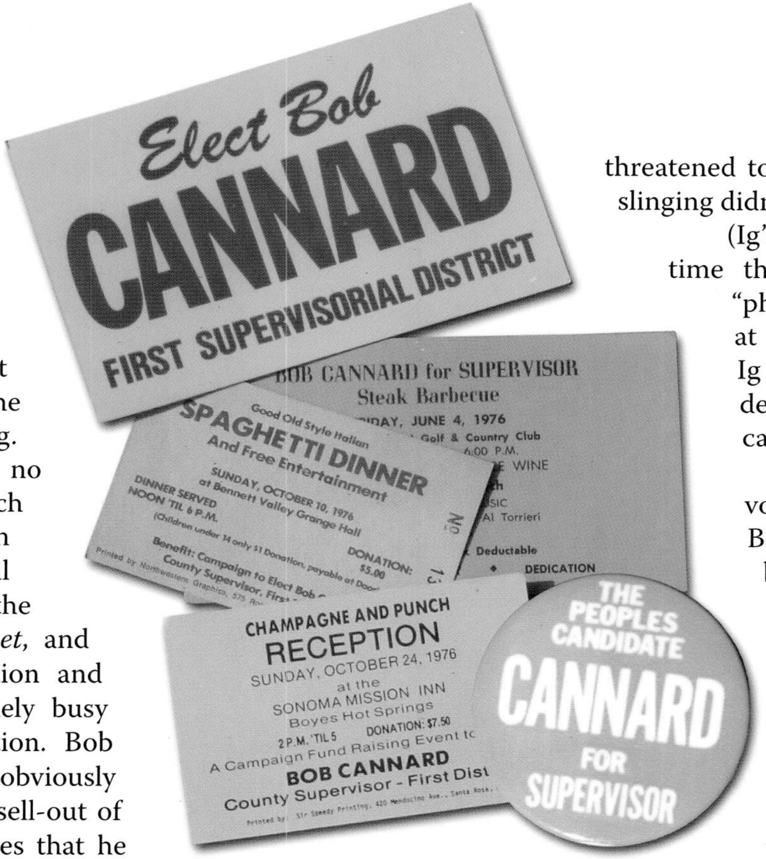

(Ig's daughter Ditty says the whole time that her father was supervisor, the "phone rang off the hook every night at home," so although Bob's claim that Ig was unresponsive to valley people is debatable, the fact that he took their calls is not.)

In the primary, Ig got the most votes but not enough to win outright. Bob failed to make the election runoff by just forty-five votes, losing out to the Rincon Valley fireman. But he did beat Ig in all but the east side of Sonoma (a fact never reported in the Sonoma newspaper), which suggests that his argument did resonate with a majority of local people. He did well in Kenwood too, but failed to make a big enough impression in Santa Rosa, where the vote tended to go for the incumbent or the local fireman. Ig also had the support of the Santa Rosa *Press Democrat.*

Such was Bob's intense dislike for Ig's politics that he supported Eby in the run-off election against Ig later in the year. Bob even stood in for the fireman in debates with Ig when the candidate was incapacitated, which he was frequently, due, Bob believes, to the fact that he was hopelessly out of his depth. Ig remarked to the assembled crowd on one occasion that if Cannard, who wasn't in the race, could do so much better than Eby, who was, then the voters had better vote for Ig.

Speaking on behalf of the reluctant Eby (who Bob considered less than ideal but nevertheless a supporter of the valley's distinct needs) left him open to public claims that he was motivated by vindictiveness, not political conviction. It's hard not to agree that some of this was true. It certainly illustrates the point that Bob is not a politician in the sense of building a consensus or engineering compromise. His style is the head on, take it or leave it variety that gets you noticed, but not necessarily voted for.

Ig won again in the runoff.

You can only imagine Bob's fury, when two years later, Ig resigned his elected position, and it was given to a Jerry Brown appointee, Brian Kahn, who Bob considered an evil disciple of the liberal left, and whose father was often accused of being a communist.

In 1976, when the popular Brian Kahn ran for re-election, Bob considered it his duty to run a token campaign against him. He knew it was a lost cause, but it gave him an opportunity to define what he saw as the grave danger of Kahn's liberal proclivities. However, despite a conservative face, Sonoma Valley and most of the adjacent areas of the San Francisco Bay Area are staunchly Democratic, which means that preaching the tenets of the Republican party may have appeared to them as extreme as Bob's view of Kahn's politics. Apparently there were other factors at work as well. Some Republican women in Oakmont told an incredulous Bob that they intended to vote for Kahn, "because he is so cute."

In any case, and not to Bob's surprise, Kahn won handily. Bob grudgingly agrees that he did represent the valley reasonably well. Eventually, after failing in a bid for a California congressional seat, Kahn left for Montana, because the rural flavor of the valley, for him at least, was gone.

Bob freely admits that Ig did an excellent job as manager of the county fairgrounds, the position he took after resigning his supervisor position, but the unpleasantness between the two men in that seminal year of 1972 makes you wonder what the atmosphere was like when in 1973 Bob's son Bobby married Ig's daughter, Maria "Ditty" Vella.

Bobby and Ditty were married in the Mission on Sonoma Plaza. A year before, marriages could not be performed there—the parks department being very much against the idea. But shortly after the elections of 1972, and the successful state purchase of the land around the Vallejo home, Bob held a reception for Senator Randy Collier behind the Mission barracks. Collier was with his new wife-to-be and Bob asked her where they intended to get married. She replied that it would probably be in front of a judge in Sacramento. So Bob took her across the street to the Mission, and she was charmed by it. Bob explained the problem with weddings there, and she replied "Randy will take care of that."

A couple of days later, Bob received a call from an

irate parks supervisor. "I must notify you Mr. Cannard that marriages in the Sonoma Mission are now approved." Bob quickly called the Bishop and the Mission was consecrated two weeks later. Collier's wedding was a semi-public affair, and any couple married for over twenty-five years was invited to attend and renew their marriage vows. The offer was taken up by about twenty-five couples, which probably guaranteed the senator fifty votes when he came up for re-election.

Part of the problem with these confrontations (that have either plagued Bob or that he has reveled in, depending on the way you look at it) is that Bob has a talent for seeing the infinite nuances and subtleties in nature but lacks the same appreciation for differences between people. For the most part people fall into two categories for him, those who agree with him and those who are wrong.

Bob wanted to have a hand in shaping the local community, but as far as he could tell, everyone was happy to sit back and let things unfold, with developers setting the pace, City Hall and the council rubber-stamping their proposals, and the other businesses getting a share of whatever growth came along. Bob couldn't tolerate this situation. There was no plan, no sense that what Sonoma was turning into was what people wanted.

In the years that he had lived in Sonoma Valley, Bob had found that affability and compromise was not the way to get things done, or at least, not the way he wanted to get things done. His experience with the Chamber of Commerce told him that nothing would ever happen without the drive and initiative of someone like himself grabbing control and sweeping forward. The local establishment looked like the old order, the people he and the pioneers were trying to get away from.

It's another irony that his schemes to energize the Chamber of Commerce were so successful in part because of the constant support provided by the *Index-Tribune,* which publicized every event. But when Bob left the Chamber, his bankable assets with the newspaper's editor were apparently gone, and from that date forward, he has rarely if ever enjoyed their support over any issue. Instead, the newspaper has seemed to look for opportunities to attack Bob, and he has obliged them with more controversial pronouncements than they could have ever hoped for. As time moved on, he had to shout even louder, and take even more extreme positions if his views were to be heard.

In January of 1974, Bob applied for the job as manager of the City of Sonoma, with strong backing from the likes of Leonard Duggan and Bob Parmalee. He wasn't hired, but was given serious consideration. It's impossible to tell if his stridency during the earlier elections affected anyone's opinion, or if his open dislike of certain aspects of the establishment were coming back to haunt him.

With the nursery gone, his stint at the Chamber of Commerce over, political aspirations on hold and only the junior college and his writing for *Sunset* to sustain him, Bob attended a conference for garden writers in San Luis Obispo. He was disenchanted with work at *Sunset Magazine* and planned to look for new contacts. He met Min Lee, the new editor at Ortho Books, the communication arm of the petro-chemical industry giant. The incredibly smart and intellectually vibrant Chinese/Native American and Bob hit it off immediately. In no time at all Min had become a regular visitor to Bob and Edna's home, wanting to learn all about practical horticulture. The editorial staff at Ortho featured great writers but not one good horticulturalist. Soon Lee was claiming to have learned more from Bob in an hour than he got from reading ten books, and Bob had become a consultant to Ortho. He contributed regularly for the next five years, creating the outline for *The Nursery Problem Solver* which has become the de facto manual in all California nurseries.

Min Lee moved on to Microsoft, and Bob continued to contribute articles to Ortho publications, but there was a not so subtle pressure to sell Ortho products at every opportunity. Bob had a hard time with this because many of their poisonous sprays he wouldn't even have allowed in his nursery. He was willing to recommend generic products for certain uses, but not wholesale use of heavily branded chemicals. There was a falling out, Bob was paid a retainer for another year, but there was no real work and the relationship petered out.

MORE PIONEER COOKING

APPLE BROWN BETTY OR APPLE PAN DOWDY

A mixture of cubed toasted bread, and apples or any other fruit at hand, sugar, and honey with a little liquor made a very tasty dessert. It could be made in a Dutch Oven alongside a campfire.

TORTILLAS

Tortillas are hand made with ground corn and water. Toasted over an open fire they were used as a combination of plate and spoon.

CHAPTER SEVEN

WATER INTO WINE

Bob continued to teach, and for the next four or five years, lived off investments, dealt in antiques, and enjoyed considerable interest income from land just to the east of Sonoma's central plaza that he had purchased and later sold to Melissa Detert, retaining the note at the extremely high interest rates prevailing in the early 1980s. And he took a keen interest in the wine industry.

At the junior college, he taught vine propagation, but insisted to his students that if they wanted to make a million dollars, "don't grow grapes, sell wine!" He had watched the market develop, seen brands proliferate, and believed that the "story" of wine was a more compelling sales tool than its quality to the rapidly growing customer base. The subjective taste rating given by experts was of little meaning to a population with unsophisticated palates and a budget of two dollars a bottle. The vast success of "Two Buck Chuck" some twenty-five years later suggests that the same is still true at the hard core volume base of the market. Maybe Bob was talking as much to himself as he was to the students, because it wasn't long before he was deep into the wine business himself.

In 1982 he met George Moller-Racke. George had been a partner in the Buena Vista Winery and was now looking for a new project. At the back of Bob's mind was an idea to produce wine using the historic name and heritage of General Vallejo, the founder of Sonoma, who was himself an avid grape grower and wine maker.

> *When William Penn Mott came to Sonoma after the purchase of the Vallejo land by the state, he emphatically said that now it was up to Dan Ruggles and myself to come up with a use that would justify its purchase but at the same time be historically appropriate.*

It had been Bob's repeated experience that whether you're in bonsais or insurance or promoting business through the Chamber of Commerce, it's the story you tell in support of the sale, rather than the inherent value of the product itself. He also knew from experience that people will joyfully exchange $10 for the daydream of a remote chance to win an exotic car, when they wouldn't freely give $10 to support the Chamber of Commerce. People want to be sold to, and the value they ascribe to the product is not just its fitness for purpose but also the emotional perceptions that surround it. Bob has always insisted that he helps people buy what they need rather than just make a sale.

You could pitch a bonsai tree with a straightforward explanation of artistic pruning, and maybe you might make a sale. But if you talk about Asian symbology, traditions developed over thousands of years, mesmerizing patterns of fluffy white clouds against a deep blue sky, and the illusions created by manipulating the eye with disguised scale, it's quite a different story. You are attaching an immediate emotional value to the tree that not only increases its perceived value and gets a sale, but also provides a memorable reminder of that value for years to come.

And with the wine industry beginning to push far beyond its generic beginnings as a cheap country beverage and into the romantic lore of artisanal craftsmanship, Bob was intrigued by the potential that existed for wrapping an agricultural product in the packaging of the area's history and creating hugely increased value for what was essentially a commodity. The added value would come from the existing story.

George Moller-Racke shared Bob's enthusiasm and as handshake partners they formulated plans to produce and sell a wine brand, as well as carbonated water from springs that still ran at the Vallejo estate near the center of Sonoma. The city council allowed Bob to use the name 'Sonoma Water Works' for the water venture. A bottling plant was set up, and Bob's son Tom devised a method for reintroducing natural carbonation to the water, which had insufficient levels when it bubbled out of the ground. The experts were convinced that theoretically Tom's method could not work, but such is Tom's genius for all things mechanical that it did, although no one could figure out how.

Bob had long-term plans to replant the Vallejo vineyard and sell wine with a concrete tie to Vallejo, but in the meantime, it could be produced elsewhere. Bob had formed a close relationship with Bruno Benziger, and it was agreed with George that the production of Vallejo wine would take place at the Benziger's Glen Ellen vineyard.

Bruno was a much decorated veteran of the war in the South Pacific who had, like Bob, come west with his family to start a new life. Their vineyards in Glen Ellen were not yet productive, and they had little production capacity. When Bob first met Bruno through Rich Thomas, the two had hit it off immediately and for two years, Bob and Bruno met nearly every morning and talked about the wine market and what it would take to build national sales. Their conversations were facilitated with copious amounts of gin. Bruno liked Bob's promotional ideas, and his focus on "depletions" from the distributors. He wanted to talk about moving the wine closer to a consumer sale rather than making it. When their meetings were over, the Benziger sons were expected to turn Bob and Bruno's ideas into action. They were not entirely happy with this arrangement, but there was little they could do about it.

George Moller-Racke, Bob, and Bruno signed a contract that made them equal partners in Vallejo wine, and although Bruno was not entirely comfortable with George, he was impressed by the latter's impressive contacts in the wine market. Capacity was not yet available to make Vallejo wine, and George was constantly pushing for them to start. But before they did, the partnership was undermined.

Bob began to sense that there was something not quite right about the water product. Tests indicated that it had no bacteria, and as Bob knew, this was impossible. He suspected that chlorine was being illegally introduced and he confronted George, who was evasive. Ultimately they could not find enough common ground to solve the problem and move on, so the partnership was dissolved, with George choosing the water operation when Bob gave him the choice of taking either water or wine.

Bruno was delighted by the decision and although the production of Vallejo wine did not start for another couple of years, Bob began to prime himself to sell it. After an analysis of the wine distribution business, he came to the conclusion that success depended a whole lot more on selling wine out of the distributors and retailers, than it did on selling it in. So he devised all sorts of promotions to provide incentives to wholesale representatives and improve the shelf presence in stores for Glen Ellen brands. He provided information about wine, about Sonoma, about the heritage of Sonoma County wines. He took every opportunity he could to get out on the road and provide stories for reps to talk about—anything that would differentiate Glen Ellen products from the rest. And even though there were protests in the Benziger family, sales increased dramatically, and it became possible to fund the introduction of the Vallejo brand. The winemaker was nominally Val Haraszthy but it was Bruce Rector who blended the first batch of Vallejo wine.

Bob oversaw production of the label designs, which leant heavily on the Vallejo heritage, and when bottling was completed, he hit the road with immediate success. Accounts that hadn't taken Glen Ellen wines took Vallejo products. They

were at a price level where the wine would not rely on subtle nuances of the varietal grape characteristic, and it was unlikely that they would have real competition with any other brand on a taste basis.

Bob knew if he could sell the story of Vallejo and California, he could sell the wine. He was absolutely in his element. The skills from the insurance business came together with his knowledge of merchandising from long before in Em's store. He could weave the story of the west, Vallejo, and California with the traditions of Sonoma and winemaking to create an overwhelming case for his wines. He used his horticultural knowledge to provide quality assurance and his infectious optimism to win people over. He provided reasons for people to buy wine where they had never existed before. And he made sure that he pushed competitive brands aside in the stores and guaranteed performance from his stacked-case displays—"The wine will sell, or I will pay your rent."

The story that Bob expounded is told in his press releases:

The Renaissance of M.G. Vallejo Wines

For the first time in over one hundred years, wines under the "M. G. Vallejo" label are in the market place. General Mariano Guadalupe Vallejo was one of California's first commercial vintners, planting grapes with his brother Salvador as early as 1836. By the time California became a state in 1850, Vallejo's winery "Qui-qui-ri-qui" (the crow of the cock) was well established. In the late 1850s when the Hungarian Count Agoston Haraszthy came to Sonoma, Vallejo was recognized as the leading winemaker. Haraszthy, also a California wine industry pioneer, planted hillsides to grapes and amicably vied with Vallejo in wine quality.

Bob Cannard, president of the M.G. Vallejo Memorial Association, recreated the Vallejo wine connection in 1980 to keep the Vallejo legacy alive. Bob is a long-time Sonoma resident who has devoted twenty-five years to preserving General Vallejo's home, Lachryma Montis, a California State Historic Park in the town of Sonoma, California, as well as saving the surrounding forty acres from becoming a housing subdivision in 1972.

The winemaker, Val, is a great great grandson of Vallejo and Haraszthy. (Count Haraszthy's son, Attila, married Vallejo's daughter, Jovita; Val is a direct descendant.)

Working together with Vallejo home officials and the State of California, they revived the historic label to generate funds from wine sales to help rebuild the old barn at the home where the General made his wine and to replant the vineyards that once flourished on the adjacent land. National sales of the wines began in June 1986. Plans also include building a working 19th century winery that would produce "estate" wines each year.

The M.G. Vallejo wines are available for public tasting and purchase at the Vallejo home chalet, as well as in stores and restaurants throughout the nation.

"General Vallejo made the people's wine," explains Bob Cannard, "and so do we." Priced at about $5, they are clean, varietal, flavorful wines. In keeping with the historic thread of this entire project, the wine is being made nearby at Glen Ellen Winery on the Wegnerville property. Originally part of General Vallejo's land grant from Mexico, Vallejo deeded the 150 acres (now Glen Ellen Winery) to Julius Wegner around 1851 for his carpentry work at Lachryma Montis.

The cream, blue and gold-foiled label includes the

same graceful rendition of Vallejo's home and barn that was on the original. The beautiful Victorian-style home where the Vallejos lived and entertained for thirty-five years is shown in all its splendor. Modern in its day, the two-story wood-frame house with verandas was fringed in lacy, carved wooden rim, painted white with dormer windows and highlighted by a tall pointed gothic window in the master bedroom. Today the building and grounds are carefully maintained with the house itself furnished with many of Vallejo's personal effects.

General Vallejo would be proud of the wines bearing his name. The strength of his personal energy and spirit are being brought to life through his favored life's work, viticulture and winemaking. Enjoy a glass of M.G. Vallejo wine and celebrate his rebirth.

With this magnificent hyperbole the introduction of the Vallejo wines was an immediate success, due mostly to Bob's marathon selling trips. In a matter of days, Bob was calling Sonoma for more shipments before the first ones had left. Vallejo wines went from zero cases sold in 1988 to the number nine producer of Sonoma County's 100-plus wineries two years later.

The wine was immaterial. They were buying history, not wine. It was the story that people were drinking up.

Part of that story

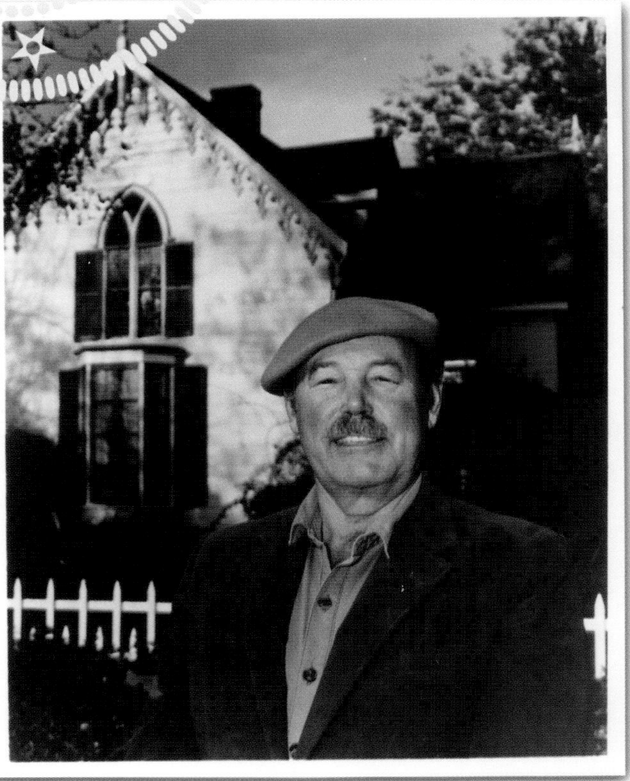

was to strengthen the link between the wine and the Vallejo heritage, with the long-term objective of having the brand declared the official wine of California. Bob had an agreement that allowed the "chalet" barn at the original Vallejo home in the state park to be used as a tasting room for Vallejo wine. Profits on wine sold through the tasting room would go to the park, and the tasting room was just the start of a plan that would resurrect the old Vallejo vineyards, start a small winery, and turn the property into a more dynamic historical showcase with income to sustain itself.

But soon after they had established themselves at the Vallejo chalet, objections were raised. The park's management did not want their location taken over by a commercial enterprise—albeit one with altruistic goals and income for the park—and religious elements objected to the general idea of serving alcohol on a state property that was regularly visited by school groups. But despite their protests, a liquor license was issued. James Brown, of Citrus Heights in Southern California lodged an appeal against the decision on "moral grounds," but that too was rejected. The license was confirmed in February of 1986.

But the state park management's objections continued, and considerable pressure came from Sacramento to stop the operation. The "prohibitionists and religionists" were threatening another round of appeals. To overcome these problems would have taken a huge amount of time and effort, and Bob was still spending the majority of his energy building sales through wholesale distributors and promoting the brand with wine writers, food critics, and anyone he believed could influence the appeal of the wine to customers and retailers.

At the same time, Bruno Benziger was handing over more and more of the Glen Ellen Winery operation to his sons. And they in turn were realizing that their true interests and the future of wine in Sonoma Valley would be at the premium end of the market and not with the everyday wines represented by the Glen Ellen and Vallejo brands.

Bob's ambitions for the Vallejo brand were as much to do with the promotion of General Vallejo and his historical significance to California and the western United States, as they were with making money. But he found himself caught between the ambitions of the Benziger family to become a force in the premium wine

Continued on page 154

In each area he visited, Bob motivated distributor salesmen by giving them something to talk about other than the taste characteristics of the wine. And he supported these efforts by pushing food and wine writers to present the same information in the columns of local newspapers and magazines.

He found writers hungry for something new to write about, and frequently lazy enough to reprint his own prepared press releases verbatim. He would do anything to get these influential people on his side. Some wanted wine, some responded to a good lunch, and some even accepted his suggestion that they invoice for their valuable "time," even though he had provided the articles written and ready to go.

As a favor to the daughter of the writer on the *Boston Globe*, he lectured the history faculty of the University of Massachusetts on the history of California at length, and without any notes. To his great delight, a member of the audience later confided, "I've written seventeen books, and have never heard this wonderful material before." Another complimented him on his memory. "Fabulous, not a single error Mr. Cannard!"

And every time articles about Glen Ellen or Vallejo brands appeared, they were reprinted and presented to the distributor salesman as sales aids, often at their Friday morning meetings when Bob gave his inspirational speeches. He backed these up by going out with salesmen on their rounds, and by his sheer

force of enthusiasm for the brands and their instant "history." He negotiated big case displays and set up promotions and tastings that pulled the stock he had sold in to the distributor through to the retail stores and out to the consumer.

At a lackluster meeting in New York, he had invited questions from a roomful of surly unresponsive salesman and was saved when an elderly man who must have known more about Bob's background took the microphone and said, "I'm having trouble with my lawn, what do you suggest?" It gave Bob the perfect opportunity to change the subject and pace of the meeting and he soon had them all on his side with advice on various horticultural subjects that had little to do with wine.

At a wine society party he organized in Florida, the participants were so enraptured, they extolled the virtues of a Vallejo white zinfandel Bob claims was close to undrinkable.

Whatever it took, Bob was ready to oblige. For over a year he entertained one "rip-snorting" buyer in Texas to hard drinking sessions that usually ended at strip shows. But on a subsequent visit realized the buyer was conducting his meeting with one hand on a bible. "I've gotten married and found religion Mr. Cannard." When Bob checked out the story with the man's secretary she confided, "Yes, and thank God for it because he doesn't chase me anymore."

Continued from page151

Mariano Guadalupe Vallejo (vä-lä'-hō), one of California's most colorful leaders of the 30s-40s, founded the town of noma in 1834. He was among West's earliest commercial tners and took great pride in ring his wines with the states- and friends he so often enter- ed. He's pictured here in front of his Sonoma home where gracious hospitality was legend.

Today, that legend lives on through the wines bearing his name. Perhaps it's the gracious spirit of the man himself which makes M.G. Vallejo wines among the most popular affordably priced premium varietals.

The wines, today, continue to be produced in the fertile Sonoma Valley where they were made over a century ago.

These quality wines complement everyday meals and are ideal for the casual entertaining style practiced by M.G. Vallejo himself and enthusiastically embraced today by his great-great grandso Vallejo Haraszthy.

Vallejo Haraszthy, a direct d dant of M.G. Vallejo and Co Agoston Haraszthy (a Hung nobleman, pioneer winema expert on wine grape variet the managing director of M Vallejo wines.

"We're proud to conti five-generation tradition c wines for today's consum reflect the ease of Califor pitality," says Haraszthy.

Smooth, full, and made in an easy-to-drink style, M.G. Vallejo wines are appropriate for casual get-togethers and compatible with everyday meals.

The wines are available in retail outlets, liquor stores and restaurants. They include two 1988 special releases: Merlot, with a rich, velvety character combining hints of coffee, plums and berries; and a limited edition 1983 Zinfandel, possessing rich berry and spicy oak flavors with excellent balance. Also: M.G. Vallejo Chardonnay *clean, with fresh fruit and vanilla flavors—ready to be enjoyed immediately.*

Cabernet Sauvignon *classically styled, revealing full, earthy flavors and soft, oak tannins with a zesty finish.*

White Zinfandel *made in nouveau style: crisp, light and with a slight spritz.*

Fume Blanc *crisp and unpretentious with rich, clean and grassy Sauvignon Blanc and melon flavors.*

MGV Red *an easy-drinking, medium-bodied dry red wine, with complexity from fruit and toasted oak.*

MGV White *a unique balance of fruit and lightly toasted oak, making it a versatile and popular house-pour wine.*

M.G. Vallejo
1883 London Ranch Road
Glen Ellen, CA 95442
(707) 996-1066

market, and the refusal of the state to allow close ties between a commercial venture and one of their parks. His frustrations are apparent in personal notes:

> *The Vallejo brand was born in a storm of protest: opposition at the state level, turmoil among the Glen Ellen partners, problems between George M. and myself, law suits from the religionists and prohibitionists, and the uncertainty of a new brand in the marketplace.*
>
> *But there has always been one factor that has made this undertaking different from any other wine*

MARIANO GUADALUPE VALLEJO'S accomplishments would read like a history of the Golden State. It was due in a large part to his efforts that California became an American territory. He made the first wines in what was to become one of the world's great wine regions — Sonoma.

Our winemaker, Vallejo Haraszthy, is the General's great-great grandson.

6 in a Series of 99

Benicia Carrillo Vallejo, wife of M.G. Vallejo, was a member of one of the first families to come to California. She and Mariano Vallejo were married in San Diego, March 2, 1832. As the city of Vallejo was so named in honor of Mariano, so was the city of Benicia (once the site of the State Capitol) so named for his wife.

18 in a Series of 99

VALLEJO BEDROOM

Vallejo paid a great deal of attentio etail, not only in his winemaking, lso in the Victorian architecture and urnishings that he brought around C Horn.

21 in a

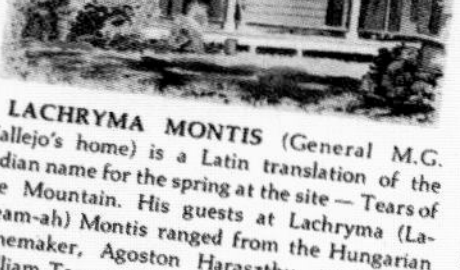

LACHRYMA MONTIS (General M.G. Vallejo's home) is a Latin translation of the Indian name for the spring at the site — Tears of the Mountain. His guests at Lachryma (La-cream-ah) Montis ranged from the Hungarian winemaker, Agoston Haraszthy, to General William Tecumseh Sherman.

Our winemaker is Vallejo Haraszthy, M.G. Vallejo's great-great grandson.

4 in a Series of 99

operation in America. And that is that as a side benefit, we were rebuilding the beginning heritage of the industry. We were bringing to the light of day the story of a great American patriot as well. We were giving something back to the consumer and the industry. A measure that no other winery or institution has ever done.

We will lose some of the validity of the brand, some of the reason to be, if we abandon the state connection. Some of the vitality will be gone. The single point that every wine writer around the country has found unique and different is that here is a winery that is doing something besides making a profit.

Bob had experienced firsthand the incredible power of the Vallejo connection when selling. He had also observed distributor representatives telling the story and rising above the constraints of subjective taste claims and price. Here was the proof that history holds the key. Bob inserts himself into history as a means of establishing his personal validity, and here was a brand of wine that was doing the same.

KITCHEN
VALLEJO FOUNTAIN
19 in a Series of 99
THE PETALUMA ADOBE, ten miles west of Sonoma was Vallejo's ranch headquarters. He imported the first pure bred beef into California in 1839 to improve the beef industry. If you enjoy fine beef and good red wine, thank General M.G. Vallejo.
Also his offspring, Vallejo Haraszthy is our winemaker.
12 in a Series of 99
THE SONOMA BARRACKS were built by Vallejo to house his cavalry. It was Mexico's last frontier against the Russians from the north. It was here that his first crop of grapes came to be made into quality wine.
And Quality is still the by-word of Vallejo wines and of our winemaker, Vallejo Haraszthy, the General's great-great grandson.
3 in a Series of 99
NAPOLEON VALLEJO'S CABIN
VALLEJO'S SWISS CHALET was shipped to him around the horn, each piece of lumber numbered for easy assembly. The building was used as a storeroom for crops and wine. Today, the Chalet is used as a tasting room for Vallejo wines.
Vallejo was renowned for fine wines. Today our winemaker, Vallejo Haraszthy, carries on this tradition of excellence begun by his great-great grandfather.
11 in a Series of 99
VALLEJO HOSPITALITY
General M.G. Vallejo enjoyed providing hospitality. This grand piano, which was brought around the horn during the Gold Rush was enjoyed with Vallejo's fine wines by his many guests. We hope you will come soon and visit us and taste our wines at the Vallejo Home.
22 in a Series of 99
0 85298 00009 3

It fitted perfectly into the Cannard scheme of things, which was to engineer a situation where his instincts, experience, skills, interests, and passions could all come together into a project that could generate income without it feeling like work. Where his personal gain was indistinguishable from his more than generous contributions to his local society. Where fun was to be had all the time because you were doing no more or less than using all your wits, all the time. He did well at school without the grind, because he could demonstrably contribute to the larger community. He graduated college

without the academic slog by having the skills to take over some of a stretched faculty's responsibilities. He excelled in the insurance business because he knew every activity that his own clients worked at, and he was already woven into the fabric of their rural community. Here was a chance to revel in the history of the city and state he lived in, provide funds to support its heritage sites, and sell a lot of wine without pulling a cork.

As he has done with his own life, he had given a wine brand an historical context. The wine venture had become a more permanent fixture, which made it difficult to give up. But the writing was on the wall and Bob would need an alternative scheme to bring the Vallejo history alive in Sonoma. He was at the time interested in a property that had come on the market, adjacent to the Vallejo Home. It included a house built for Vallejo's daughter Natalia called "Willows Wild." The property had once been the site of one of Sonoma's first wineries.

With the kernel of an idea forming for Willows Wild, Bob was reluctantly able to give up on the original plan at the Vallejo home chalet, and when the Benzigers decided to sell the Glen Ellen brands in order to fund their premium winery expansion plans, he did not object, even though it meant they could no longer maintain the Vallejo brand.

His reward was a share of the millions of dollars that the sale generated—along with a longer lasting tribute to his sales ability. If he stayed out of the wine business, the Benzigers would pay him $10,000 a month for a considerable period.

Bob remained close friends with Bruno. Sometime after Bob left the winery, Bruno was hospitalized for a heart problem. The doctors told him he had to give up drinking. Helen, his wife, and Bob were in the habit of going to the hospital every day about five o'clock. On the day Bruno was told he had to give up the gin and scotch, they met in Bruno's room, Helen bringing a martini and Bob a bottle of scotch. Bruno gave them the news. Bob suggested to Bruno that he had to look at it in a positive way, "You must say to yourself, Bruno, every time you want a drink 'I have had my share.'" They enjoyed several drinks that day as a celebration. Bob took the bottle of scotch home. Bruno died quietly in his bed less than two month later at home. Bob had visited with Bruno and Helen over breakfast the day before.

CHAPTER EIGHT

THE VALLEJO HERITAGE

Bob was now secure financially, and free of the commitment that had taken him on the road for so many months in the preceding three or four years. He was sixty years old, and his thoughts returned to the Vallejo legacy and how best he could preserve it. The General's life is well documented elsewhere, but Bob has a unique view of his significance, revealing it in a Fourth of July address given some years later.

Sonoma and Manifest Destiny:

I'm sure you have all heard the stirring words "Listen my children and you shall hear of the midnight ride of Paul Revere. On the eighteenth of April in seventy-five; hardly a man is now alive who remembers that famous day and ride..." No, Paul Revere did not ride into Sonoma, but his grandson did on July 7, 1846. He raised the American flag on the Bear Flag pole right here in the Sonoma Plaza. Manifest Destiny had been achieved. America had truly become a nation from sea to shining sea. What started in Philadelphia in 1776, ended in Sonoma in 1846.

The early history of California and the history of

Sonoma are one and the same. Much of what happened in the early years of California started in Sonoma.

It is fair to say that without General M.G. Vallejo, who laid out the town and built his home across the street, California could be a province of England rather than the greatest state in the Union.

In 1830 the United States did not have six Americans west of the Sierras. The only claim we had on the West Coast was by Lewis and Clark floating down the Columbia River in 1805. McKenzie had already come across Canada to the mouth of the Columbia River. The Russians had their trapping outpost on the Sonoma Coast at Fort Ross. The French had a thriving agriculture colony in the Los Angeles area growing grapes and making wine.

It was through the efforts of one man—M.G. Vallejo—who through determination and skill kept California from becoming aligned with any of these foreign nations. He regularly made that famous statement, which made him equal to any of the earlier heroes of the republic, at the conference of California dons in Monterey. That statement is, "Let us join with our fellow Americans where we will be fellow citizens rather than subjects of the King or the Queen or the Czar." This statement ranks him with all of the earlier heroes of our nation.

And it was his judgment that kept California free from foreign entanglements even though offered great inducement, until Manifest Destiny could catch up in time. Without M.G. Vallejo and Sonoma, there is a good chance that California would be a province of England like Canada.

Today as we celebrate the birth of our nation and the Fourth of July, let us remember June 14, 1846, when our nation became whole by stretching from the Atlantic to the Pacific.

Also, let us work for and pray for freedom and justice for all people, not only in this great nation but also in all nations around the world.

Thank you

Read Bob's Founder's Day speech to the Daughters of the California Pioneers on December 7, 1991, and you not only get an idea of the great esteem and admiration that he has for the General and the State of California, but hints of the parallels he sees in his own life.

Daughters of the California Pioneers—Founders Day Luncheon
December 7, 1991—Palace Hotel
Guest Speaker, Robert H. Cannard
"Mariano G. Vallejo, Lord of the North"

Occasionally in history there has been a favored place that has all of the ingredients to foster and promote great changes throughout the world. People, land, climate, and resources in a unique combination and proportion so that everything seems to work together. Great things happen. California was such a place during the last century.

Also, occasionally history has seen a man or a few people living in that area that just naturally do great things. People who otherwise might be quite ordinary, but because of the special circumstances of the moment stand out as great contributions to mankind and effect great changes. M.G. Vallejo was such a man.

The Spanish people in California in 1800 were little changed from the people of Moorish Spain that came to the New World starting at around 1500. They had come from a country that had just shed the yoke of Muslim control. But the Muslim customs still were a dominant factor in their lives. The layout of their towns with their great plazas, their architecture open to the air were very similar to the Arabic Middle East. The customs in their homes were all reminiscent of their Muslim past.

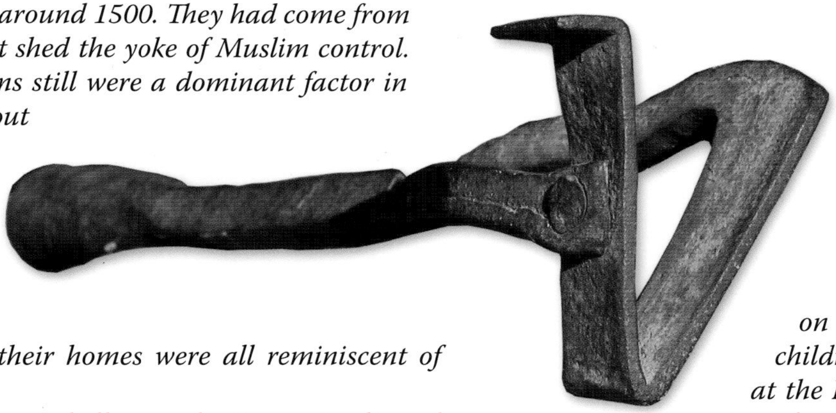

When Queen Isabella and King Ferdinand successfully drove the Moors from Spain about 1490, they had a few great supporters. And these supporters were rewarded by favored positions in the New World. The Vallejos were one of these families. One was an admiral in the Spanish navy. Another was later to become governor of Mexico. Later generations managed the mines and wealth in Mexico and Peru for Spain. In other words, the Vallejos moved west from the Indies to Mexico and later north into California ahead of the European civilization that followed them. The Californians of 1800 were little different in custom and thinking than the ones that came from Spain centuries earlier.

You will see later how these customs and this training helped shape the future of our state and in most instances worked against the Spanish people. As is often the case in history, the benefactors are not the ones who made these changes happen. In a great many cases, the Californians lost their land, their wealth, and their status in the new state. Curiously, they have never lost their allure or social status to the newer immigrants to California.

M.G. Vallejo was born in Monterey on July 4, 1807, the eighth of thirteen children. His father was a soldier stationed at the Presidio in Monterey. His mother was a Lugo from San Luis Obispo. Interestingly the priest that baptized Maria Lugo, Father Pablo Mugartegui, probably made the first wine ever made in California while he was stationed at the Mission at San Juan Capistrano. My research on the history of wine shows the year 1782 or 1783 as the first vintage in this state. The Italians not withstanding, it was the Spanish padres who laid the foundation for the present wine industry.

Mariano's early life in Monterey was much like any other young boy of a favored class. He received some tutored schooling, attended church and received some instruction from the padres but nothing terribly unusual happened to the lad. It was then that events of the day took over that were to shape his life. When he was fourteen, Mexico became independent of Spain. By the time he was fifteen, he had become secretary to Governor Arguello. He learned much from this association. Beside a practical education, he became aware of the larger role of politics. He formed friendships and acquaintances that were important to him all his life.

He became a cadet at the Presidio in Monterey when he was seventeen and rose through the ranks quickly. He had numerous encounters in the field with various Indian problems. He learned lessons that were to be of great value to him in Sonoma. By the time he was twenty-four he had been promoted to lieutenant and was in charge of the Presidio at San Francisco.

As an aside...

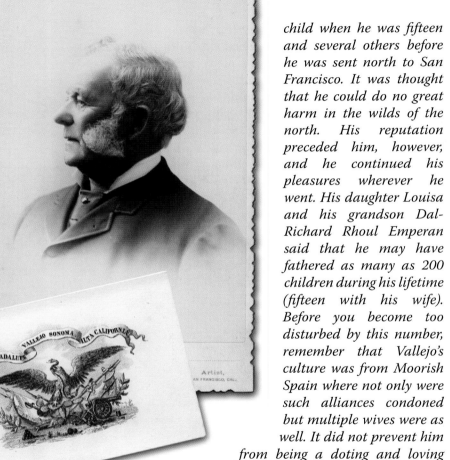

While in Monterey he acquired a reputation as a ladies man. He fathered one child when he was fifteen and several others before he was sent north to San Francisco. It was thought that he could do no great harm in the wilds of the north. His reputation preceded him, however, and he continued his pleasures wherever he went. His daughter Louisa and his grandson Dal-Richard Rhoul Emperan said that he may have fathered as many as 200 children during his lifetime (fifteen with his wife). Before you become too disturbed by this number, remember that Vallejo's culture was from Moorish Spain where not only were such alliances condoned but multiple wives were as well. It did not prevent him from being a doting and loving husband to his wife and family. Vallejo was yet to confront European (Victorian)

morality that much of the world lived by. He was a product of the past. I used to tell Dal Emparan, a rake in his own right, that Vallejo's first words on meeting a woman must have been, "Lay down, I want to talk to you." There were not too many women in California, Spanish or otherwise. There are many people living in California today with the name of Vallejo. I have the names of several.

M.G. and Dona Francisco Benicia Carrillo were married in 1832. He was twenty-five and she seventeen. The ceremony was performed at the Presidio's chapel in San Diego. They came north to the Presidio in San Francisco soon after the wedding.

It was a very good match. She had descended from a highly talented Spanish family and he from a rough border heritage that extended back 300 years. They were both physically and mentally tough, products of the time. They had fifteen children, many of them highly talented musically and in the arts. But alas, good fortune had passed them by with the coming of the Americans. Dona and Mariano were great contributors to the future of California, but received little in return. Like many others of their class they sowed the seeds of future greatness but did not reap the benefits of their efforts. They had been bred into and lived by the standards of the middle ages where they felt responsibility for all that they saw and cared for. Hospitality and responsibility went hand in hand. The Vallejos gave away land, cattle, seed, and help to nearly all Americans and newcomers who arrived. They probably expected, but did not receive, a reciprocal bond with those whom they had helped. Alas, their domains crumbled around them as competition and new law prevailed. But as M.G. said late in life, "I've had a very good life and would not want to change very much if I could."

Yes, he had a good life, and I would just like to recall for you a few of the milestones of that long and illustrious career.

- *He came to Sonoma in 1834-1835 with instructions.*
- *He argued in the councils at Monterey during late 1830s and early 1840s.*
- *He planted the grapes that were to become the foundation of the wine industry in 1838-1839.*
- *He built the presidio and barracks in Sonoma, laid out the town in 1835-41, and tamed the Indians with Solano becoming his great ally.*
- *He built the first public utility in California at Martinez —The Benicia Ferry.*
- *He gave land in Benicia and Vallejo for state capitals.*
- *He and Benicia are the only couple in U.S. history that each had a state capital named after them.*
- *Presided over Sonoma when the Bear Flag was raised and manifest destiny realized.*
- *Operated the first agricultural experiment station west of the Mississippi, one of first in the nation. He and John Bidwell of Chico introduced it.*
- *Imported the first purebred cattle into the west in 1839.*

• He served as secretary to California's Horticultural Society.
• He was the first California senator from Sonoma County.
• He was honored by both the Native Sons and the California Pioneers as a Patron Saint and largely responsible for many of them being successful.
• He served on the Constitutional Committee that wrote our basic laws and set the tone for our judicial system in the state.
• He was an idealist who believed that California was better off determining its own destiny with the U.S. rather than the then dominant forms of monarchy that mostly prevailed in the world.

Yes, he and Benicia made great additions to what has become the leading edge of change here in California, the nation and the world. They saw and participated in the change from Moorish feudal Spanish culture to the dawn of modern times, from 1500 to 1900 in one lifetime. M.G. died in January of 1890, Benicia a year later.

M.G. Vallejo left his mark on California. His legacy has endured. After all how many men can say they may have fathered 200 children?

Bob may well have been sitting on the porch of Vallejo's daughter Natalia's Pink House—now a restaurant—surrounded by his six boys and their families, when he formed the idea for his most ambitious project to date.

With the help of architect Adrian Martinez, he prepared plans to develop the lot by converting the house into a museum and offices. There would be a small winery demonstrating traditional techniques and a tasting room inside a replica of the Vallejo barn, with a token vineyard. The tasting room would be run as a not for profit operation to generate funds for other restoration projects through the Vallejo Association.

In his presentation piece to the city, Bob described how he and Edna had purchased the property from owners reluctant to see it go to residential developers and more drawn to Bob's emerging ideas. The house would become home to other societies as well as a museum. And it would include an office for M.G. Vallejo Wine Inc. He described a Victorian garden, orchards, a gazebo, swan pond with fishing for children, and picnic tables for visitors. He envisioned every family in Sonoma Valley having the opportunity to sign

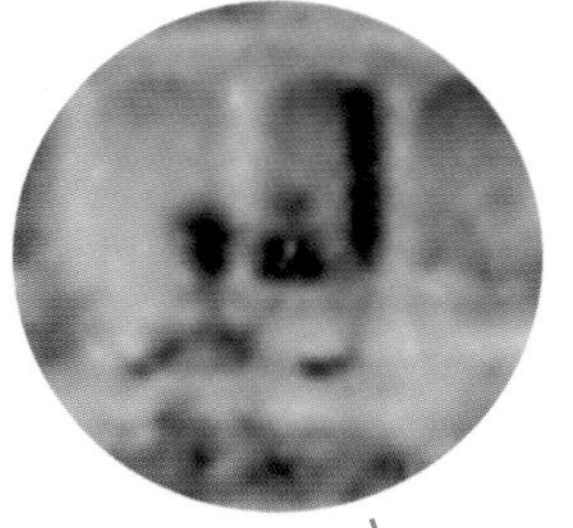

The Pink House is clearly visible in this century old photograph of early Sonoma, and it may be Vallejo's daughter Natalia on the veranda

up to live for a day as the Haraszthys did in the 1860s, eating the same fruit and vegetable varieties, cooking the same way with the same recipes. Through the Willows Wild project, the people of Sonoma could have experienced living a day as it was lived 125 years before.

As I see the project, it would become an extension of the agricultural and historic nature of the area. It would add to the open space in the center of the town, and the Vallejo-Haraszthy house would viably become once again a part of the Vallejo estate.

Bob knew that there would need to be rezoning but had seen it happen plenty of times before in the city and didn't believe it would be a problem. But just in case, he included a paragraph at the end that read:

In short, what we propose, I think, will be of great benefit to the future of Sonoma. If you agree, and reach a positive decision, I will be happy for the future. On the other hand, if you believe the negatives are there, we will have to sell the property and would expect it to be subdivided.

Although Bob is adamant that his plans had been transparent and unchanged from the start, some say that he made some late changes and additions that made the project less acceptable.

After consideration by the City's planning commission, it was decided that Bob's plans warranted a full EIR (Environmental Impact Review). This was unusual. There had been voices of compromise at the commission meeting, but the city attorney, Klein, pushed the members toward a

Continued on page 166

Bob is the proud owner of both the official ring worn by General Vallejo in this photograph, and Chief Solano's ceremonial war club, which is over two feet long.

General Vallejo's home, Lachryma Montis, as it is today, and how it appeared in photographs taken by the renowned Carleton Watkins of San Francisco in the 1880s for a book intended to publicize the lifestyle and real estate opportunities in Sonoma Valley. Vallejo's widow Benicia sits on the porch with some of her family posed carefully around her.

GENERAL VALLEJO'S GRANDCHILDREN.

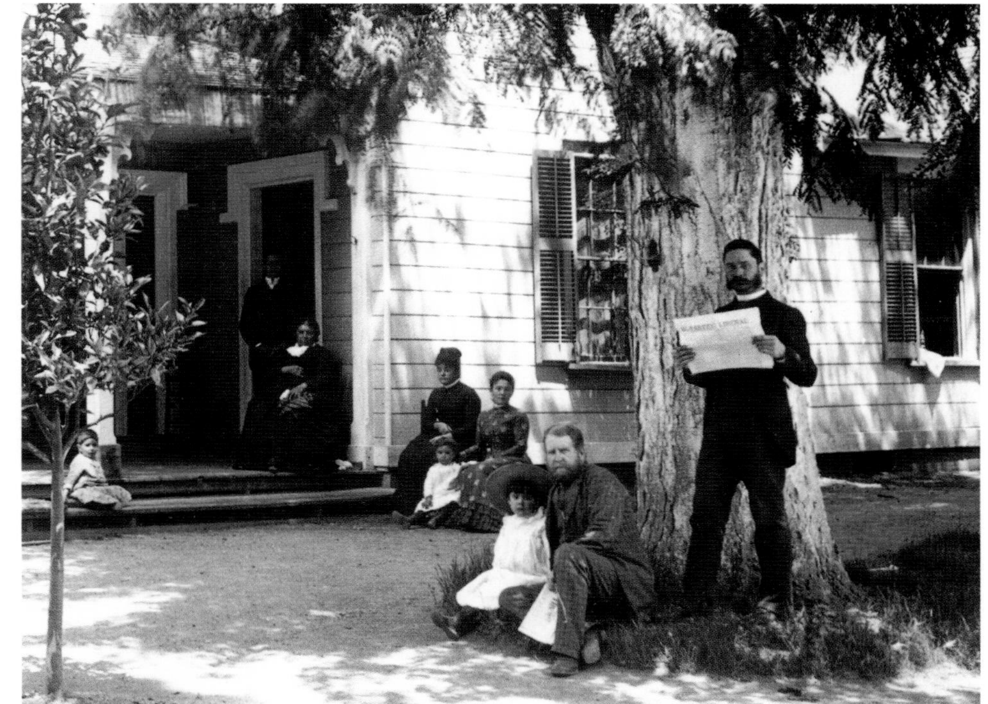

Continued from page163

full review. There were fierce debates in the council chambers when Bob appealed the ruling, and accusations that he was being singled out for "go slow" treatment by the City. Certainly it seems strange that people would argue that a winery might produce noxious smells and upset the neighbors, when the Sebastiani Winery had been operating for years in the heart of the most upscale residential part of the city. And as Bob said at the time, why would the traffic be any worse than it had been when they operated the tasting room at the nearby Vallejo property. Besides, most of the information required by an EIR was already on record.

But the City was adamant. A full EIR was required and it would cost Bob some $20,000. It probably didn't help that Ig Vella was on the planning commission. It probably didn't help that Bob's first encounter with the Sonoma city manager Brock Arner a few years before led to a shouting match on the telephone. Bob had driven into a hole created by a city construction project and wanted insurance information from Arner, who was less than cooperative. Arner asked Bob who he thought he was to demand the information. Bob replied that he was one of the people who paid Arner's salary with his taxes—and made a few other choice rejoinders.

It also probably didn't help that Bob had made his alliances with similar outspoken iconoclasts, fought and beaten city hall and local developers before, and had an open feud with the local newspaper. The latter was only important in the sense that the *Index-Tribune* was part of the self-protective network of business people who preferred to accomplish their plans through the normal process of quiet social alliances and strong support for the city bureaucracy. Although Bob had been an integral part of most business and social associations, he remained an "outsider" because he was not given to the superficial civility, self-congratulation, and compromise that such organizations tacitly demanded for "real" membership.

To Bob, the demand for an EIR was not just unreasonable, unfair and unnecessary; it represented the part of the establishment he had scant regard for getting back at him for being enterprising and bold without regard to the "unwritten code." He was right about the unfair, unnecessary, and unreasonable. Within a very short time of Bob selling the property, the City, planning commission, and City Council approved a restaurant (The General's Daughter) and a cooking school (Ramekins) on exactly the same site. Both are fully commercial, open until midnight, and neither offer public utility. No EIR was demanded, there was no problem with rezoning, and no traffic issues were raised. The City even provided development money to the project's owner Suzanne Brangham, who also had no problem raising funds from local private investors.

It's hard to see the rejection of Bob's plans for Willows Wild as anything other than a move to penalize him for being an assumptive and outspoken outsider who didn't play the game. But it wasn't a cohesive plan, a conspiracy in the true sense. It was more likely the accumulation of individual gripes, old scores, and new feuds that set a general tone of disapproval for Bob's style of doing things.

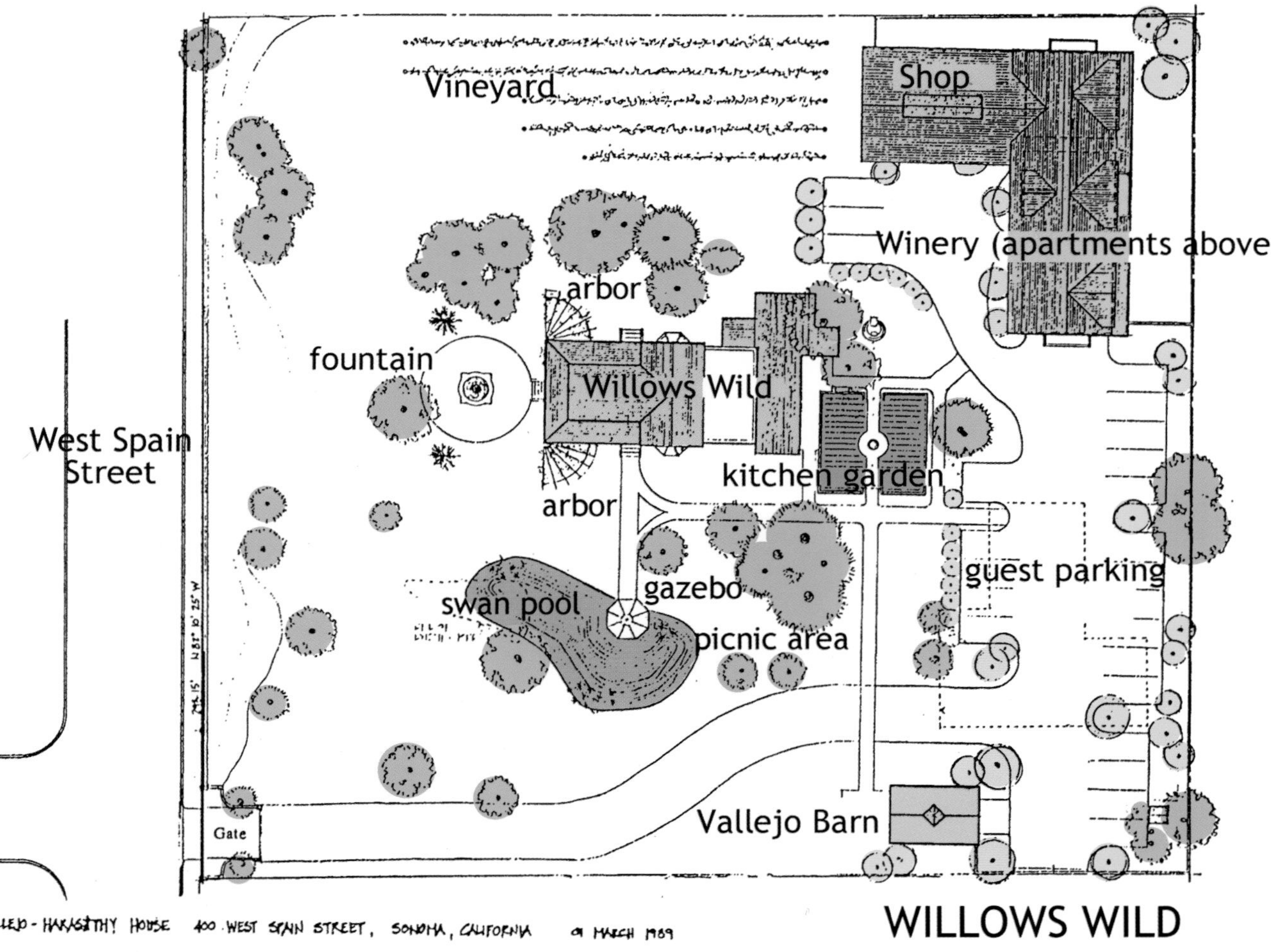

WILLOWS WILD

But he was a Cannard, and he preferred to promote the benefits of his ideas and not ask the permission of the bureaucrats.

Part of the problem was that Bob tends to completely finish projects in his mind before starting them in practice. It's why he can make complex pieces of furniture without a drawing. He simply repeats with his hands what he has already done in his mind. So he could see the museum flourishing, he could hear the children at the picnic tables and the tinkle of glasses in the tasting room, and he could smell the delicious aromas of aging wine, all with the image of General Vallejo looming large over a busy property. So as far as he was concerned "they" (whoever comprised that shadowy group) had snatched away something he had already created.

He was incensed. The $20,000 price tag for an EIR was immaterial; he could have covered it easily. It was the principle, and he was damned if he was going to fall into line. He pulled his plans, and while not actually listing Willows Wild, he offered it for subdivision in his own advertisements, castigating the forces that be.

As far as Bob is concerned, there is no question that his detractors in the City got together and deliberately stonewalled his plans; the only debate concerns degrees of culpability. If you lived in Sonoma for any length of time, you would know that of course there is an establishment, and anyone who decides to buck the system, usually by calling a spade a spade, suffers the social and commercial effects of not having anyone to grease the wheels. It's not so much what people do, it's what they don't do. And they chose not to get behind Bob's plans.

The more he drew attention to the City, council and newspaper's "favoritism," the less his ideas were favored. It wasn't illegal, it's what all establishments do. Bob has fought the establishment whenever it tried to overstep its mandate in order to support commercial enterprise at the expense of citizens, or pander to its own police and fire departments' expansive and unneccessary empire building. There was the Maxwell Farms retail development, when the City tried to ignore the terms of the legacy that made the location available only for limited commercial use. He argued loudly for an eminently accessible site on West Napa Street when the police department chose to locate their headquarters off the plaza on first Street West. Each time he has suffered the similar effects of taking a stand. But he said out loud what an awful lot of people were thinking. He made the wilder accusation that flushed out the smaller injustice. His extreme point of view gave credibility to compromise. It doesn't matter what side you're on, you have to admire someone like that—someone who challenges the system.

It gets you on to the newspaper's shit list—which may be bad thing, but then they omit you from their official version of history, which is probably a good thing, given their inclination to deride you.

It is a bad thing when you want to build a barn.

WILLOWS · WILD
HARASZTHY-VALLEJO HOUSE
On the Vallejo Estate in Sonoma
400 West Spain Street (Vallejo Street) • Sonoma, CA 95476

CHAPTER NINE

BARNRAISING. OR BEATING CITY HALL THEN JOINING IT

Shelving his plans for Willows Wild, Bob applied to the City for a permit to build a barn at the back of the property to use as a workshop for himself and his sons. It would replace an old barn that was no longer sound.

The City's reply was that before they could comment on the new barn, he must improve a fifty by three hundred foot section of an unpaved track on the edge of his property designated in old plans as part of a city street. He must then dedicate it to the City and promptly remove his old barn, which intruded a couple of feet into what would then be the city's "Fourth Street West."

It went downhill from there.

The City's claim to Fourth Street was nonsense, and they probably knew it, but it took time, effort, and legal research on Bob's part to build a case against the City. It was a totally fanciful fabrication on the part of the city management, led by Brock Arner who together with certain members of his staff stretched their authority to the limits. It seems probable in the light of their treatment of others that their action was a deliberate time- and money-wasting strategy against someone they had decided was to be singled out for special treatment. And while on the one hand denying that their actions were vindictive, the City's public works manager Wayne Wirick continued to throw up roadblocks one after the other. First it was improvements to the entrance to what was no more than a field, then it was a gravel driveway, then a hammerhead turn around for fire trucks. When these were taken care of they started on the barn design features, refusing to give a building permit until all sorts of modifications were included, and each time it was costing Bob fees to have his plans turned down.

The city management engaged in bureaucratic inanity to foil Bob's plans. They seemed content to pay for the city staff to waste time filing report after report, objection after objection—on a barn. And they continued to demand that the older barn be removed and the non-existent street dedicated to the City. After six months of time wasting, Bob appeared for the umpteenth time in front of the city council to argue his case. The mayor was developer and attorney Ken McTaggart. Bob finally lost it. He told the council that the City had no legal basis for their demands for him to dedicate a major part of his property to them, and that he would start work on the barn the following day, permit or no permit. He added that he

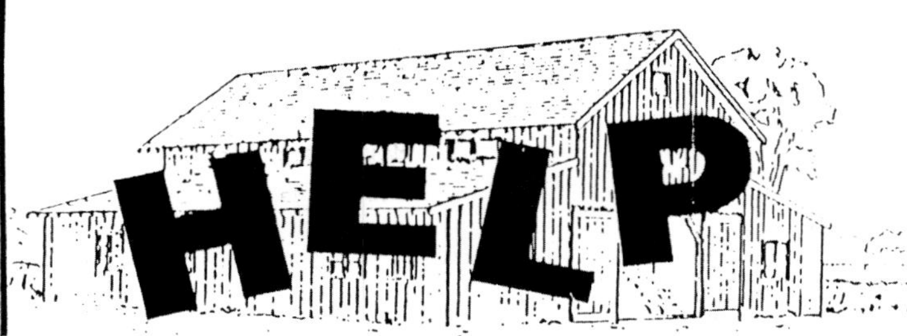

The Cannard Family wants you to express your opinion on whether you prefer a barn, agriculture and open space at the pink Victorian on Spain St. or the City's alternative of a street, houses and more traffic.

The City Council has no legal grounds whatsoever. Fourth Street West is not even in the General Plan of 1985. However, they seem determined to collect this $160,000 in taxes that 40 homes on this site will generate. They want us to dedicate a street where no street is planned or needed.

We need your help. Thank you.

Send your opinion to:

Sonoma City Council
No. 1 on the Plaza
Sonoma, CA 95476

Hearing August 15 at 7:30 p.m.
Council Chambers

You are cordially invited to be present and be heard. Thank you.

Bob Cannard

would simultaneously file suit against the City for their false claim.

City attorney Wilson, perhaps realizing that the City had pushed it as far as they dare, interjected and suggested an immediate closed executive session. The council returned in under two minutes and Mayor McTaggart announced between clenched teeth that Cannard could pick up his permit the following day.

The promise was not fulfilled. It took another month of time wasting and niggling by Wirick before the permit was issued. It was a pyrrhic victory for Bob, and he continued to pay dearly as the City watched every nut and bolt and two-by-four used as the barn took shape, making a shower of objections at the slightest variance from code. He and his sons built the barn in two months, however it would be another two years before the issue was settled, and the acrimony flew as more and more people were obliged to take sides.

Bob never admitted that there were code violations, that work had been done without the necessary permits because of the City's delays, or that he had been argumentative and difficult. He justified events on the basis that through their illegal demands and unreasonable objections, the City had deliberately provoked his responses. The newspaper enjoyed the controversy and supported the City's position.

Bob briefly resurrected scaled down plans for Willows Wild and received tentative approvals, but sensing that a repeat of the City's barn tactics on a more ambitious project would probably drive him mad, he folded the plans and began discussions to sell part of the property to Suzanne Brangham. As mentioned before, Suzanne's plans for a restaurant and subsequently a cooking school were more ambitious and generated more traffic—and yet required no environmental impact report and sailed through the approval procedure.

There should have been no difference in the way two parties were treated, and yet there was.

The newspaper and City continued to treat Bob with disdain as his barn project staggered toward its acrimonious completion, and perhaps because of this, his popularity increased. A significant number of people were similarly outraged that a city and council given to rubber-stamping the plans of developers and insiders should act so objectionably towards a single resident's small project. It didn't help that city manager Brock Arner and newspaper editor Bill Lynch were tight.

In an attempt to find out whether he could affect the system from the inside, Bob decided in 1990 that he would run for a place on the Sonoma City Council. His campaign material proposed change, more fiscal responsibility and less meddling. It drew attention to his record of public service in support of just about every organization in the city and valley. It was well known that whatever his stand on local issues might be, he never hesitated to contribute time and money freely and without favor throughout the community. He was the first person contacted when a fundraiser was planned, and could be relied on for ideas, enthusiasm, organizational skills and energy. Any person down on his luck that Bob knew about would be looked

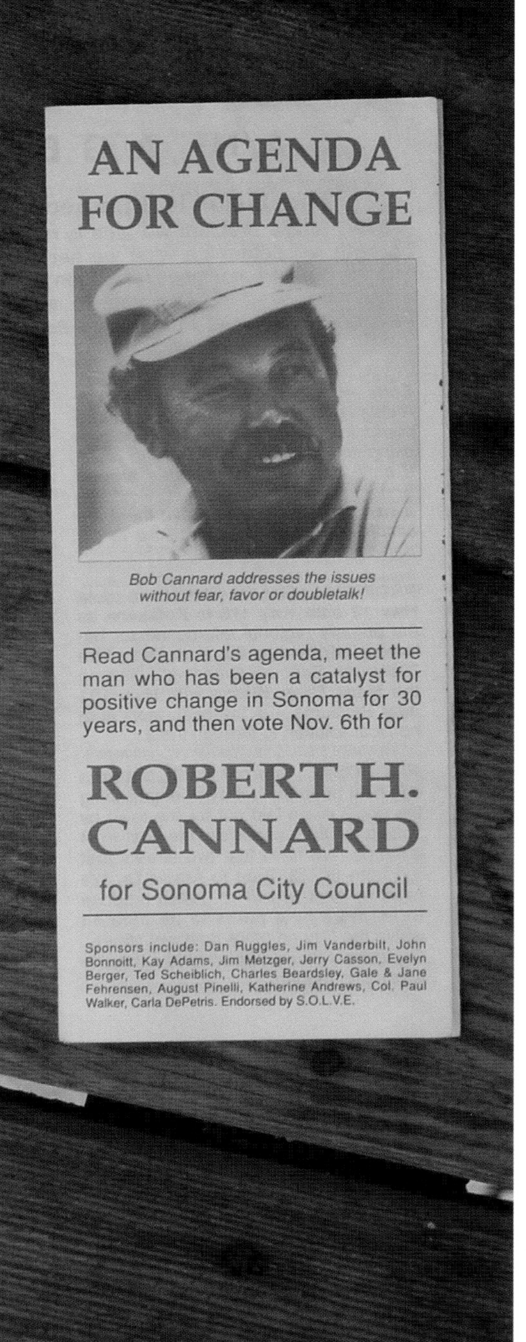

after—with company and food and advice. If Bob Cannard promised to be a guardian of the fabric of true community, and a person who stood for conservative values and individual rights, then the supporting evidence was all around for everyone to see. And then his showmanship emerged when, just before the election, he invited all the thousands of residents of the City of Sonoma to a free old-fashioned ox roast at the nearly completed barn. It was a great event attended by many hundreds of people, including his opponents. Bob's entire family and a host of friends turned out to make sure that there was food and drink for everyone. Apart from being a wonderful example of old-style hospitality and a great community get-together, it probably worked too, because Bob won a seat on the council in the election two days later.

The problems with the barn ran on into his period of tenure as a council member, but soon were lost to the more pressing issue of city finances, which he was determined to make the central issue.

Bob's take on the overall situation was that Brock Arner spent too freely and was putting the city in hock at an alarming rate. To offset the growing disparity between revenue and expenditure, Arner was encouraging residential development (to get future tax income) by stretching the general plan's declared limits as far as he could. Not surprisingly, any business venture that benefited from a rapidly increasing population supported what others saw as irresponsible and unaffordable expansion, without a thought to the character and heritage of the city.

It is true that somehow Brock Arner ushered through more residential development during a declared moratorium than had ever been built over a similar period without a moratorium. He was also willing to put city resources into providing

When Sonoma's civic groups need help, they call on Cannard

Cannard's innovative ideas and hands-on approach have raised literally millions of dollars for Vintage House, the Vintage Festival, Depot Museum, Red Cross, Catholic Social Services, Hospital Auxiliary, Veterans, Chamber of Commerce and other good causes.

Effective Leadership, Community Service

Founder, president, or board member:

• Chamber of Commerce • Vintage House • Sonoma Community Center • Valley of the Moon Vintage Festival • Depot Museum • Plaza Merchants Assoc. • Sonoma Garden Club • various Historical Societies • Boy Scouts • Firemen's Association • Highway 12 committees • Recycling Center • Environmental Council • Hospital Auxillary • Sonoma Valley Arts Association • Kenwood Fire Department

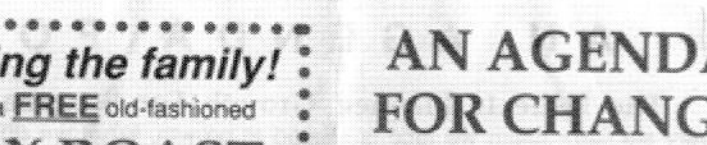

Bring the family!

to a **FREE** old-fashioned

OX ROAST

Sunday Nov. 4th, 5 to 7 p.m. at the "Pink Victorian"
400 West Spain Street

Cannard has been roasting whole steer since 1947. In '67 he held the first Ox Roast at The Plaza as a fundraiser to revitalize the Chamber of Commerce.

Come & enjoy fresh roasted beef, garden vegetables & live entertainment, including the American tradition of a political parade – bring your pots & pans! This will be a final opportunity to meet the candidates for City Council, as all will be invited to this community event, hosted by Bob Cannard.

AN AGENDA FOR CHANGE

Bob Cannard addresses the issues without fear, favor or doubletalk!

Read Cannard's agenda, meet the man who has been a catalyst for positive change in Sonoma for 30 years, and then vote Nov. 6th for

ROBERT H. CANNARD

for Sonoma City Council

Sponsors include: Dan Ruggles, Jim Vanderbilt, John Bonnoitt, Kay Adams, Jim Metzger, Jerry Casson, Evelyn Berger, Ted Scheiblich, Charles Beardsley, Gale & Jane Fehrensen, August Pinelli, Katherine Andrews, Col. Paul Walker, Carla DePetris. Endorsed by S.O.L.V.E.

utilities to undeveloped sites, even if those properties wouldn't be developed for years, with the result that the City carried the loss while the value of the lots dramatically increased for the owner. And he was happy to wildly increase city employees remuneration packages and benefits despite a poor financial position.

None of this could have happened without the compliance of council members, who were all invited to be "brought up to speed" by city manager Arner at individual meetings with him just before the regular council meetings. Bob refused to attend those meetings. Some council members were comfortable with whatever city hall recommended. In four years, Phyllis Carter only voted against staff recommendations once. With the exception of Anthony Cermack, it was a rubber-stamp council that Bob served on.

The financial situation had forced Arner to raid funds that were not supposed to be used to shore up the general fund. He emptied the cemetery fund and borrowed at an alarming rate. When Bob started shouting about the growing financial deficit, he was told by the newspaper, city staff, and some of the other council members that he didn't understand city finances. The basic profit and loss situation is fine, they said, it's just short-term cash requirements that look bad—but aren't really. At one point, Bob was criticized in an *Index-Tribune* editorial for talking about city finances in public instead of airing differences in Arner's office.

It is perfectly true to say that, provided the city was growing and tax revenues were slowly growing, cash flow problems could be considered no more than a short-term irritant.

But if the deficit grew at a faster rate than revenue, which it did at the time, and the general growth rate slowed, which it ultimately did, there would come a point at which it would be dangerous to proceed with the City's rate of spending. Bob and councilman Anthony Cermak felt that time had come, and that Arner had appallingly little concern for risk management. In fact, the City was actually bankrupt for a time. The other three councilmembers disagreed, and most of Bob's tenure was hallmarked by fierce debates punctuated by three-to-two votes.

When the true nature of the City's finances came to light later, Bob claims city staff tried to point the finger at city clerk Eleanor Berto, saying she used antiquated bookkeeping methods. But the city clerk could not spend one penny or transfer a dollar without the direction of the city council or city manager.

Anthony Cermak and Bob did stall some of the more egregious salary deals that Arner cut for city staff, and they fought and won some degree of rent protection for mobile home owners. Cermak frequently cautioned the council that they

were discussing public issues in private sessions. When Bob went public with some of his complaints about the operation of the council and City that had been discussed in private, the City countered with a proposal for a code of conduct for councilmembers. When Bob retorted that it was much more likely that the City and other council members were breaking more than ethical rules at their closed sessions, the proposal for a code of conduct was hastily dropped.

Bob continued his withering attacks on Arner's profligacy, his nurturing of relationships with developers, and his generosity with salary packages to police and fire departments. He and Cermak were repeatedly pilloried in the pages of the *Index-Tribune*, but true to form, Bob let it roll off, like water off a duck's back. Together with Anthony Cermak, Bob did manage to raise water rates to improve the lines and pipes which were antiquated, and they did curtail some of the proposed salary packages to city employees.

Bob maintains to this day that Arner ran the City into a debt of well over a million dollars with the cooperation and complicity of the council, and the acquiescence of the local newspaper. When you have the vast majority of the city budget going to the police department and the fire department, where employees get regular pay raises irrespective of the state of the economy and retire early with great pension packages, there are bound to be problems. The repercussions of these fiscal practices continued after Arner's departure. Arner resigned in the summer of 1994 and was replaced by Pam Gibson who was forced to borrow from water revenues to cover cash shortages. By legislative action, water cannot be sold to make profit, only to cover the cost of its supply. Whether or not the short-term use of water fund money to cover other costs is also prohibited is a matter of debate among some. However, when a municipality grows dependent on water revenue, albeit to cover short-term cash problems, it invites allegations that its fiscal needs conflict with water conservation aims.

Since Bob left the council in 1994, the City has severely curtailed development through an urban growth boundary, given up the police department, and is left to fuss over the last few parcels available for subdivision. The landlords around the charming center of Sonoma—it's historic plaza—have seen fit to raise rents to the point that soon only real estate offices, gift shops and wine tasting rooms (in other words businesses focused on non-residents) will be able to afford to stay. Despite setting as its target the protection of its rural and historic heritage, successive councils have failed to do so, and have never taken the lead even when developers have threatened to change the very essence of the city, preferring to let private citizens fight for what they didn't have the guts for. Bob ran again for city council in 2002, when he saw lots being built out to their extremities for trophy homes, and the lack of consideration given to the needs of lower income families, not to mention a disastrous water situation, and little attention to traffic problems. He came dangerously close to winning. Any disappointment on his part over the outcome was more than offset by his relief at not having to serve, a feeling probably shared by all those around him.

Besides his run for council, Bob maintained his involvement in community causes and controversies. He turned out to lend his support to those campaigning for the return of chickens to Sonoma Plaza, a campaign highlighted with coverage in the *Wall Street Journal* in May 2002. He drew considerable fire in 2001 for his opposition to the public hospital's plan to build a big new medical center outside of town because of their failure to engage the public's input. And he fought his own battles with developers who tried unsuccessfully to foist a plan to put twenty-eight homes on a lot fit for fifteen right next to the barn where he spends a lot of his time, and where his neighbors are feeling that they are being crowded out.

Mayor Ken Brown appointed Bob Sonoma Alcalde in 2001. The appointment was celebrated at a luncheon attended by all of Bob's family, friends, dignitaries, and city officials in the largest turnout for an Alcalde luncheon on record. Bob handed out copies of a short address to avoid making a speech, but when newspaperman Bob Lynch said he was relieved that Cannard had chosen not to make a speech, Bob gave it anyway, extending it well beyond the following written comments.

Alcalde Lunch, February 23, 2001

I would like to thank our councilmen for selecting me as the Alcalde for this year.

There has been controversy in my life. As Dan Ruggles used to say, "Bob, you and I will outlive our critics. They will be long gone, and you and I will still be here preaching the same sermon."

One thing there is no controversy about is who is the "better half" of the Cannard family. I would like to introduce and thank Edna for training me so well over the past fifty-nine years. She and I met in the summer of 1942 while I was a lifeguard at the local pool. I don't know if she saved me or I saved her. We have six sons, six grandsons, one grand daughter, and two great-granddaughters, some of whom are here today. A rugged bunch of individualists.

I have here in my hand a copy of a note that I wrote

to Tally Bean when he was mayor of Sonoma. It says, "How about changing the title of the Mayor of Sonoma to the Alcalde of Sonoma? We would have the only Alcalde in the state and that in itself would be a distinction in this historic town." He liked to be called mayor. I still think it's a good idea.

I don't expect I will be an Alcalde in the usual mode of most of the people who have had this honor in the past. For the most part they have been reserved, distinguished persons who have presided over parades and public celebrations with great dignity. I expect to add to these duties an ongoing report to the council and the public on the state of our town as I see it. If I can add one small measure of understanding to help Sonoma retain the agricultural flavor of the past century and a half, I will consider it worthwhile.

In one generation, Sonoma has lost so much. Ask Dorothy Castagnasso about horse races on Spain Street or Pete Viviani's mother staking out her cows in the plaza. There was regular train service in and out of town as well as barges on Sonoma Creek at Schellville to haul hay and produce to San Francisco. The Conti brothers will tell you of the bridge over Fryer Creek on Napa Street about where the Exchange Bank is today. Loren Sims or Bill Lynch will tell you about catching trout and steelhead in Nathanson Creek when they were boys. Don Eraldi will tell you about mail delivery on First Street East by boat. Hans Kornell had a champagne winery where Safeway is today. Bill Wyle and Don Eraldi will tell you of the pigeon shoots that August Sebastiani held in the plaza. Don says they didn't bag many birds but made a lot of noise. Milt Castagnasso will tell you of the family dairy where his horses are today. There was a major feed store on the corner opposite the plaza on the southwest side. There were two chicken and turkey hatcheries on Broadway that supplied the big poultry businesses in the valley and the poultry shows that went with it.

Sonoma has changed in one generation from an agricultural backwater of the Bay Area into an avant garde City of Tomorrow with four homes on every lot. Change is not all bad, because only through change can we improve. But Sonoma has changed as much in one generation as most of the country did over two hundred years. Sometimes the best thing we can do is nothing.

I look forward to the future and hope that I can contribute to saving what is left of the best of Old Sonoma. The Cannards came to Sonoma after several years of study and travel. We determined that this was the best place in California to live and raise our family. Luther Burbank was only twenty-two miles off when he said the same thing about Santa Rosa.

I want to leave all of you with a blessing. We know that all life comes from the sun. From the sun to the earth, the plants, animals and vineyards, to the kitchen, to the table, and to the family and good friends. Good wine. Good food. To the good life. To the goodness of life. May all of us share in the goodness of life in Sonoma.

Bob took his year as Alcalde very seriously, providing the following report to the city council less than two months later, on April 1, 2001.

To: Mayor Ken Brown and the Sonoma City Council

Please consider this a quarterly report from your Alcalde. Shortly after my appointment in January, I determined to try to be a useful help to the City. One of the things I decided to do was to gather information from the citizens that you might not hear directly from them.

I have met with many people on the streets, coffee shops, parks, grocery stores, club meetings and others and listened to what they had to say. Mostly these people would not write letters to the newspaper or attend pubic meetings. However, most of them vote regularly. Their voice is important to Sonoma. Consider this report as coming directly from the sidewalks of Sonoma.

I just listened to what was being said. It seems that in January there were two overwhelming topics on most people's minds. One was the upgrade of the Sonoma Valley Hospital and the other was the further development of the Sonoma Golf Course by the Sonoma Mission Inn.

The plan of the SMI to further develop a complex on Arnold Drive at the golf course was very unpopular. The basic question as I heard it had to do with fairness. Why should a big corporation get preference when people in the same area had been waiting twenty years for the same services? Since SMI has changed their plans, the controversy has died down, but the issue remains for the future. One seventy-year-old native suggested that a way to take care of the car problem on Arnold Drive was to double deck the road!

The Sonoma Valley Hospital question is a different matter. If anything I have heard more about this than any other public issue since the school bond controversy of the early 1990s.

The city and valley residents clearly understand that this problem will not be solved in Washington, Sacramento, or by Sutter Health Care. They know instinctively that it will be solved by the people of Sonoma Valley or not at all. As I have listened to the people, I have not heard one voice against keeping and upgrading the current situation. The overwhelming concern, including of members of Kaiser, is that the emergency room service be continued. People will go to great lengths to see that Sonoma Valley Hospital remains in Sonoma.

What I hear are questions, questions, questions. Perhaps the most frequent is, "Why can't we upgrade the present hospital?" This usually begins a discussion of many other questions and almost always ends with the comment, "Didn't the people on the hospital board learn anything from the school bond issue?" In short, fewer than 50 percent of the people at the present time would vote yes on a hospital bond or parcel tax regardless of what it promised if it means the hospital moves from its present site. In fact, I doubt that moving the hospital to a site out of town would get one vote out of three.

In the past, the people of this valley have had great confidence in the board of the hospital. At the present time this is not so. In fact, many people think this is a one-man show. I hear no opposition to the questions that the new director, Mike Smith, has asked because some of these questions are the same ones many people have. Until the citizens of Sonoma Valley feel included in the hospital decision any further action by the board is meaningless. The people simply will not vote for something that excludes them. Some regular questions in this regard are: "Why are there not more people who have lived here more than ten or fifteen years on the committees? What about the viticulture families that control most of the land?"

In the past it was the old-time families, the doctors, and long-term residents who organized, built, and ran the hospital. Mostly these people have been excluded and the person on the street knows it and will not go along with this board's decisions. As an example, nearly everyone knows that we would not have this present hospital without the generous donations of August Sebastiani.

Everyone knows that, like the schools, the hospital is a separate political district and the city council has no direct control over what happens. However, everyone looks to you to help solve this dilemma (mess) at the hospital. Maybe you and the hospital board can agree on a group of citizens that can put something together that the voters will support. If not, there is no chance that the situation will improve at this vital part of the community.

One other point: To help improve communication between the council and the citizens of Sonoma, I have long advocated neighborhood meetings. I will be glad to help organize these informal meetings if you like so that specific concerns of each part of town can be heard. If nothing more is accomplished, the people will get to know who they voted for. I look forward to helping.

If there are specific questions, you want me to pursue, let me know. I consider it a great honor to be your Alcalde.

It is impossible when reading this report and his other letters not to be impressed by the great affection that Bob Cannard has for his hometown. The vehemence of his attack on those he saw as a threat to its character and viability is more than matched by his huge interest in the well being of its citizens, even if his ideas on how they might achieve happiness and fulfillment are not always coincident with their own.

Although the subjects do not loom large in Bob's life, he has strong views on religion and national politics. He describes his father as having been a "rock-ribbed Republican," yet Bob registered as a Democrat when he became eligible to vote in 1947 while at Penn State. You might think his gratitude for the opportunity to get an education under the GI bill prompted him to vote for its champion Harry Truman in 1948, but Bob voted to re-elect the Democratic president "because he had the guts to drop the atomic bomb and end the war with Japan."

It was the first and only Democrat that Bob has ever voted for as president, and he has been doggedly Republican ever since. His reasons are predictably rooted in history rather than contemporary experience.

> *In looking at the platforms of the Democratic Party for the previous century, it did not take me long to come to several conclusions. It was an appeal for power for the wrong reasons. First of all, nearly all the poor people were Democrats and lived in the slums of the cities; I did not expect to be poor. They depended on the government to redistribute the wealth of the nation. The leaders of the Democratic Party saw their chance for votes. It was obvious that a considerable segment of our population was becoming dependent on the national government to take care of them. This is not what I wanted. That is why I am a Republican.*
>
> *This dependency discouraged the very qualities in our people that had made this country so great. In many of the battles of World War II, the individual initiative of our troops was the difference between victory and defeat. This was a true pioneer quality. Government support programs were killing this quality of independence in working citizens. The pioneer spirit was replaced by lethargy. That's not what I wanted. That's why I am a Republican.*
>
> *Nothing in nature is equal. The very survival of mankind and every other species depends on the genetic diversity that occurs in every generation. There are, and hopefully always will be, superior individuals in every generation that will do better than their fellow men. This leveling by government is destructive of the very first law of nature that has allowed mankind to survive through the ages. That's why I am a Republican.*
>
> *While I was in college, it did not take me long to realize that I was not one of the people that the Democratic leaders hoped would follow the carrot of government programs. The elitist Democratic Party leaders thought that they could spend the people's money better than the people themselves. These leaders, often very wealthy and well educated, thought themselves above the common man. Wealth and education were the very qualities that every pioneer and frontiersman did not have, but they had something far superior—the ability to survive under difficult circumstances anywhere, asking no one for anything, depending entirely on themselves for everything. The intellectuals would, and very often did, perish when confronted with life on the frontier.*
>
> *The pioneer held the better-educated Easterner in*

contempt. Our freedom as individuals was achieved by these pioneers. The Constitution and Bill of Rights were written by Eastern intellectuals but freedom and democracy in reality were achieved by the families that went over the mountains. They would have none of the hogwash that these educated easterners were better than they were. We are very fortunate that they did not form a nation of their own in the Ohio and Mississippi valleys. They built and produced; they did not inherit. Every one of them became a farmer of sorts. They carved a life out of the wilderness.

Today the Democratic Party gets only the urban vote. Ninety percent of the counties in the U.S. voted Republican in the 2000 election. People occupying less than 10 percent of the land area of the country can elect a president and our national legislature. It is against the Constitution; is it any wonder that we have massive problems? Yet these city Democrats overrun the rural counties for every reason—including the tax base to support their social programs. When they move to the country, they try to bring the city with them. Land will always be the basis of life. The farmer, the man that feeds will always be the most important man in society. I never met a man that didn't eat. That is why I am a Republican.

My advice to every person who works for a living is to pay your union dues and vote Republican. That way you can have it both ways. The Republican Party has always stood for cutting taxes and the unions look for higher wages. Higher wages and lower taxes are the only possible way for the working person to get ahead.

That is why I am a Republican.

If you push people to summarize their political views, it is inevitable that the result will be an over-simplification. It would be wrong to assume that Bob hates all intellectuals —perhaps just those that come from New England and write history textbooks. It would be wrong to believe his true understanding of evolution is as narrow as that suggested here, but he is comfortable with the notion of a fair portion of society "falling through the cracks."

He knows perfectly well that the inbreeding in the families of isolated mountain people represented the antithesis of genetic diversity.

He seems to harbor a suspicion of educated people, yet he has always courted their company. And although he frequently describes himself as the dumbest in the family, he took the trouble to educate himself extensively in the subjects close to his heart.

He claims that city dwellers have an unconstitutional advantage over the rural population, and advocates low income housing on the edges of cities, yet he chooses to live in the middle of town himself. He draws no parallel between social programs and farm subsidies.

The dogma he apparently espouses could be a simple provocation, or more likely it is evidence that his view of the political landscape needs to be as certain and unchanging as his own solid and definite placement in the natural world.

Continued on page 183

In the fall of 1972, the Cannard garden was being picked over by peacocks that were destroying his young plants. The only person who kept peacocks was winery owner August Sebastiani at his home on the hill less than half a mile away. But when Bob told August that peacocks were raiding his garden, the patriarch vehemently denied that his birds were to blame. Bob insisted that there were no other peacocks around, but August claimed his birds were well penned. "Well they better be," says Bob, "because I'm going to shoot 'em next time."

Bob and a close friend Joe Cannuli nailed two young male birds a few days later with a .22, and in short order they were plucked, dressed and in the freezer. A short time after Christmas, the usual early morning crowd —including Bob—sat round a big breakfast table at the Lazy D in nearby Schelleville, then a regular haunt for many Sonoma old timers. August Sebastiani was at the bar.

"How're your peacocks doing August?" said one of his friends. August grumbled into his coffee but didn't respond.

"What about those two you had for Christmas, Bob?"

"Terrible. I don't know where they came from but they were as tough as hell."

"You missin' any birds August?"

With that, August slammed down his knife and fork, stormed out, and didn't speak to Bob for four months. When I asked Bob what they really tasted like, he looked sideways, grinned, and said, "As a matter of fact, they were pretty good."

Thirty-five years ago, the hot topic in Sonoma Valley was a proposed new highway running down the valley. Bob was one of many who were in strong opposition to the plan. Many public meetings were held, inlcuding one at Dunbar School, which he remembers with great amusement. At a noisy and animated stage of the proceedings, an opponent of the scheme rose to complain bitterly about one-sided newspaper coverage of the issue in the *Index-Tribune* (not an unusual occurrance).

His speech was interrupted by the commanding tones of an eighty-five year old woman by the name of Mrs. Murgatroyd —who claimed to be the not-so-secret daughter of Lake County's notorious Black Bart.

"Listen sonny," said Mrs. Murgatroyd, shaking a bony finger at the middle-aged complainer. "I say the same to you about the newspaper as I say to those that complain about the smell from my outhouse.

It's the only one we got!"

CHAPTER TEN

PROMOTING THE PAST WITH AN EYE TO THE FUTURE

In 1988, while working on his plans for Willows Wild, Bob proposed a plan to rebuild the old Sonoma adobe jail that had stood on First Street West to the northeast of the central plaza. He offered period wood (which was to come from the old barn on the Pink House property), and he knew where to locate period adobe bricks and whatever else was needed. Support came from preservationists, but the City was cool to the idea, having earmarked the location for a small utility building—the one that stands today next to the dog park. It may be truer to say the City was cool to Bob Cannard, and he might well have been using the offer to sweeten the Willows Wild proposal. Either way neither project went ahead, and sadly, personal animosities left Sonoma's historic heritage all the poorer. But it wasn't long before Bob turned his attention to a project that would not require the same level of approval. Planning was under way for a new community facility—The Vintage House—which would primarily provide daytime services for Sonoma's seniors, but also be available for a variety of local functions. (Bob's own Alcalde luncheon was held there.) Incredible efforts by volunteers had made the Vintage House possible and Bob wondered what he might do besides donate money to honor these volunteers.

> *They had announced that the Vintage House design would be Mission Style, and as constuction proceeded, I felt I could enhance the concept by contibuting an authentic Mission fountain in front of the building.*

Over the years Bob had visited all of the California Missions, and come to the conclusion that the fountain at the Mission San Carlos in Carmel was the most beautiful. There had never been a fountain at Mission Solano in Sonoma, so he would replicate the one at Carmel for the Vintage House.

Then followed a month of research, which revealed that the best stonework was done in Morelia, the capital of Michoacan province in Mexico. Morelia is also the source for rosa contera, the pink stone used for most of Mexico's important civic buildings.

And it just so happened that a short time earlier that year Enrico Maron, from Morelia no less, had turned up at Bob's door in Sonoma expaining that his father Ramon was a great grandson of General Vallejo. (Bob had spent a lot of time trying to locate Vallejo's descendants as part of his historical research. Somehow, Enrico had got to hear of his efforts, visited Bob in Sonoma and stayed a month with the Cannards.)

So when the fountain project came up, Bob called Mexico and was immediately invited to visit Morelia, where Enrico would help all he could with the arrangements to produce and ship the fountain to Sonoma.

In mid-November Bob flew to Mexico City, armed with four cases of M.G. Vallejo wine and a check for $104 that the Mexican Consulate in San Francisco had assured Bob would cover the duty on the wine.

Declaring the wine and presenting the check was a big mistake. The check seemed of little interest to the customs official, so with the translation assistance of the man behind Bob in the line, and a half hour of haggling, they agreed to $50 cash, which to Bob's amazement went straight into the officials pocket.

Minutes later he was met at the gate by Enrico, whose car was just outside, "guarded" by a policeman who also took some folding money for his trouble. Then followed one of the most hair raising rides Bob had ever experienced, with Enrico weaving at high speed through heavy traffic, with total disregard for any traffic regulations.

> *"Nobody else stops at stop signs so why should I?"*

After several hours, they arrived at Ramon Moran's estate, which was surrounded by high walls with broken glass embedded in the top, and guarded round the clock. It seemed to Bob that the large home and its staff of gardeners, maids and servants ran on the basis of plenty of showers, clean clothes and petty theft, tolerated and even encouraged by the owners.

The following day, Ramon took Bob in a borrowed truck to find the stone quarry and negiotiate a price for what they needed. While loading the truck, one of the stones rolled away down the hill, and another trip had to be made the following day after it had been dragged back up.

All the stone was then delivered to the side of the road near a busy intersection where Ramon had agreed to meet a stone cutter the next day. At the meeting, Bob showed the pictures of the San Carlos fountain, and after several hours of haggling, they signed a contract that Ramon drew up—for two fountains (three and five meters in diameter,) two birdbaths, two stone water filters and a duck, to be completed in twenty days. They signed the contract and Bob handed over a portion of the total price. The stone cutter's crew promptly put up tents right there by the roadside and set to work.

Things were going well until on one of Bob's daily visits the workers seemed to be drunk. Because he was concerned that the job would fall behind, he reported the problem to Ramon. In no time at all Ramon was down at the worksite with a hired policeman threatening the stonecutters with jail if the job wasn't finished on time.

It was, and in good order too. The stones were soon on their way north. Needing a certificate of origin for the border crossing into the United States, Bob headed for the nearest government offices, where he was told that the person handling such requests was on vacation and wouldn't be back until after Christmas. It was then early December, and getting used to the routine, Bob asked how much it would cost for a certificate. Soon he was presented with a fancy looking twelve-dollar certificate, signed, sealed and bearing the impression of a large iron stamp.

When Bob started to pull out his contract to confirm what was being shipped, the official told him to fill in anything he wanted.

In Mexicali, where he caught up with the fountains, Bob took the advice of the Morans and hired a policeman rather than a taxi to drive him around various government offices for more paperwork, and to meet his broker from California who would handle the cross border transaction. The broker confirmed that regulations then in effect meant that the stonework would need to be loaded on to a Mexican truck using Mexican labor for the hundred yard trip to the border for inspection by both sides, before being transferred to another truck on the US side. This required yet more cash payments to grease the wheels.

Part way through the loading operation, the workers were rolling the stones end over end to move them from one vehicle to another, and Bob saw that some of their corners were being knocked off. When he instructed the men to pick up the stones they refused on the basis they were too heavy. But by this time, Bob had been joined by son Tom and a friend from Sonoma, and these two immediately hoisted stones and began to carry them to the broker's truck. There was a brief discussion about the quality of US versus Mexican workers, and eventually all the stones were carried not so carefully by the then furious Mexicans.

Somewhere along the line, the two stone water filters disappeared, but everything else made it to Sonoma, and Tom Cannard installed the fountain outside the completed Vintage House. As a fitting postscript, the stone cutters had failed to number the stones, and before the installation could be started, Bob and Tom had to first solve a giant stone jig-saw puzzle. It is a beautiful fountain, but the experience in Mexico left Bob extremely cynical about the entire country, which he now believes runs on nothing but a pervasive web of corruption. Being an historian, his subsequent researches revealed the reasons why, and he expresses them in a uniquely simple way.

Human sacrifice of the brightest and best of the Mayan civilization left the native Mexican population genetically depleted, the rapacious Spanish crown paid no salaries to its colonial officials who plundered the country, and the Catholic church finished the native people off with the brutal extraction of their very life blood to build churches and cathedrals. QED.

In 1931, the non-profit M.G.Vallejo Memorial Association was formed to improve the historic representation of General Vallejo. Three of its trustees (including Bob) managed the Cannard Fund, which was created by him to provide resources for projects in support of the MGVMA mission.

In 1994 the Sonoma City Opera applied for a grant to fund the composition and first performance of an operatic work, which was seemingly committed to the ideals of the Association. The trustees willingly approved a sum of $100,000. The opera was to be performed in the summer/fall of 1996, coincident with the season of celebrations in the City of Sonoma to mark the sesquicentennial (150th) anniversary of the Bear Flag Revolt.

Bob and the other trustees saw the opera as the perfect alternative to bricks and mortar memorials. It would be a lasting artistic tribute to the historic significance of events revolving around General Vallejo, the opera agreeing to maintain historical accuracy as to characters and events, within the context of "a viable theatrical piece" . . . with a "universal scope."

Sonoma City Opera and MGVMA entered into a commissioning agreement with the noted librettist Phillip Littell and composer David Conte. The artistic director of the SCO, Antoinette Kuhry, would oversee the project, and around a year later, presented a first look at the opera *The Dreamers*. The directors of the Association were soon horrified to discover that instead of focusing directly on Sonoma and the role of General Vallejo, the opera featured the broader problems of the ethnically diverse population of the new state of California as they struggled to realize their dreams, with only loose adherence to actual historical events. To Bob and the other GVMA directors it was a huge and totally unexpected affront. In their terms, the libretto was historically inaccurate and portrayed General Vallejo and the people of Sonoma in a bad light, using them only as stereotypes in a different story to the one they believed was to be told.

"Instead of a historically accurate opera and a lasting memorial to Vallejo, we have a bizarre fantasy that trivializes the memory of General Vallejo," complained Bob

Bullock. The Vallejo Association demanded changes, but the City Opera dug in their heels and the composer and librettist declared that nothing would be altered. It transpired that they were were within their rights. Unfortunately, the details of the contract giving them these rights (negotiated by the artistic director and her attorney husband) were not disclosed to the board of the MGVMA until it was too late to make changes.

This was particularly frustrating to the Association, which had deliberately stayed out of the process to allow the creative freedom requested, and assumed that the opera's artistic director would act on their behalf. Her commitment, however, was more to the theatrical appeal of the piece overall, which left the Association feeling that history was being perverted for artistic gain.

With nothing to see yet, the public could only watch the debate rage in "letters to the editor" and remain blissfully unaware of what it was all about. In the end, Bob and the directors of the Vallejo Association decided not to take legal action, preferring instead to boycott the opera, and bow out with some grace and a bit of humor with an ad of their own.

The opera went ahead, and by all accounts was theatrically impressive. Bob did not attend and has not sought descriptions from those who did. He remains embittered by the experience, but his anger remains more directed at those responsible for the contract that gave him no room to negotiate change than at the writer and composer of *The Dreamers*. As the provider of the funds that paid not only for the opera, but its production costs and

IN MEMORIUM

To avoid further public controversy during the Sesquicentennial Celebration of the Bear Flag Revolt, and in honor of that great Sonoman and American.

GENERAL MARIANO VALLEJO

whose memory our Association was formed to celebrate, we Directors have elected to take no legal or other action enjoining Sonoma City opera's presentation of "The Dreamers."

We regret that our funding of this opera made possible a story that trashes equally the event itself and all who took part. As its author admits, "Absolutely everyone . . . is portrayed in a bad light."

General Vallejo Memorial Association

Robert H. Cannard **Daniel T. Ruggles**
James C. Vanderbilt **Robert D. Bullock**

IN MEMORIUM

its artistic director's fee too, he must have been deeply hurt when the librettist publicly expressed scant regard for Vallejo, describing the General's life achievements as "rather slim."

Perhaps it was this statement that had provoked Bob to declare "there'll be blood in the streets" if the production went ahead.

There was no blood in the streets, but there was a lot of bad blood. It didn't help that the wife of Vallejo's close confidant, Chief Solano, was portrayed as a drunken whore turning tricks with the soldiers in Vallejo's barracks. Bob had accepted that the Vallejos may not be shown in the best of lights, and that many of the events of those early days of Mexican rule could now be viewed as brutal and unsavory, but he was personally and deeply offended by the creative treatment of this hapless woman, who had done little more than fall prey to the seedier habits of a more "advanced" culture.

> *My god, this woman was expected to move straight from the stone-age into the modern world. She was a victim of lifestyles and habits she was totally unprepared for. How dare they treat a woman like that. It was a travesty, a travesty!*

If the *The Dreamers* turned out not to be the musical tribute to Sonoma and the Vallejos he had hoped and planned for, the no strings payment of $100,000 to the opera was certainly a tribute to Bob's generosity. As an avid student of history and fierce upholder of the heritage of the Vallejos, but not a student of the performing arts, it was perhaps inevitable that he would be disatisfied with the result. It wasn't the first time that history had taken a back seat to artistic expression, and it wasn't the first time that Bob had freely donated money for a cause that he would have little control over.

When Pauline Bond, a longtime Sonoma resident died, she bequeathed her property on 7th Street East to the city she loved—with conditions that it be used as an agricultural community resource. In 1994 City Hall set about evading those conditions, and tried to push through a quick plan to use the property to generate income, but vigilant residents including Bob cried foul and the City backed off.

The Sonoma Ecology Center then saw an opportunity to use the land for a Community Farm. They had the best possible motives—to champion sustainable growing methods and produce fine organic produce for altruistic uses. They had found a committed and apparently qualified person to lead the effort, and obtained the approval of the Sonoma City Council. But they still needed seed money—literally.

About that time, Bob had been turned down by the City to use the land around the Pink House for his version of community development, and he had sold his interest in the M.J. Vallejo wine brand. It had been his publicly stated intent to donate profits from the direct sale of Vallejo wine from the Pink House or Vallejo home—had it been approved. So the idea of a community garden where the traditions of self-sufficiency would be preserved looked like a good alternative and something that Bob would support enthusiastically. In his words, the Ecology Center personnel talked a good line and insisted that the management of the farm would be in good hands.

Bob agreed to provide $25,000 to help get the project started. He placed no conditions on the donation, but occasionally drove past the property to see what was happening, usually first thing in the morning. Having spent so many years in the growing business himself, Bob knew how much hard work was involved and just how early you had to start to get farming work all done in a day. But at 10:00 a.m. there was rarely anybody to be seen. Apparently the "farmer" had to come out from Forestville and generally didn't make it until later. This didn't seem like the kind of commitment that would make the plans work.

The money somehow got swallowed up pretty quickly. So did thousands of gallons of city water. The City ended up having to forgive a $10,000 water bill, and Bob pumped another $25,000 into the project before it became obvious that the plan wouldn't work. Even the attempts to provide a regular supply of veggies to people who paid an upfront fee didn't materialize either. The project dwindled away until it consisted of little more than a single volunteer doing mostly what he felt like with no real output.

Bob describes the Ecology Center's staff as good at grant writing—which enables them to conduct their own academic scientific studies—but lacking the expertise to handle outreach projects when real output is expected. So the unfortunate experience with the community garden has colored his view of the entire purpose of the Ecology Center. He maintains that folks learned a hell of a lot more about natural resources from his walks with the jaycee students along Nathanson Creek, than they ever did from lengthy Ecology Center studies that never seemed to result in useful information for regular people.

> *They are more interested in the symptoms than the cause of ecological problems. They spend all this time and effort ripping out invasive species when we should be attacking the underlying reason—a dislocated and collapsed watershed. I mean, it's obvious to anyone with common sense that they're wrong.*

Therein lies the problem that some people have with Bob. His ideas are so grandiose, so sweeping and so ambitious that there's no half-committing to them. It's the full Cannard package or nothing. And whether you like it not, he *has* roasted the steer, raised the barn, beat Santa Rosa, saved the Chamber of Commerce, excelled in horticulture, sold the insurance, built the multi-million dollar brand, acquired wealth, mobilized political effort—and if he could do all that, well, shouldn't you believe that his way is the right way on everything?

Having tried to achieve his aims through charitable contributions with at best mixed results, Bob turned his attention to more direct ways to preserve and promote the local historic heritage. A growing friendship with neighbor Fred Cline provided an ideal opportunity for Bob to create a new monument to history, without the problem of committees and boards of directors or creative consultants.

It was at the Cline family winery at the south end of the valley that the City of Sonoma and the northernmost Mexican mission of San Francisco De Solano was originally planned to be built. It was then the location of an Indian camp with hot and cold springs. Padre Altimira had consecrated the spot on the fourth of July 1823, but subsequent tensions between local authorities, the Catholic church and the Mexican government conspired to move the site a few miles northeast to its current location. Bob and Fred decided that they would construct a memorial at the original site.

The secularization of the Mexican missions took place in 1835, and the ambitious plan for the Sonoma mission was curtailed, leaving thousands of unused adobe bricks. These were picked up by General Vallejo's brother Salvador for his own home, the General's home, and what is now the Swiss Hotel, just half a block from the current mission on Sonoma Plaza. When the Swiss was retrofitted and modernized, the owner Helen Dunlap donated the same adobe bricks to the Cannard Cline project, so they could use authentic materials contemporary to the period. Bob supervised the construction of a small commemorative mission-like structure designed by him and Fred near the spot chosen by Altimira in the grounds of the Cline family winery. He used period building techniques, architectural proportions and raw materials, and even used unskilled field labor to do all the building and carpentry work, as would have been the case during the construction of the original Mission in Sonoma a hundred

In adode bricks over a hundred and fifty years old, you can see the print of an animal and what looks like a soldiers boot.

Following the end of the U. S. - Mexican War (1846-1848), the cannon was left at one of the Mexican outposts when that portion of Mexico was taken over by the United States.

e photograph, located on the Cline Ranch, was
lobe bricks from Mission San Francisco Solano
al Mariano Vallejo came to Sonoma in 1834,
the unfinished
uct his home,
rother's home,
Swiss Hotel.
ake, the hotel
safety and in
vere set aside.
s given the
lly with the
e them for
ma. In sort-
ound some
, an animal
. Note the
ce of Bob
ed by un-
the same
uld have

ar
on
as
a t
of
Ruc
Vist
on S
cann
Augu
nard
tised
if it w
Canna

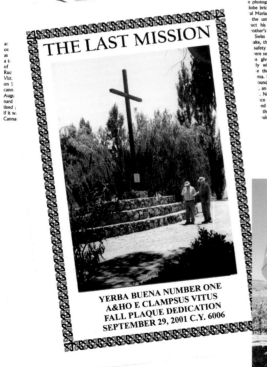

THE LAST MISSION

YERBA BUENA NUMBER ONE
A&HO E CLAMPSUS VITUS
FALL PLAQUE DEDICATION
SEPTEMBER 29, 2001 C.Y. 6006

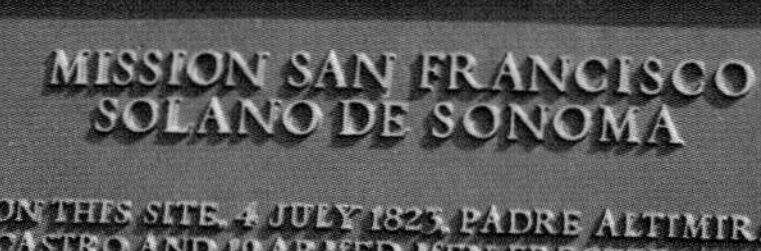

SOLANO DE SONOMA
ON THIS SITE, 4 JULY 1823, PADRE ALTIMIRA,
LT. CASTRO AND 19 ARMED MEN ERECTED A CROSS
SET A CAMP ALTAR, CONSECRATED THE GROUND
WITH A MASS AND FIRED A VOLLEY. CLINE RANC
WAS THEN USED AS A PRELIMINARY SCOUTING SIT
AND DEPARTURE POINT FOR NORTHERN CALIFORN
EXPLORATION. COAST MIWOKS WOULD LATER BUIL
A PERMANENT MISSION IN SONOMA. BRICKS USED
IN THE NEARBY SHRINE ARE FROM SONOMA MISSION
THE 21ST AND LAST OF THE CALIFORNIA MISSIONS.
DEDICATED SEPTEMBER 29, 2001 C.Y. 6006
BY CAPITULUS REDIVIVUS YERBA BUENA NUMBER ONE
ANCIENT AND HONORABLE ORDER OF E CLAMPSUS VITUS
CREDO QUIA ABSURDUM

and sixty years before. The doors were made from relief carved planks retrieved from Professor Cowan's yard in Kenwood thirty years previously—beautifully mellowed California pepperwood. Even handmade hinges and other fixtures were made to period designs.

There were some not so small irritants like disputes with the county over permits, and supposed code violations. Bob is adamant that the structure was hugely strong, but because it didn't perfectly comply with code, they were required to add steel-cored buttresses.

Nancy Cline worked with the California Historical Society to locate a period bell, an original 19th century Camino Real Bell, and it stands to the left of the mission.

During a visit to Robert Parmelee's cabin in the Sierras, Bob met an official of the E Clampus Vitis organization, which after a history largely dedicated to drinking and carousing has become a fierce protector of California's historic heritage. Bob provided the locations of some fifteen significant sites in Sonoma County that would be of interest to them, and also mentioned his own efforts with the Cline family to commemorate the first selected site for the Sonoma Mission. E Clampus soon threw their weight behind the project, organizing the cross, plaque and an opening ceremony to consecrate the new mission. They also made Bob an honorary member of the organization. The site has now become a part of the visitor experience to the Cline family winery and gardens.

The local preservation establishment was initially reluctant to accept Bob's version of the past, but after an appropriate number of years, the League for Historic Preservation finally acknowledged Bob's efforts and awarded the mission one of its commendations in 2004.

Not too many people are aware that there is a "Sonoma" rose. While at the Chamber of Commerce, Bob contacted Armstrong Nursery, the second biggest producer of backyard roses with the idea that the name Sonoma would be a good marketing device to sell roses. After some initial resistance, the name was approved. Bob recommended a yellow or gold color to tie in with the Spanish connection, but the decision came back for pink. Five hundred pink Sonoma rosebushes subsequently arrived at the Chamber. Bob gave them away, and turned distribution over to local nurseryman Frank Wedekind. Appropriately, you will find Sonoma roses right in front of City Hall on Sonoma's Plaza.

It was another example of Bob's ability to recognize trends. Here we are thirty-five years later and the commercial world now attaches the name Sonoma to any product with an image synonymous with quality and the good life, from trucks to garden furniture.

Bob went on to build another period structure at one of the local Cline family ranches. It is a log cabin that originated in Virginia, and dates from 1827. It was carefully dismantled and transported to Sonoma, where Bob supervised its rebuilding at a location carefully selected in a private and remote spot. Huge trees tower overhead and the place has no modern references to break the illusion that as you approach the building you are stepping back in time and could be, say, a pioneer woodsman pushing the frontier westwards somewhere between the Atlantic and Pacific.

The setting is no different to the scene that would

have greeted Padre Altimira almost two hundred years ago. It's a Bob Cannard kind of place, and although it would be practically impossible, he would like to think that some of his final years could be spent there, among the trees that have been his constant and favorite companions—next to his family. Trees don't talk back, don't run and hide; and they rarely hold opinions that could be at odds with Bob's. But they do offer quiet conversation, about the wind and sun and rain and seasons, and of course about history. Bob can see it in the color, bark, size, height, shape, structure and leaf texture. He reads the thickness and length and posture of the branches and analyzes the scars the way a forensic scientist might. In his mind, he sees the tree as a seedling, a young sapling, and all the changes that occurred over the centuries, building a history as detailed and vivid as any you might read in a book. Friendship with a whole host of particular trees throughout California and Pennsylvania have provided Bob with a huge library of biographies—volumes of historical data and memories. Books whose pages can be turned, a few at a time, when he visits them, as he does every year, in a series of ritual reunions.

He has seen trees that were born centuries before him fall and die and be recycled in a powerful display of nature's resolute regenerative processes. He has seen trees taken before their time by mishandling, ignorance, disinterest and fear—and he cannot understand our callousness toward the earth's penultimate apex species—the one we depend on for our ultimate survival.

But he has planted hundreds of thousands of replacements and sleeps secure in the knowledge that they will stand proud centuries after he has been recycled, as silent testaments to his own noisy life.

Trees and plants convert the energy of the stars into every single thing we depend on to exist, and to Bob, they are not abstract natural history, but integral to his personal survival.

CHAPTER ELEVEN

TREES

Trees have played a lead role in Bob Cannard's life and he in theirs. Since those early neighborhood walks with his mother on summer evenings as a boy, past maple and dogwood, chestnut and beech, his interest grew as the trees grew with him. On college graduation day he made a promise to himself to give away a million trees. He estimates 300,000 so far, and many times more than that sold and planted through his landscaping and nursery businesses. And every year he continues to start new trees from seed and cutting, while harvesting olives, cherries, apples, peaches, plums, pomegranates, pluots, quince, lemons and oranges from May to October. His message to children on Arbor Day in 1993 provides some of the reasons.

THE IMPORTANCE OF TREES

Today we are going to talk about how you and trees help each other every day. Most of the oxygen we breathe in comes from trees and other green plants. And the air that we breathe out is what the trees need to breathe—to give us back the oxygen we must have to live. So you see, trees are very important to us, and we are very important to trees.

It's nice to know that each of us breathes out enough CO_2 *for a big tree to live and grow. Each big tree breathes out enough oxygen for one of us. It's like each one of us has a*

—it's why it always feels cooler when we are near trees. And the shade is also nice on a hot day.

Trees give us wood—for our homes, our furniture, cardboard, paper—and it is woven into our lives in a hundred other ways. That is why it's very, very important for us to recycle anything we can that is made from trees. The more we recycle, the fewer trees will be cut down, and the more oxygen we will have to breathe.

If you count all the people in the world and all the trees that are cut down in a year, it's about one tree each. Which is why it is so important that every one of us should plant at least two trees a year—one to use and one that will grow so we can breathe.

special friend in a tree.

Trees help us in so many other ways. They clean the air of pollutants. As the wind blows air through the branches of a tree, it slows down, and the heavier dirt in the air drops to the ground. The air absorbs moisture given off by the trees

Bob's love of trees and belief that they are vital to our well-being has gotten him into frequent battles with anyone who has planned to remove them for development projects and the like.

In early 1978, there was a series of very heavy overnight freezes, and soon after, Caltrans announced that they would be cutting down 247 eucalyptus trees between Sonoma and Oakmont along Highway 12 because they had serious splitting, were dead or dying, and represented a threat to motorists. They had put out a contract on the trees for $275,000. A public hearing was held and Bob went along, but not before consulting a couple of local old-timers.

Farmers Quile Ubaldi and Cliff Rich, whose combined ages exceeded 170 years, confirmed that in their living memory, and even after the disastrously harsh frosts of 1933, not a tree had been lost in the valley in this way. There were plenty of perfectly healthy trees, they said, where you could see the scars from those frosts, and damage would be taken care of by the natural healing process. Armed with this information, Bob vociferously disagreed with Caltrans' consulting arborist at the public hearing, who maintained that the trees would certainly die and be a major threat to public safety. But his protests were ignored and the trees were condemned.

A couple of days before the tree-felling was to start, Bob drove the section of highway where the eucalyptus trees lined the road, and found that the frosts had been highly selective. First, the majority of trees on only one side of the road were marked for removal. Then, for a distance, only trees on the other side of the road were marked, before switching back again. This arrangement was evident everywhere. The reason became apparent when Bob saw that the electricity lines followed exactly the same pattern.

It would be hard to come to any other conclusion than that there was some kind of deal between Caltrans and the electricity company. It seemed that Caltrans was more interested in the safety of the PG&E electricity lines than the safety of the public.

Soon, Bob was at the Caltrans offices in San Francisco, demanding to see the district supervisor, a Mr. Hart—the man who had chaired the public hearing. After checking, the secretary told Bob that Mr. Hart would not see him and the trees were coming down.

"Tell him if he doesn't see me, I'll go straight from here to the TV stations," was Bob's response.

Minutes later, he was leaning over a desk, staring down the furious Hart who was big and heavy. As Bob recalls it, his large bald head was glowing red.

"So who's getting paid off Mr. Hart?"

"What do you mean?" bellowed Hart.

Bob told him in no uncertain terms that mysteriously, only trees under power lines were marked for cutting, and that if something wasn't done to put things right he would tell the story to every newspaper and TV station in the Bay Area.

Hart got on the phone right away, and by the time Bob had driven the forty miles back home, there was a Caltrans engineer at his door explaining that the decision had been reversed and no trees would come down.

Only two very young trees later proved to be frost damaged to the point that they had to be removed, and to this day not one of the other 245 has caused a serious problem. In the twenty-five years since, Bob is quick to point out, they have absorbed the carbon dioxide breathed out by the same number of the valley's human population, and returned to them their daily oxygen needs.

When the Community Center removed some of the trees from around the building, they took down two spruce memorial trees that were planted in honor of a local resident who had founded the Community Center and died during the Korean War. There was a blistering response from Bob, who considered the sculptures that replaced them "junkyard art on concrete slabs."

November 13, 1997
Pulse of the Public

Editor, *Index-Tribune*:

It would be nice to be able to give the President of the Board of Directors of the Community Center the benefit of the doubt and say he is new in town and does not know what he is talking about. That is not possible because nearly every statement he makes is untrue. Why anyone would consider trading two beautiful spruces for two slabs of concrete is more than I can understand. These trees were in perfect health and at the height of their glory. I have every reason to believe they would have lived for another hundred years. What do we get in return? Two slabs of concrete replacing the lawn, and two concrete benches. City people making city-type decisions in Sonoma.

Makes you think of the person who buys property next to a pasture because they want the open space and then complains about the cows. Or in my case, the person who comes from San Francisco to be in the country and then complains about my chickens. No wonder that Sonoma has changed. The City of Sonoma's official Vision Statement says, "more trees, less concrete." But it doesn't mean a thing.

The president promised the Garden Club that the memorial trees would not be removed. That there would be no more trees cut at the Community Center. Obviously this statement is untrue. The facts show that all of the trees on the west side foundation have been removed. The special planting of rare trees on the east property line have been removed. The Italian cypress have been removed. The new plantings will quickly grow to obscure the light that they seem to want. They have planted a Liquidambar eighteen inches from the foundation. This is the same species as the mammoth trees in the front lawn. What do you think will happen there? Don't blame the landscape architect. He is a professional with a job to do. In much the same position as a surgeon who is asked to do cosmetic surgery. I sat on the Tree Committee with him; he does not hate trees.

The Community Center is important to Sonoma. What is the answer to this dilemma? The only answer as I see it is to put the financial squeeze on the Center by withholding all financial support. This board of directors is not to be trusted and until they realize that Sonoma is not San Francisco, we must take drastic measures. Perhaps the directors will shape up or ship out. The Community Center must remain a viable part of Sonoma.

Bob Cannard.

Bob lives only half a block from the Community Center and has strong connections to it. At the front are a pair of trees with their trunks intertwined. Bob planted these as "wedding trees."

The practice of planting two trees together in the same hole has its origin in colonial American farm culture. When a Pennsylvania Dutch couple was married, they would plant, on their wedding day, the trees in front, usually, of their new farm home.

Today many of these trees are still around. You can see them in southeastern Pennsylvania. Since these trees have grown together and been pruned over the years by nature and man and as a single tree, their great size is the only distinguishing character. I know of many of these trees that are more than 200 years old.

To carry on this custom, I sometimes give a newly married couple two trees planted in a large patio container so that they can move it around with them as they move in our changing society.

Bob believes that trees are a whole lot more than pretty plants that provide shade from sun and shelter from the rain. As he repeated prosely-

tizes, they are air filters and windbreaks; they pull up moisture and minerals from deep below the surface; an average size tree will provide one person's daily oxygen needs, removing harmful carbon dioxide as it does so, and provide a means to put carbon and other beneficial elements back in the topsoil through the annual leaf drop. They provide shelter and food for birds that balance bug populations and also fertilize the soil. We despair at the rate that rainforest in other parts of the world are being destroyed, but accept it on a daily basis here. The City of Sonoma repeatedly fails to protect old oaks from developers who cut down first and apologize afterwards.

During Brock Arner's tenure as city manager, Bob tried to get the City to consider a tree ordinance that would engage an arborist to look after "heritage trees" (dating prior to 1823) from a resident's property line to the property setback. The city-sponsored Tree Committee thought it was a good approach, but the idea was rejected out of hand by Arner, with no objection from then Councillors McTaggart, Murphy and Carter.

The City was later willing for the Tree Committee to conduct a survey of the plaza trees and recommend a maintenance plan. Bob hired James McNair, and footed the $12,500 bill for the survey, which the City accepted. But they never used the survey. Bob gave another $12,500 for a survey of the street trees in Sonoma.

At the south side of the plaza, there used to be two really unique looking small eucalyptus trees, with beautifully burled trunks. Both were left six feet out in the street when the sidewalk was moved back to widen the street. One of them leaned at an unsafe angle. Bob paid the City $1,000 and they agreed to prop the trunk. In fact they let the tree fall down and promptly cut it up for firewood, never even apologizing to Bob. The episode produced a "Letter to the editor" response from him that revealed a deeper concern for the disappearance of familiar landmarks.

December 11, 1997
Pulse of the Public,
Editor, *Index-Tribune*

The loss of the eucalyptus tree in the roadway of Napa Street need not have happened. This is the tree that was in the parking space across from the Church Mouse. A couple of years ago, the Cannard Fund gave the City of Sonoma a thousand dollars to install a steel post with a yoke to prevent this tree from falling over in a wind. The post and yoke were never installed. The tree went down over Thanksgiving. Another part of the Sonoma Heritage is gone. I'll ask the City to return the thousand dollars.

Of greater concern than the loss of this historic part of our town is the fact that not one person in city government cares a whit. Don't blame the city staff. The responsibility lays squarely on the City Council. During the past sixty years, nearly fifty percent of the Plaza has been paved over. You might say how could this happen? The sidewalks have been moved back twice to widen the streets, concrete walks have been installed, the amphitheater and playgrounds have been built, the U-driveway in front of City Hall has been doubled in size, new walkways have been added, slabs of concrete have been installed under all benches and tables, parking areas behind City Hall were paved, a bus shelter has been built, restrooms have been added, and the paved area around the Carnegie Library has been increased. All in sixty years. Add them up and you will see that nearly fifty percent of the Plaza is under paving.

Sixty years ago, Pete Viviani's mother pastured her cows in the Plaza; likely there are several hundred Sonomans who remember. In 1937, if you had asked Judge Grinstead—who the Grinstead Memorial is named after—if he thought fifty percent of the Plaza would be paved in sixty years, he may well have said, "I don't think that could happen." It has happened.

Not all of these "improvements" are all bad, but the Plaza is a National Historic Monument, of importance to everyone in this town, state and nation. This mind-numbing tragedy of what we have allowed to happen is beyond reason. Unless things change, it is entirely possible that the grandchildren of those who saw Mrs. Viviani's cows in the Plaza, will see the other half of the Plaza paved over.

The current City Council will scoff at such an idea. Again, don't blame the city staff. It is up to us to make sure that the three people elected to the City Council next year understand the seriousness of the problem. We need three people with the guts and gumption to say we have had enough. It's our responsibility to protect this national treasure. M.G. Vallejo had the vision to lay out the Plaza as a part of his town plan for Sonoma. We are slowly but surely destroying that legacy.

The eucalyptus is gone. I expect I'll get the money back, but the desecration of the Plaza continues.

Bob Cannard.

The City never did return the $1,000.

Only a couple of months earlier, Bob had been firecely opposed to moving a Victorian home near the plaza to make way for a parking lot. In his "Fellow Citizens" appeal, he described the house as "not only one of the historic shrines of our nation, but the very lifeblood of Sonoma."

When a camphor tree planted by Vallejo became distressed, Bob found that an irrigation line had broken nearby and the roots were being drowned. He pleaded with the state parks for three years to do something about it, even offering to pay whatever it cost to repair the irrigation line. But they refused every plea and eventually the tree died. The state parks hired someone from UC Davis who declared that the tree had died of disease—which to Bob was nonsense as proved when the tree was cut down and the wood was found to be perfectly clean. It sits in Bob's barn in neat boards ready for one of his furniture projects. Whatever he decides to make, chair, box or tabletop, it will be a permanent reminder of his connection to a tree that is in turn connected to the history of a revered character in a more expansive story. And the tree will thus never need to die.

Which is exactly why trees that may have only passing significance to many people, have huge importance to Bob. They connect him to the past events of his own life just as vividly as do his family and friends.

Considering that Bob's love affair with trees has been going on for most of his conscious existence, he's had remarkably few bad experiences. On the following pages, you'll find a selection of trees that for one reason or another, figure prominently and happily in Bob Cannard's personal history. He visits them every year.

TREES EAST

Memorial Park, Danville, PA, where Bob's father gave the Memorial Day address on the day Bob was born, and where later Bob would spend many hours as a child quizzing the old veterans of numerous wars who sat on the benches and whiled away the hours among majestic trees older than the United States of America itself.

With his mother, and sometimes aunt Vi, Bob would walk past this house with its two magnolia trees on summer evenings in the early 1930s.

A Pin Oak planted by Bob almost sixty years ago in downtown Danville, in front of the old family home of his lifelong friend, Bill Cole.

Trees in the driveway of a church where the graves are mostly of soldiers who fell in revolutionary and civil wars.

Bob probably planted the tree in the foreground when he worked as a life-guard. It's in the grounds of the swim club. Just upsteam was where a young boy dived headfirst into deep mud and drowned before he could free himself. And round the corner downstream is a deep hole where the police had Bob dive in to recover the body of a motorist who crashed into the creek

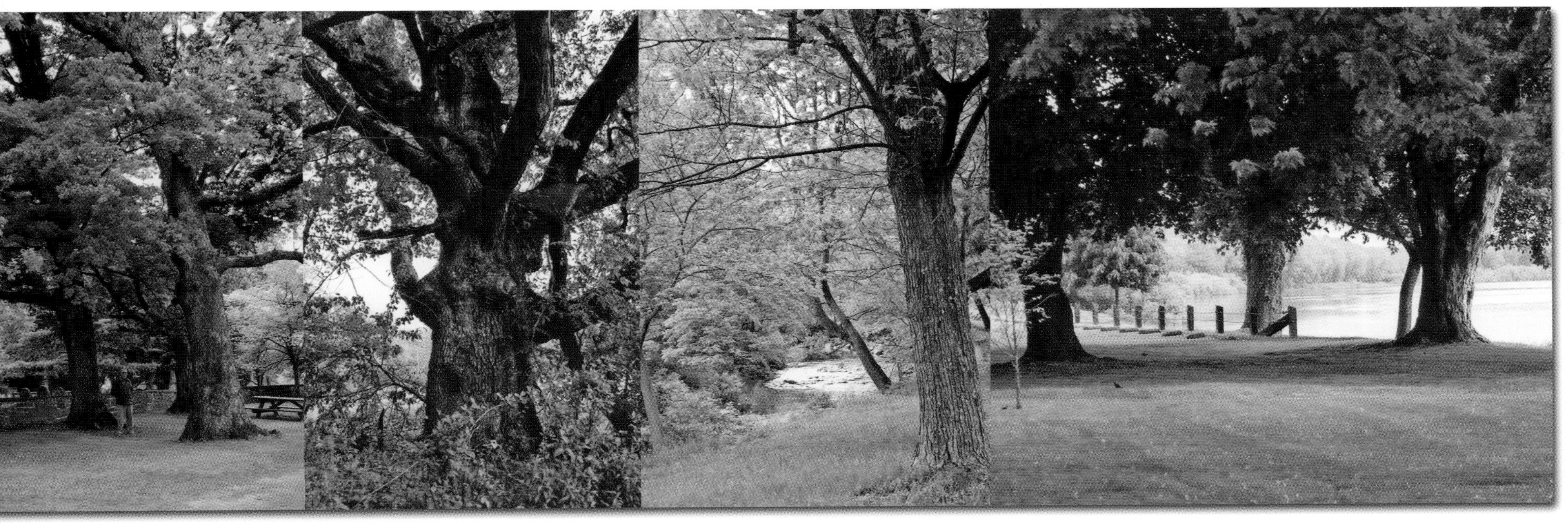

An old favorite on the edge of a small wood a few miles east of Danville.

On the banks of the Susquehannah where Bob swam and fished and grew up.

TREES WEST

In the hills to the west of Sonoma are some of the oldest trees in the valley. The trunk of this myrtle is fifteen feet across, which means that it is more than 1200 years old. Countless generations of native Americans have sheltered under its branches. It was around before Lief Ericson reached the east coast of North America, or Sir Francis Drake the west. It has lived through the entire modern history of the United States, California and what we call the civilized world.

On a summer evening in 1992, Bob and Edna were taking a turn around Sonoma Plaza, when out of the doors of the Eldorado Hotel staggered a man who despite his state recognized Bob and clung to his arm. "You're the man who came with the tree to the extension school in Boyes and made us search all over for leaf mold to throw in the hole—took us hours with the sun beating down. About fifteen years ago."
He paused in thought, then continued . . .
"It's the only time I ever really accomplished anything in my life. I felt good about that tree."
The man lurched off. This is the Pin Oak he talked about. It's now about fifty feet tall.

These redwoods were planted by Bob in 1978, near the police department. He had hoped to rebuild the original adobe jailhouse just beyond the trees, but the proposal fell on deaf ears at City Hall. Far from being resentful, Bob cheerily comments that it probably gives the city's ex-manager great delight every time one of the pets in the new dog park cocks its leg at the base of Bob's redwoods.

Imagine the imposing shape of this old, old cemetery oak if it had been allowed to grow naturally.

One of remaining original valley oaks remaining in the City of Sonoma. Maybe 600-700 years old. Many fall victim to developers that chop first and ask questions afterwards. That, and careless enforcement of the regulations by city staff.

This magnificent yet battered redwood, on the western slope of Sonoma Valley is one of the few remaining old growth trees that covered huge swaths of Sonoma County.

Another huge myrtle tree bearing the scars of a long life in the California sunshine.

The trees that Bob reveres when they are alive continue to provide for him long after they are chopped down. Over the years, he has gathered together an impressive collection of hardwood, and converted much of it into all manner of useful devices and furniture that now grace the homes of his large extended family and friends alike. He is as instinctive when constructing furniture as he is when growing trees. He uses no drawings, preferring to visualize the entire process in the minutest detail, from the selection of the figuring in the wood to the dimensions of every component and on to the logical sequence of work and even the decorative treatment he intends for the finished item. The actual work is then a replay of what he has already done in his mind, and the results, as you can see, are striking, solid, full of personality and made, of course, to last.

He loves making boxes, and is adept at taking a thick piece of wood and turning it into successively smaller boxes, nesting one inside another. He made the rustic box at the top from a fence post. It was for a family that leaves a key by the front door, near firewood. Bob thought what better way to disguise the whereabouts of the key in the pile of wood. It was so well disguised that the box was thrown on the fire.

As you can see by the decorated benches to the right, he paints well in oils. None of his pieces is as fine as the "Rocking Duck of Sonoma" he made for grandson Ross It is a masterful combination of different woods—shaped, molded, inlaid and upholstered in as fine an example of Americana as you will find anywhere.

The dowry chest above, inlaid with the heart and flower motif, was made for his grand daughter Coleen. Son Tim filled it with money for her!

Much of the wood Bob has collected comes from Sonoma Valley and long time friends Denny and Monty Farr in Millville, Pennsylvania have always been helpful finding hardwoods and other rarities, such as the twenty-five foot antique flagpole they recently shipped from the East Coast.

Despite never using drawings, Bob rarely, if ever, has made a mistake with a woodworking or any other construction project. He has a unique way of allowing his subconscious to work for him.

People often ask how I am able to do so many things well the first time I try, and I reply...

We are creatures of our minds. I believe we can do almost anything we want to if we let our minds work out the problem. The trick is to learn how to put the problem or idea before your brain and then forget about the details. Our mind can sort through the many ways to achieve the results and then come up with a plan that works.

When I decide to make a piece of furniture or paint a picture or get involved in a project, my mind does all the practice work in advance. I see the final piece as I want it and then proceed. As the project develops through each step, I have already done all the practice in my head. My hands then do what my brain tells them to do. Practice makes perfect they say, and my brain has done all the practice. I suppose that is why the country carpenter says "measure twice and cut once." This approach works for most any thing we face in life.

The workshop in the barn has everything the woodworker might need—somewhere. If you look closely, you will see a tray of pheasant eggs waiting to be incubated (under the drill press).

CANNARD CANDY

"ASK FATHER TO MAKE US SOME QUINCE."

1 or more quince peeled, cored and sliced in 1/2" thick slices

Boil in sugar syrup (2 cups of water to 1 cup of sugar) until nearly transparent. Dry in a warmed oven for a few minutes and sprinkle with sugar. Store in a closed container. The leftover syrup is great on waffles or pancakes.

CHAPTER TWELVE

FAMILY ALBUM

In 1981 or 1982, Rich Thomas, who was running the viticulture program at Santa Rosa Junior College asked Bob if he would like to help with a major wine tasting and competition to be held at Treasure Island in San Francisco Bay. Rich went on to develop the wine tastings for the Sonoma County Harvest Fair and other West Coast competitions. Many of Bob's students were now in Rich's class, and Bob decided to go.

Bob went down to San Francisco the day before to set up and prepare the wine. Late in the morning he asked a security guard where the telephones were and was directed outside to a phone near the edge of the Bay.

As soon as I got to the telephone, I realized I had been there before. In May of 1946 I sailed under the Golden Gate Bridge in a troopship from oversdeas and landed right there at Treasure Island. The building where we were doing the wine tasting was the debarcation assembly point for troops returning from the Pacific. Outside there was a field filled with telephone booths and each of us was allowed to make one five-minute call. By then my father and mother were both dead, and I didn't know where my brothers and sisters were, so I called Edna Taylor. I distinctly remembered looking out at the famous San Francisco skyline while I made my call. And there I was, thirty-five years later, being trans-

ported back to that point in time in 1946, calling Edna again.

When I went back inside the building I told the students that I had just made a call to the same girl from the same phone and place I had called her from thirty-five years before when I came home from World War II. There were tears in the eyes of many of the young women in the class.

Bob follows this line by asking "I wonder why?" He knows of course, but it is one of Bob's idiosyncracies that he rarely admits to emotion, even if he feels it. Another is that although he is given to spontaneous and overt gestures of affection, they are rarely, if ever, directed toward his sons. Much of that must have come from his own need to be in control, and six headstrong boys with at least as powerful a physical presence as himself in the home must have required one firm leader. To instill his principles of self-reliance and toughness he probably found it necessary to maintain authority with some loss of closeness. That would be a sacrifice a mountain man might be prepared to make. He is as effusive as any father might be when praising the talents of his sons, even if he has a hard time telling them personally. But it's certainly not unusual for fathers to be this way.

Most people would describe Edna as an amazing person, to have held her own in a household not just of men, but of big, physical, boisterous, opinionated men. And on top of that she has welcomed an endless succession of students, friends, visitors, girlfriends, co-workers and political co-conspirators for short and extended stays at the family home, even if it did mean bouts of migraine in between. The fights between the boys were apparently epic, but the home is now relatively quiet with just the two of them. Edna has her routine and Bob has his. The food is always fabulous, whether cooked by Edna or Bob, and the conversation is bright, witty and full of humor. Edna remains the quiet partner on the whole, but if Bob tries to push his luck, her response is a sharp and emphatic "bull****!" that suggests no room for negotiation.

Bob is still canning and bottling and preserving for a family of eight, even though the boys are long gone, and the cellar is filling up. His vast collection of papers and books and

Edna on her mother's knee in a family picture, and with one of her grandchildren. Her father had been an engineer on the Empire State Building before the Depression.

the barn, or cellar or garage, and it will soon be delivered to you with a cake, or fresh eggs or tomatoes or peaches by the boxful. If you are fortunate enough to be invited to one of the great family parties, you will be swept up in the embrace of a glorious celebration of good will, good food and good people.

Somehow, Edna has found time to paint, and her work is careful, deliberate and fresh.

documents and art and artifacts fills the spare spaces. But Edna has her nook at the breakfast table, and sits in peace with her crossword in the morning when Bob is off at the barn, taking care of garden and orchard and chickens and pheasants, to return near noon for lunch and his regular as clockwork afternoon nap. They enjoy Hawaii in the spring, the big redwoods in northern California in the fall, and San Diego for Thanksgiving when Edna is thankfully free of hosting the enormous family get-togethers that occur on other holidays and birthdays for sons and grandchildren and daughters-in-law and anyone else orbiting in the general area of the Cannards.

They are generous to a fault, and if there's anything you may be short of, it will be in their house somewhere—or

With so many noisy people all with a point of view and no reluctance to express it, order was difficult to maintain at family gatherings. So Bob took a walking staff made for him by son Bobby (carved with the names of all family members and regularly updated) and declared it to be the Cannard Speaking Staff. He also prepared a set of informal rules for its use.

THE COUNCIL OF CANNARDS

Established under Robert and Edna the First to ensure the continued peaceful and serene life as enjoyed by the California Cannards since migrating west in 1959.

Of equal importance is to provide for a tranquil transition to the succeeding generations and on into the future.

The following dictum and laws should not be changed or eliminated. However, modifications and additions can be adopted at any properly scheduled Council meeting. A proper meeting is defined as one that all living descendants have been notified of, with a reasonable time for attendance scheduled.

Law I. A Council should not convene until everyone has had plenty of food and libations.

Law II. The Cannard Speaking Staff will be the symbol of the Council and will be used to both open and close each Council meeting.

The head of the Council will hold the staff in his possession for life.

Each succeeding generation shall elect a new Staff Holder who is a direct descendant of Robert and Edna the First.

Any member of the Council can request the Staff to speak to the Council. This person will be given total respect and allowed to speak without interruptions. When he or she is done, another person can request the Staff for a reply. As many can speak at each council meeting until all are satisfied.

A majority vote of the Council will decide any issue. The voting members will be all descendants of Robert and Edna the First and their consorts. Once a member of the Council means that person is a member for life.

Law III. REMEMBER THE REASON FOR THE COUNCIL IS TO ENSURE PEACE, PROSPERITY AND HAPPINESS FOR ALL CANNARDS.

The rules and the speaking staff do work. At Bob's 75th birthday celebrations held in the garden of the Cline family home in Sonoma, a few bales of hay made a small stage, and taking the staff from each other, Bob's sons stepped up on the stage one at a time and delivered their own birthday speeches. They called him father, not dad, which is kind of old-fashioned and kind of nice, proving that politeness does not detract from affection. And each had an endearing shy respect for "father" that contrasted sharply with their size.

Bob may not be comfortable praising his sons directly, and that may have have upset a few people, but he has no problem talking to the rest of the world about them, and that should make up for it.

Let me tell you about the boys. Every one of them learned how to do something with their hands. I mean do something. If you can do something, or make something with your own hands, you'll never go hungry.

When Tom was 11 or 12, he could fix just about anything mechanical you could imagine. Bicycles, model plane engines, motorcycles, you name it. Why, this place was swarming with kids. I must have lost a couple of thousand dollars worth of tools. And a year or two later it was automobiles, pickups, etc. They brought 'em here broke, and Tom would fix 'em. You ask Tom Vella, he'll tell you. "If Tom Cannard can't fix it, you might as well throw it away" that's what he'd tell you. And it's still true today. I don't care if it's a septic system or winery equipment or a truck or a watch, clock, pump, tractor. Anything, I mean anything, and Tom can figure it out in a few minutes. He's a mechanical genius, nothing less.

In the spring, when I put down the pots of colors from the nursery all over the garden here, Jim could immediately—I mean without hesitation—turn them all the right way round before planting! He knew instinctively which was the front and which was the back of the plant. Not many people even know that plants have fronts and backs, let alone find 'em, but it's true. And Jim is a master. Just like my mother, and to a certain extent myself. It's why James' color gardens around town here attract such attention today. Every plant is perfectly oriented to show its best. And what a cook! He was taught by one of the best chefs this valley has ever seen, Harry Marston, at Au Relais, now Deuce on Broadway. Jim came to me in the 8th grade and asked what he should do with the year's 1099 tax form he'd received from Harry. It was for $13,000! Can you imagine that he'd earned that much. He'd learned and done every job at the restaurant while he was still in high school, earning more than regular workers. He frequently took over the kitchen when Harry was away.

The things I could tell you about these boys!

Within a month of going to ag school in Fresno, Bobby was calling to say they couldn't teach him much he didn't already know. And he left soon after. You see Bobby has the gift my mother had. He knows plants. I may have given him a start, but by his own observations and instinct, he could make plants want to grow their best, and before he was a teenager! He was confident too. I remember once when he was showing a customer around a table of grafted bonsai trees at the nursery in Kenwood. He came to a bunch of trees that didn't quite meet his standards and I overheard him saying "father did them." He was probably right too.

Let me tell you, when it comes to agriculture I may be a link to the past, but Bobby is the link to the future. He's the only person that's figured out how to truly integrate his produce growing into the natural system of things, and I can tell you the way it's going with food production in the world, they're going to need Bobby's ideas. He has already had a huge impact. The ag schools and all kinds of world travellers come to his farms on a regular basis. And he has a compulsion totally unique to him and my mother, to help any needy person that crosses his path.

Did you see the furniture in Bobby's new kitchen up at Sobre Vista? You should take a look. The stand for the kitchen sink, and the worktable and dressers. Beautiful, sturdy,

perfect workmanship and fine designs—all made by my youngest son Jack. Right off the top of his head. He cut the tree, sawed the wood, dried the planks and milled the lumber. I mean he can make anything. And he can cook too. He took over at Au Relais when James decided he didn't want to spend his life working indoors.

My oldest Tim is a wizard with mechanical things too, but more toward electronics. When he was about thirteen years old, I showed him the circuits in an old radio. Took him through, step by step, even though I didn't know it all myself. And within a week do you know that he had it all figured out. Not long after he went to the dump and got five old TV sets—we didn't have one in those days—five broken sets. Well in no time at all he had made one good one out of the five. It used to cost someone $25 to get a TV repairman from Santa Rosa out to Kenwood. Tim would do it for $10, while he was still in high school! A genius with electronics. Self taught. He's another one that said after a few weeks at the Jaycee, "Father, they can't teach me anything. I know this stuff." He set up a cable system in Kenwood, California. Became chief engineer of cable systems for nine western states, and no college degree. Retired at forty-five because he didn't

want to move to the new company HQ in Denver. When the MBAs he hired asked him where he went to school, he would say "on the streets."

Marian Brackenridge, the sculptor from across the street said that Edward was a "natural artist." He modeled for her a lot. Well, he's the best looking. Tall and with big hands, he has amazing manual dexterity and an incredible eye for form and shape and color. He could pick up any old piece of wood, turn it around to look at, run his hands over it, and know what it could become. I remember dropping a few rounds of wood—slices from a large cedar trunk—in the yard one day. A couple of hours later I saw that Ed had taken one and made a complete set of children's patio furniture, chairs, table, etc, using only an axe and an awl. Can you believe it? All done by eye—no measuring, with just an axe and awl.

He went on to make many sets like that one for sale. When he was fourteen, he attended a class in Glen Ellen learning stained glass, but it only lasted a few weeks. When I asked his teacher why, he said that Ed had already picked up everything he could teach him. After a trip to Wales, Scotland and Ireland, and knowing that we needed a section of new fence at the house on Third Street, he built an amazing creation of grooved redwood posts and slate slabs inspired by the walls in Wales. Bobby went on a similar trip studying horticulture.

Every one of these boys is better that I am at what they do. I can make furniture—made some fine pieces too—but not like Jack. You've seen my paintings, I can get a likeness, but I'm not an instinctive artist like Ed. I can grow plants, trees, shrubs, but not the way James and Bobby do. I've been a landscaper, but James' gardens are masterpieces of color. Have you seen Tom at a lathe—he's a genius with anything mechanical. No, these boys can do things. I may have started them off—like showing Tim the radio circuits—but they ran with the information, figured it out for themselves, made their own way. Edna and I encouraged them, gave them the tools or books or materials, but they taught themselves.

That's what I intended, and that's what has happened.

Jack had more to contend with than the other boys. Being the youngest in a family like the Cannards was not easy, and just short of his twenty-first birthday he suffered a devastating blow the day he was due to leave on a ski trip to Tahoe. Sudden excruciating pain took him to the emergency at Sonoma Valley Hospital. A blood test confirmed leukemia. It was recommended that he leave immediately for the nearest hospital with expertise in the subject—at UC San Francisco. Bobby would take him. They stopped briefly for Jack to see his dog, and again at Black Point where he went off for a walk up the hill on his own. "I just wanted to look at the sky one more time," said Jack on his return.

The family reassembled at the hospital after Jack's examination and the doctor announced that he might not last another twenty minutes. Bob was pretty sure he wouldn't survive the day. But after some drastic therapy to clear away the vast excess of white blood cells, Jack was temporarily stabilized. He spent the next few weeks in hospital while options were considered.

These were limited to doing nothing, with an estimated life expectancy of six months, or take a chance with a new procedure—a bone marrow graft—and chemotherapy.

Jack wanted to go ahead, and his older brother Tom turned out to be an almost perfect donor match. It was scheduled for early March. There were two other kids in what was really an experiment. The doctors told us there were considerable risks, but Jack turned round and told them not to worry because it was the time of year that his father grafted trees, and a transplant was not that different. When they told him to visualize red blood cells eating up the white cells, he told 'em that he'd already started doing it. He was determined to beat the rap! And he did too. The other two girls in the experiment died, but not Jack, he's a fighter. And when his hair grew back it was darker, like Tom's. And the most remarkable thing was he began to develop Tom's taste too. Damndest thing I ever heard.

Edna believes that Jack is most like me. Tom and Tim are the engineers like their two grandfathers. Nothing baffles them, nothing. Bobby and James are growers, like my mother, instinctive. Ed and Jack are a mixture of Edna and me. Artists and craftsmen. You've seen Edna's oil paintings—wonderful—and all her restoration work. You've seen my efforts on those two benches for the grandsons I decorated. That's where it comes from. And they're all tough too, like Edna's father, Charles Taylor, who became a vocational instructor at Lewisburg Penitentiary. He was a calm man, but if he was pushed too far he had a temper you never wanted to see again. That's why he had no problem with the convicts. He could walk freely among them because they knew if they started anything, he would knock 'em down. There's a bit of him in all the boys.

If Tim throws down his glasses, watch out. He was just off the school bus one day in Kenwood, with five or six other boys, and out of the corner of my eye, I saw him throw off his glasses. Do you know that before I could get across the nursery, four of them were down, one was running away and I had to pull Tim off the other one still swinging. Pull him off! They were making fun off him having to do his watering chores in the nursery as soon as he got home from school. I'll guarantee you they never made fun of him again.

Yes, independent bastards all of them. Survivors every one. They may not be intellectuals—neither am I—but they know how to get on in the world.

Yes, the children have been the most unifying part of my and Edna's lives. We are expressed more through our children than we are in our own lives. And without Edna, I should not have been such a good person, or as happy. She is the anchor of the family.

Bob's commitment to civic affairs, his iconoclasm, cavalier reluctance at certain times to take steady employment and his huge capacity for gin must have put a great strain on his relationship with Edna. She is not the kind of person who would enjoy drawing public attention to herself. She is financially conservative too, and worries when the checking account gets down to ten thousand dollars.

His tendencies must have been apparent to Edna when she first met him at the swim club over sixty years ago, and even Bob admits that her first impression was that he was far too full of himself. Over time one assumes that their commitment to each other and the family gave them the strength to deal with adversities that might have defeated lesser people. No matter what problems have surfaced, Bob and Edna Cannard have figured their way through them. They are not quitters. They make commitments and they stick to them. They have treated their lives as if they had been isolated in remote wilderness. You break a leg, you fix it; there's no furniture, you make it; there's no food, you grow it. You argue and fight and stray and disagree, you fix it the same way.

It's probable that Bob's absence from the home because of all his community activities actually made it easier for Edna to find her own patterns and habits independently, and the likelihood of confrontation more remote simply because they just didn't have that much time together. It seems to have helped them find a deep acceptance of each other's basic nature and that has sustained them through ups and downs. But there's no doubt that Edna must have had the same kind of spirit and strength possessed by pioneer women to have handled seven men like her husband and boys.

They are all big. They are all solid. And if there are other common characteristics, they stem from Bob's own odd blend of rough-hewn mountain man and academic. His knowledge of history is breathtaking and his ability to draw from it expansive ideas about the motion and impetus of America in all its variety is freewheeling, wonderful and unique. His knowledge of horticulture is encyclopedic. Yet he will measure himself and you by whether the plants are watered, food is stashed for the winter, wood is sawn and you could repair a worn harness if you had to.

Edna and Bob's boys are undoubtedly products of discipline on the one hand, and enormous freedom on the other. All the freedom and encouragement to pursue their own interests, with the constant reminder of what he expected of them in the nursery, at home, at the barn and in the yard.

Whatever their formula for success has been, it is undeniably apparent in the faces of Bob and Edna Cannard in their fiftieth wedding anniversary picture.

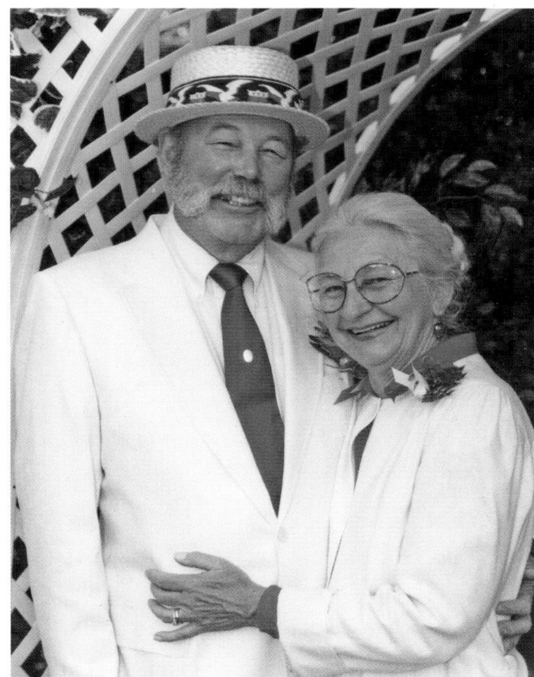

The Cannard family would not be complete without Stephanie. She and her mother came into the offices of the Chamber of Commerce back in the early seventies when Bob was manager. Stephanie's mother was looking for a motel in Sonoma where she could cook for her sick husband and was very distressed because she wasn't having any luck. Bob sent them off with some suggestions, but on his drive home to Kenwood later that day, he saw them at the side of the road, and it didn't look like they were too happy. So Bob picked them up and took them back to their motel. Subsequently the family found a home, Edna became very close friends with Stephanie's mother and Stepanie became a fixture at Bob and Edna's as part of the wide circle of their sons' high school friends. She was tall and striking and charming and vivacious, and Bob of course remembers that she rarely wore shoes and her feet were always dirty. For some reason he responded to her "strong jaw and good teeth," and all these attributes combined to make her exactly the kind of woman that would have made a perfect wife for his ideal of the classic pioneer woodsman.

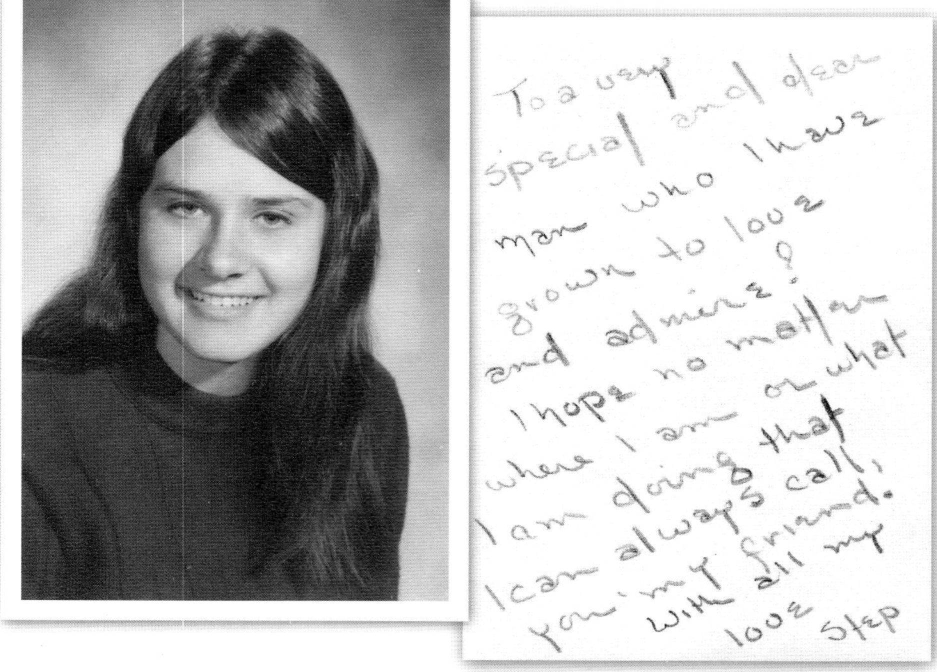

To a very
special and dear
man who I have
grown to love
and admire!
I hope no matter
where I am or what
I am doing that
I can always call
you "my friend."
With all my
love Step

In fact, during a stint with the Peace Corps when she was twenty years old in a remote corner of Central America, Steph performed a successful appendectomy on a local man. She had no medical training and the instructions came live over the cb radio as she operated!

Bob must have hoped that Stephanie would join his family, and although she was briefly close to Bobby to the point of planning to draft dodge together in Australia, she met her attorney husband Jim at UC Davis and now lives in Bakersfield. Together with their children, Jenner and Colin, Stephanie and Jim have remained the closest of friends with the Cannard family.

THE CANNARDS

Edward

Linda & James

Jack & Anne Marie

Tom & Julie

Bobby & Charlene

Tim & Bonnie

Tim's daughter Colleen & husband David

Tim's son Timmy & wife Joanne

Bob & Edna with
Tom & Julie's twin sons Oliver & Edison
(or is it Edison and Oliver?)

Tim's son Chris

Colleen and David's daughters
Christina and Adrianna

Bobby's sons Ross & Marius

CHAPTER THIRTEEN

RECOGNITION

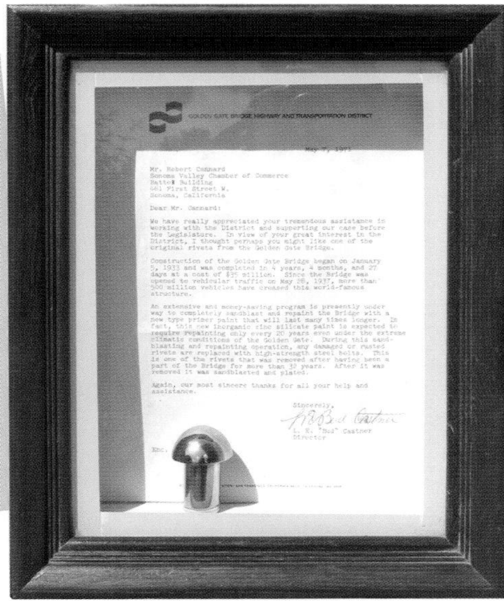

Mr. Robert Cannard
Sonoma Valley Chamber of Commerce
Batto Building
661 First Street W.
Sonoma, California

Dear Mr. Cannard:

We have really appreciated your tremendous assistance in working with the District and supporting our case before the Legislature. In view of your great interest in the District, I thought perhaps you might like one of the original rivets from the Golden Gate Bridge.

Construction of the Golden Gate Bridge began on January 5, 1933 and was completed in 4 years, 4 months, and 27 days at a cost of $35 million. Since the Bridge was opened to vehicular traffic on May 28, 1937, more than 500 million vehicles have crossed this world-famous structure.

An extensive and money-saving program is presently under way to completely sandblast and repaint the Bridge with a new type primer paint that will last many times longer. In fact, this new inorganic zinc silicate paint is expected to require repainting only every 20 years even under the extreme climatic conditions of the Golden Gate. During this sand-blasting and repainting operation, any damaged or rusted rivets are replaced with high-strength steel bolts. This is one of the rivets that was removed after having been a part of the Bridge for more than [illegible] years. After it was removed it was sandblasted and plated.

Again, our most sincere thanks for all your help and assistance.

Sincerely,

L. E. "Bud" Castner
Director

Enc.

Over the years Bob has received a variety of awards for civic activities, including Citizen of the Day from San Francisco's KGO Radio Station and the Golden Gate Bridge Authority.

In 1971 there had been a move in the state capitol to turn over the toll income and operation of the bridge to Caltrans. Bob lobbied hard in Sacramento, writing, calling and meeting with state senators to maintain the Bridge Authority's independence from the state treasury. Efforts were successful, and Bob's award features a rivet from the Golden Gate Bridge appropriately gold plated.

It was in 1997 that the highest accolade came, and one that he treasures most—an honorary professorship at Penn State for his contributions to horticulture. On that occasion he addressed the students in the Department of Hotel Management. His speech about food encompasses many of the principles that have guided his life and work, and provides a wealth of common sense advice to anyone involved in food service.

It was Bob's opportunity to pull together all his beliefs and convictions about the human condition in relation to offerings of the natural world. It was his chance to make a plea for good nutritious food, produced in harmony with nature rather than against it, and produced in a way that benefits the structure of society. It's a plea that we hear more and more today, with the incredible growth in appeal of "organic" food, and the equally fast growing problem of obesity from over promotion of processed comfort food. It's really an appeal for a return to our local communities for sustenance of all kinds. And it's based on his continued belief that happiness and contentment, individual and family, can only come from redeveloping our conscious contact with the natural world.

"THE GOODNESS OF LIFE"

Where have we been? Where are you going? A century ago the majority of Americans ate one-pot meals. Two hundred years ago President John Adams lit his fireplace every morning with a flint and steel to heat water for his morning tea. My father, an immigrant from England, born 125 years ago, was raised in a home where they cooked over an open fireplace. If asked today, how many people would know what a crane, a spider, or a spit was used for?

The standard cooking equipment for the westward movement from the Atlantic to the Pacific was a black iron kettle and, if they were lucky, an iron skillet. Think about cooking a meal tonight for a big hungry family with just one pot and a frying pan and not much time. We are just one generation away from those who lived that way.

The changes that have occurred in the last century are only the beginning. During the past fifty years, pioneers in your field like Water Conti, the man for whom this chair is named, and others have started a revolution. They have been in the forefront of the changes of how America eats. Much of the credit for improved nutrition and a longer life span goes to schools like this. We have a long way to go. These people have set the standard for change. What happens in the next fifty years depends on you. Remember that only through change can you improve.

In 1930, about 25 percent of Americans lived on farms. More important, the other 75 percent had a heritage of agriculture. Their parents were familiar with the production of food or were immigrants from Europe with a rural background. This was an agricultural nation. Today only 3 percent of the population produces the food we eat.

The decline and fall of the family farm is not difficult to trace. But that is another story for another day.

All energy on the earth comes from the sun and sustains all life. As I say about wine: From the sun to the land—to the vine—to the wine—to the family—to the table —to good friends—to good food—to the good life—the goodness of life.

This link with the sun is important to understand. The life cycle of plants is regulated by the sun. The various foods that we eat come from different parts of the life cycle. The level and amount of nutrition is different throughout this cycle.

For instance, think about all the different vegetable foods you have eaten in the past couple of days. And this would include all of the fruits and grains as well

as what we think of as the typical vegetables.

If you ate sprouts, they were germinated seeds. Seeds are the stored energy of the sun to start the next generation.

If you ate the next stage of growth, like lettuce, cabbage, celery, or carrots, you ate the vegetative stage. Strong in minerals and vitamins because the plant had converted the sun's energy, with water and minerals from the earth, into the leafy vegetative part of the plant we eat.

The next stage is the early part of the reproductive stage. Broccoli, young squash, sweet corn, and cauliflower are good examples. The latter part of the reproductive stage is represented by tomatoes, cucumbers, peppers, and melons.

The last stage of the life cycle that we eat is the dried hard seeds. All of the grains, wheat, rice, corn, and beans, fall in this category. These seeds are all high in proteins. Although not the balanced proteins that we need, they have the highest food value of any vegetables. The energy of the sun has been stored for the next generation. After a rest period, the cycle can begin again.

You can see why I think that every chef should be a farmer or gardener, and why every chef should start his day in the garden. I have seen the cooks at the Greystone Campus of the C.I.A. in Napa, California, go out in the morning to the large organic garden to plan their menu for the day. They can see what vegetables are at the peak of perfection. We all know that fresh food is better for us and tastes better too.

The labs can bring you up to date, but we used to say that spinach lost 50 percent of its vitamin C five hours after it was picked. How much spinach can you get in the market that has been picked less than five hours? There is a way to bring the production of food closer to the people who prepare, cook, and eat it. I have no argument with supplements. I have taken vitamins and minerals for years.

Production and profit are the only real criteria in our national food supply. Quality and nutrition run a distant second. Take the production of corn as an example. When I was a boy, almost no farmer could produce 100 bushels of corn per acre. Now almost every farmer produces 200-300 bushels per acre. Advancement? What they don't tell you is the 100 bushels per acre corn had 20 percent more protein than the 200 bushels per acre corn produced today. Less nutrition but more profit for the corporate farm.

Do you ever wonder why tomatoes in the winter time taste like cardboard? It is because they have been picked green and bred to be handled by machine from the field to the supermarket. Where can a chef or the people get good food? Is there an answer to this dilemma? Yes, there is an answer. Is there a better way? Yes, there is a better way. Buy locally produced food. The cook in the home and the cook in the restaurant should not settle for the good looking garbage that is offered today. Most of it should be composted and returned to the soil.

If all of you would buy only locally grown products, our national health would continue to improve. If each of us spent just a dollar a day on locally grown food, $225 million a day would be pumped into our local economy. They say this local dollar turns over seven times before it leaves the area. Think of it, $1.5 billion a day circulating locally. Thousands of local businesses would begin from vegetable growers, to gristmills, local bakeries, egg producers, and others. The family unit, the family farm would return. Our social structure would change. Our highways would be less crowded. Commuting would decrease. The family would be kept closer together.

Everything in its season should be the rule for all cooks. Why do we need cardboard tomatoes with our salad in the winter when a few slices of apple would both look and taste better? Ninety-nine percent of all foods in every supermarket have been hauled long distances from someplace else.

There are not many places in the United States where a person with a plot of ground (20' x 20'), 400 square feet, cannot grow enough vegetables for themselves. During most of the year you can have from 10-20 available every day. During the coldest part of the winter the numbers will decrease but with careful storage you can eat well.

When I was a student here at Penn State during the late 1940s, we kept a garden at Boalsburg where we had available in the winter carrots, beets, cabbage, rutabagas, potatoes, parsnips, salsify, celery, parsley in a cold frame, apples, and winter pears. We had already canned tomatoes and many fruits: dried corn, huckleberries, and apricots. With our chickens and eggs, we ate very well. Growing your own food is not difficult. We have six sons and together we raised most of the food we ate.

If I were in State College, we would set up four 5' x 20' (400 square foot) raised beds. Two with tunnel-type plastic covers. I would show you how you could pick all the vegetables you could eat every day of the year. You would spend less than twenty minutes a day to have a very healthy diet and the cost would be less than a dollar a day. You could call it your personal 20-20 plan.

There are hundreds of cookbooks available on every subject. How many of them tell you when to plant to have your crop on a certain date? Each of you should write every year, " A Year in the Garden and A Year in the Kitchen." It should be a creed that you could live and work by. If you and every other college student expanded this creed just a little, this country would change in a hurry. The creed is simple and has five steps:

1. Plant a garden. Grow as much of your food as possible. If not a career, it is a great hobby—something you can get your teeth into. Taste your own grown tomatoes or corn and you will know what I mean.

2. Keep three chickens for each person. Chickens are the greatest recylcers alive. They can eat anything including the surplus from your garden. The eggs and meat and manure produced would give the national petro-chemical industry fits. The local producer would thrive. Arrange your pens so the chickens roost over the compost pile. It will be returned to the garden and eliminate the need for commercial fertilizer.

3. Support public education. More effort must be made to educate every person to his or her highest potential from the cradle to the grave. No investment will pay a greater return. Our present system must be changed and improved.

4. Recycle. Never buy anything new that you can get second hand. We have become a throwaway society. Most products today are designed to become obsolete, broken, or useless in a short time. Look at almost any product produced today. How long will it last? Industries would be forced to produce better products.

5. Never vote for an incumbent politician. This is supposed to be a government by the people. There are thousands of potential candidates that are equally qualified as any in office. We do not need professional rulers. If you don't know much about the candidates, vote for he youngest. They have to live with their mistakes longer.

This creed will work. If every college student lived by it or something similar, this country would change for the better. Many of our problems would disappear.

If we want to return the family to a dominant position in our social organization, we must allow it to function. Children must help grow their own food, work together, help cook the food, and eat together with shared benefits and responsibilities. Our children will develop confidence and self-worth as the first steps of pride in themselves, their families, and their communities. We will no longer hear the most common reply we hear from them today: "I'm bored, there is nothing to do." Our present system of indolence, indulgence, and TV is just not working. Back to the subject at hand.

Understanding hospitality is where your study begins. Food and shelter are basic human needs. To provide food and shelter in a changing world has become very complex. Hospitality in a mobile society is the challenge you face. You can expect that more and more people will eat and sleep away from home. Because of improved communication, business travel may decrease but overall more people will be on the road than ever. The only glitch as I see it is that communication may make it possible for our minds to travel while our bodies remain at home. There may be a generation of college students soon where their minds spend a weekend on the moon while their bodies remain behind. Total communication is not far down the road. We may be able to plug our minds into a computer. Maybe then you will not have to listen to people like me.

However, hospitality—food and shelter—will always be important. Let me tell you a story where hospitality changed the course of this nation. M.G. Vallejo, whose ancestors came to America with Columbus, was born in Monterey, California, in 1806. He became the Mexican governor's secretary at fifteen, then joined the military and became commander of the Presidio of San Francisco at twenty-four. In 1834 he was ordered to develop an outpost north of the bay to check the expansion of the Russians who had built Fort Ross on the California coast in 1812. He established his own home at Sonoma in 1835. This is where hospitality changed history. Vallejo believed that the future of California was in its land and people. He gave "all that came" land, seed, cattle, and help in building a house. But the statements that rank him with the founding fathers were his repeated declarations at the convention of California dons at the capital at Monterey where he said, "Let us join with the Americans where we will be fellow citizens rather than subjects of the King, the Queen, or the Czar." The United States had no valid claim to the West Coast. England, France, and Russia had a strong presence there. The United States had M.G. Vallejo. He held California neutral until the manifest destiny could catch up in time. California became part of the United States. Vallejo's hospitality was a primary factor. As a host, he had no equal.

At his death in 1890, he had gone from the richest man in California in 1846 to a man of modest means. The United State Land Claims Commission had taken most of his land. He was not bitter. He wrote late in life, "What more could a man desire but a piece of land to grow good food, poultry, and animals, a wood lot to heat his home, with family and the respect of his fellow men." He was a man of great wisdom.

In this field you have chosen to study there are careers as diverse as the people here are today. Some of these careers are not open to anyone today simply because you have not thought them up yet. Change will continue at a faster pace. You must learn to change one step ahead of the times.

From my point of view, the most important thing you can do for yourself, your profession, and your country is to force the issue of locally grown food. Sell your roommate on the idea, your neighbor, your boss, and anyone else you can influence. This is the one point that can save us from corporations without conscience.

Do I think you can make a difference? You bet I do. If each of us will do our part, we will change the way America eats. We will improve health, revitalize our citizens and families, and, best of all, we will have time to slow down and enjoy life. We will be a well-fed and happy nation. We need only the will to change. Our work has just begun. Yours is a very important job. How important? I'll answer by paraphrasing Will Rogers: "I never met a man

that didn't eat."

The goodness of life is yours.
Thank you.

Bob Cannard. 10/20/97. State College, PA

A week later, Bob received this letter from the faculty at Penn State, indicating that his speech had made its point.

Dear Professor Cannard:

It was great having you here at Penn State this week. Thank you for spending so much time with our students. The feedback we've received already tells us that your presentations had quite an impact. It's very exciting to see your enthusiasm for our wonderful industry. We are proud to have you as a Conti Distinguished Professor.

I hope that you can return to Penn State in May. We are also excited about the possibility of working more closely with the Culinary Institute of America in the future. Best regards to your lovely wife, Edna.

Cordially,

Fred J. Demicco, Ph.D., FMP
Associate Professor of HR&IM, Associate Director of HR&IM

The Culinary Institute of America came to California in 1976 looking to establish a campus in Northern California. They had arranged to present their requirements to interested Sonoma County groups at the Round Barn Inn in Santa Rosa. A small group of people went from Sonoma, including Bob, to the afternoon meeting. There were a couple of people from Napa, but the vast majority of the audience was from Santa Rosa.

The board of directors gave an hour long presentation that detailed their plans and objectives, told of how much land they were looking for, and finished by discussing the benefits to the local wine and food industry that would result from locating their institution in Sonoma County.

Bob was really impressed—it was exactly what they needed to put Sonoma on the map. He thought it was a great way to boost the profile of the county with a prestigious establishment that was already providing chefs and administrators to the growing list of world-class restaurants throughout the North Bay.

But when the audience was asked for comments at the end of the presentations, there was absolutely none, and the room was quiet. Bob was astounded. From the back of the room he raised his hand and immediately exclaimed that this was the chance of a lifetime. It was a huge opportunity for the county to establish its credentials as the premier location for fine food and wine. He admonished the crowd, telling them that they should have begged the CIA to come to Sonoma County, never mind waiting for them to show up. (He actually said "you're sitting there on your asses like you're all dead!")

He may not have made much impression on the crowd, but he certainly got the attention of the CIA Board of Trustees. The very next morning he received a call from its president, Walter Conti, thanking him for his contribution. They hit it off immediately, and from then on Bob was consulted on a regular basis. Walter Conti was president of the American Restaurant Association, president of the Board of Trustees of Bob's alma mater, Penn State, and president of the CIA all at the same time. Bob and he had also been at Penn State at the same time, and soon realized that Walter may well have been one of the students made fun of by Bob and his pals as "waiters" when students in the hotel management department used the same building as those enrolled in horticulture.

Bob worked hard to promote the interests of the Culinary Institute, and tried to get them interested in Sonoma Valley. But Greystone, the former location of the Christian Brothers Winery in the Napa Valley became available, and was the natural choice for the new facility. In 1995 the CIA dedicated the herb garden located right in front of the impressive façade to Bob and Edna Cannard in recognition of his services to the school in particular, and horticulture in general.

If this had not occurred, it is possible that the Kunde Winery in Kenwood may have been the chosen location.

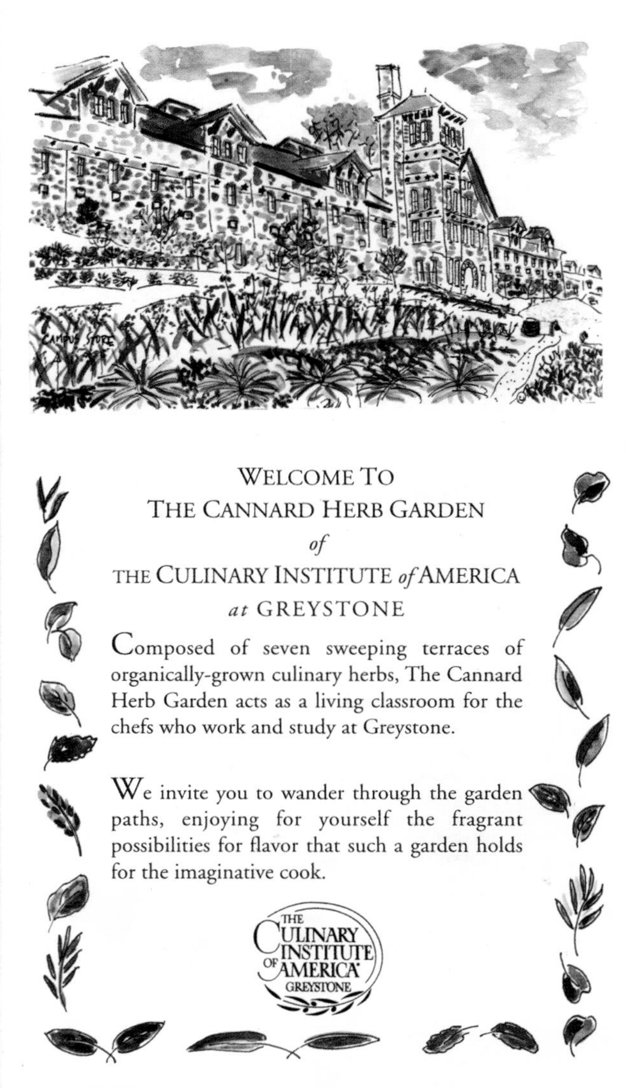

WELCOME TO
THE CANNARD HERB GARDEN
of
THE CULINARY INSTITUTE *of* AMERICA
at GREYSTONE

Composed of seven sweeping terraces of organically-grown culinary herbs, The Cannard Herb Garden acts as a living classroom for the chefs who work and study at Greystone.

We invite you to wander through the garden paths, enjoying for yourself the fragrant possibilities for flavor that such a garden holds for the imaginative cook.

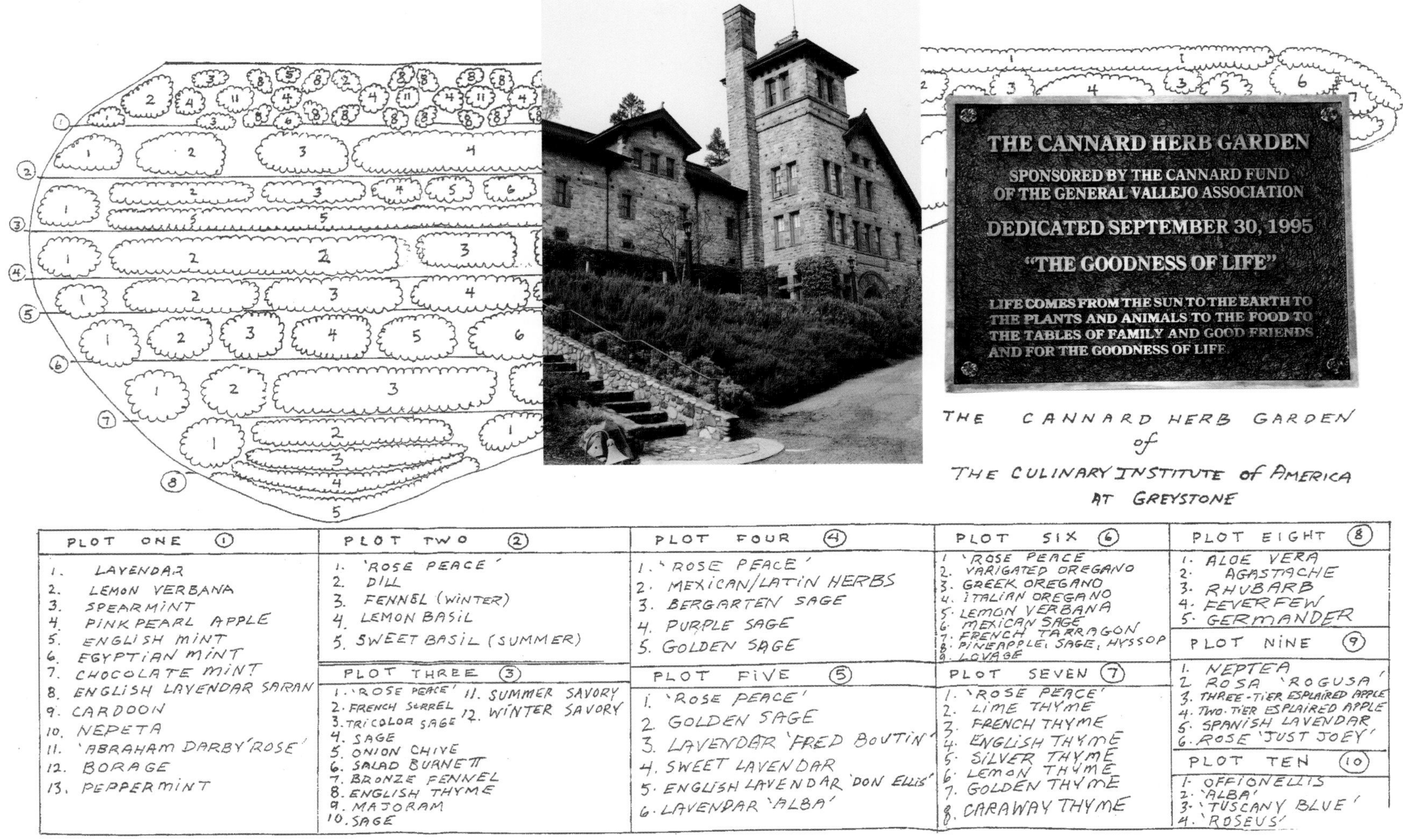
THE CANNARD HERB GARDEN
SPONSORED BY THE CANNARD FUND OF THE GENERAL VALLEJO ASSOCIATION
DEDICATED SEPTEMBER 30, 1995
"THE GOODNESS OF LIFE"
LIFE COMES FROM THE SUN TO THE EARTH TO THE PLANTS AND ANIMALS TO THE FOOD TO THE TABLES OF FAMILY AND GOOD FRIENDS AND FOR THE GOODNESS OF LIFE
THE CANNARD HERB GARDEN of THE CULINARY INSTITUTE of AMERICA AT GREYSTONE
PLOT ONE ①
1. LAVENDAR
2. LEMON VERBANA
3. SPEARMINT
4. PINKPEARL APPLE
5. ENGLISH MINT
6. EGYPTIAN MINT
7. CHOCOLATE MINT
8. ENGLISH LAVENDAR SARAN
9. CARDOON
10. NEPETA
11. 'ABRAHAM DARBY' ROSE'
12. BORAGE
13. PEPPERMINT
PLOT TWO ②
1. 'ROSE PEACE'
2. DILL
3. FENNEL (WINTER)
4. LEMON BASIL
5. SWEET BASIL (SUMMER)
PLOT THREE ③
1. 'ROSE PEACE'
2. FRENCH SORREL
3. TRICOLOR SAGE
4. SAGE
5. ONION CHIVE
6. SALAD BURNETT
7. BRONZE FENNEL
8. ENGLISH THYME
9. MAJORAM
10. SAGE
11. SUMMER SAVORY
12. WINTER SAVORY
PLOT FOUR ④
1. 'ROSE PEACE'
2. MEXICAN/LATIN HERBS
3. BERGARTEN SAGE
4. PURPLE SAGE
5. GOLDEN SAGE
PLOT FIVE ⑤
1. 'ROSE PEACE'
2. GOLDEN SAGE
3. LAVENDAR 'FRED BOUTIN'
4. SWEET LAVENDAR
5. ENGLISH LAVENDAR 'DON ELLIS'
6. LAVENDAR 'ALBA'
PLOT SIX ⑥
1 'ROSE PEACE
2. VARIGATED OREGANO
3. GREEK OREGANO
4. ITALIAN OREGANO
5. LEMON VERBANA
6. MEXICAN SAGE
7. FRENCH TARRAGON
8. PINEAPPLE, SAGE, HYSSOP
9. LOVAGE
PLOT SEVEN ⑦
1. 'ROSE PEACE'
2. LIME THYME
3. FRENCH THYME
4. ENGLISH THYME
5. SILVER THYME
6. LEMON THYME
7. GOLDEN THYME
8. CARAWAY THYME
PLOT EIGHT ⑧
1. ALOE VERA
2. AGASTACHE
3. RHUBARB
4. FEVERFEW
5. GERMANDER
PLOT NINE ⑨
1. NEPTEA
2. ROSA 'ROGUSA'
3. THREE-TIER ESPLAIRED APPLE
4. TWO-TIER ESPLAIRED APPLE
5. SPANISH LAVENDAR
6. ROSE 'JUST JOEY'
PLOT TEN ⑩
1. OFFIONELLIS
2. 'ALBA'
3. 'TUSCANY BLUE'
4. 'ROSEUS'

CHAPTER FOURTEEN

EPILOGUE

When Bob first came to California, he was expecting to find that people here would be no different to those in Pennsylvania, or any other state. His experiences during WWII with service people from all over the country led him to believe that the similarities far outweighed the differences. Americans are Americans, regardless of location. So he expected to find people in Sonoma County as friendly and helpful as his neighbors had been back east. Sadly he found this to be far from the truth. And years of contemplation have never quite provided the reason. He is drawn to the idea that there is a pervasive provinciality with its attendant take-care-of-yourself attitude that stems from the dominating influence of the first immigrants. At the same time, he recalls that California has been described as "the home of the descendents of malcontents and ne'er-do-wells." He admits that among the pioneers that he admires so much were many who never quite managed to make it. They repeatedly put discontent and failure behind them, and moved west a few miles more for yet another chance to improve their circumstances. By Bob's account, the gold rush accelerated this phenomenon, but having reached the western limit of North America, the Pacific Ocean, people had nowhere else to go, and a population of hardy social misfits piled up.

Of course, he recognizes that hope, optimism, opportunity and success piled up in California too, counting the Cannards as fortunate beneficiaries. Perhaps Sonoma County is a place where the differences between the elements of a bipolar community are more apparent than in most places.

Whatever the truth and however Bob fits into it, he has shrugged off the barbs and petty hatreds and feuds, preferring to see their humorous side, and who knows, taking a perverse delight in provoking some of them.

Well, it's not entirely true to say that the feuds that have involved Bob over the years failed to leave their mark. In fact, some hurt to the extent that Bob would love to have filled these pages with stories of some of the protagonists and their forebears who probably deserve to have their names dragged in the mud.

For example, it's Bob's view that the *Index-Tribune* has printed outrageously one-sided analyses, blatant lies and twisted half-truths in support of its friends in "the establishment," frequently at Bob's expense.

Editor Bill Lynch has frequently claimed that the *Index Tribune* is "vigilant" when it comes to the Brown Act which demands transparency from elected bodies, yet neither he nor his journalists have been remotely interested in many egregious violations. In fact the opposite is true. He laid into members of the school board for the heinous crime of sending "serial emails." But he never took up the same cause when Bob tried to reveal that the City Council were holding blatantly illegal closed sessions under the auspices of city manager Brock Arner.

Bill was happy to slam Bob for suggesting publicly that the Sonoma Valley Hospital board were acting inappropriately in their dealings on the ill-fated Sutter Health agreement, but when the same board was ripped by the District Attorney's office for holding a blatantly illegal closed meeting (at which it was decided to spend taxpayer's money on an advertisement in Lynch's own newspaper,) his editorial comment was "They were just trying to have a marketing meeting."

In the face of such transparent double standards, it's hardly worth upping the ante by attempting to redress the balance of argument on any number of issues where Bob feels he was slighted by the Lynches—as much for omitting his side of the story as by touting their own as the true version.

The fact is, the *Index-Tribune* is an establishment newspaper that relies on ad expenditure by the establishment, and it would be naïve to expect it not to support establishment causes, the status quo, and any development that might provide the opportunity to sell more newspapers.

By comparison, Bob is one of those rare people that even when he joined the establishment—lecturing at the Jaycee, heading the Chamber of Commerce, as Alcalde, or on the City Council—he has no more acquiesced to "the system" than when he was on the outside, and that is his great charm, and his great value, to the residents of Sonoma.

Far better that Bob gets lambasted and ostracized for having a point of view, than become one of the endless succession of elected representatives that fall in line for fear of not being made mayor when it's their turn.

Bob's running battles with the City of Sonoma and the social club that frequently masqueraded as its council are chronicled in other chapters. And as much as the establishment often bridles at the sound of his name, the truth is, the city would be poorer if it hadn't had Bob Cannard to keep it on its toes and provide a target when they were bored. And as much as Bob himself professes disgust and contempt for a succession of its members, this is well tempered with humor.

In a complimentary letter to the *Index-Tribune* that *was* printed—perhaps proving Bob is not always right — Will Shonbrun, a noted progressive and therefore one who vigorously rejects Bob's Republican conservatism said it perfectly . . .

Tuesday, November 16, 1993
One reader's year-end awards
Editor, *Index-Tribune*

Uh oh, they're upon us again, like a plague of locusts or a blessing depending on your perspective ... the dreaded holidays. Bookended by Halloween and New Year's they run the gamut between secular, religious, and mystical. On the positive side, they're a great excuse for getting out of school, getting out of work, getting out of ... anything.

On the negative, it's a demand for jocularity, and you may not be feeling particularly jolly. I suppose it's a mixed bag; a little bit of hell, a little bit of heaven.

At their best they can be reminders about those in need and less fortunate than ourselves, and the long-lasting joy in giving and helping.

Which brings me to the first annual presentation of my year-end awards, for...Sonoma's Most Interesting Character—Bob Cannard. Hands down our hands on man. He's eccentric, wonderful, and wily; what a guy! Every town needs at least one

Will Shonbrun.

Some of the opposition to Bob's ideas have come simply because he is Bob Cannard. This is more than just unfortunate. If people had listened to him, there would be no water shortage and dry wells in the valley because there would be series of lakes along Sonoma Creek to recharge the system and offer recreation as well as utility.

If people had listened to Bob there would be thousands more trees in the neighborhoods.

If people had listened to Bob there would be less of a traffic problem up and down the valley because there would be a rail line and a "southern crossing."

The police department would have been centrally located at Fifth West and West Napa instead of isolated up a single egress road. It would have two or three fewer officers but be more visible.

The fire department wouldn't be a nonsensically located boondoggle of a monument to excess, the City would have two million dollars in the bank, kids would be better provided for, there would be vegetable gardens with affordable housing, fewer trophy houses built to the edges of the lots on the east side, and far greater prominence given to historical sites. There would be chickens on the plaza, and part of it would be pedestrian only. And perhaps most important of all, the valley would be municipally consolidated, and represented exclusively, not by people whose major interests lie outside the valley in Santa Rosa.

These may not seem a big deal to city folks or part-time residents, but for the people that came to the valley for its slow charm, rural heritage, natural beauty and immense ecological wealth, they are.

The positive side, however, more than compensates, because if people *hadn't* listened to Bob, there would be no magnificent Fourth of July fireworks in the fields by Vallejo's home because it would be covered with houses. Urban Santa Rosa would have smothered Kenwood and the valley south to El Verano. The Chamber of Commerce and the Vintage Festival would certainly not exist, there would be no annual Ox Roast and no fountain at the Vintage House. The Historical Society that sponsored this book may well have expired, and the population would not have had his constant reminders that our wonderful history can and does enrich our lives. There may never have been a horticulture department at the Santa Rosa JC, and Sonoma County may not have the incredible base of fine growers that bolster its reputation for producing the most fabulous wine and fresh foods in the world.

And for at least a couple of decades, the front page of the *Index-Tribune* newspaper would have been short of headlines.

At the beginning of this book, Bob pays tribute to the many people that shared his opinions and shouldered the work that made some of these accomplishments a reality. But it has been his hard charging no compromise leadership, and willingness to be the public target for the opposition that gave authority to the plan—whatever it was.

For more than a few, it is the personal contribution that Bob and his family have made to their lives that will be the true tribute to his existence.

For every public rant there have been a thousand private kindnesses, and for every harsh criticism of our major institutions, hundreds of gifts in money, time and effort to the clubs and societies that form the real fabric of our existence.

Bob Cannard is monumentally generous, and if the only downside is that you have to listen to his advice, it's a tiny price to pay for a man of the earth who on a daily basis brings its great bounty, spiritual and otherwise, into the homes of those he adopts.

In the fall of 2004, Bob was diagnosed with colon cancer and immediately went for the most aggressive surgical treatment, which appears to have been entirely successful. The event briefly had him pondering his mortality, but six months later it is long forgotten.

It's his intention to be cremated when the time comes, and trusts the family to carry out his wishes to have half his ashes placed here in Sonoma and the other half under a designated tree he planted in Pennsylvania, where he still takes two trips every year.

His belief that his component atoms will go on for infinite time in one form of life or another, and his acute sense of his own place in a history that will always exist is profoundly satisfying to him. He is frequently called on to give eulogies, partly because he knows the history of almost everyone around and has a fluent and captivating vocal delivery, but also because his own convictions enable him to place others on his timeless continuum, and he communicates this in a vital and comforting manner. He has a knack for making other people's lives significant.

While accomodating the religious convictions of others with magnanimity, Bob is nevertheless clear about his own.

Evolution is the God that all religions should respect, not worship—respect. This is the God of Mother Nature. In every generation of every species in the world there are a group of individuals that are best suited to the conditions existing at that time. These are the ones that reproduce and carry the species into the future. Those individuals in each generation that are least suited to the current conditions are soon eliminated from the gene pool of the future. This is true of every species on the land, sea, or air. The pendulum swings back and forth as we evolve. Some species evolve, others disappear.

We must always remember that the positives in each species always triumph over the negatives or that species disappears. That is why in the assent of man we have gradually improved. We no longer consider it sport for men to kill each other in combat in the Coliseum. Hockey and football may be close but death is not the object.

Man's climb toward improvement and perfection has been greatly helped by the many superior individual minds that have been produced. All major religions, and probably all minor ones as well, have been oriented around genius minds of the past. The prophets of the Old Testament in Judaism, Allah in Islam, Jesus in Christianity, Buddha in the East as well as hundreds of others throughout our time on Earth.

Religion and faith are two different things. Faith is personal and has very little to do with religion. One can have great faith and still disapprove of what that organized religion you belong to practices. The best recent example is the Catholic Church's handling of the priests' child abuse problem. Most Catholics I know have maintained great faith while disagreeing with the church leadership in how they handled the problem.

I have often been asked if I am a Christian. My reply is that I consider myself a First Century Christian. And to the question as to whether Jesus was the Son of God, my reply is that I believe we are all the sons and daughters of God. Jesus was the greatest teacher of all time.

The recorded miracles that Jesus performed may very well all have happened. Natural phenomena occur everyday that we cannot understand. The Bible has been rewritten and shuffled so many times, especially during the first centuries, that no one knows exactly what happened. I am a small part of the cycle of nature and am perfectly content with my infinitely minute place. I know where I came from and I know where I'm going and could not be more at peace.

My philosophy has always been to enjoy every minute of life. Life is the true miracle that we all enjoy. With a few drops of the pure blood, I will live forever in one form or another.

The beauty of Bob's views on religion is that they are expressed as deeply held personal convictions and not Truth to be prosyletized.

For many years, Bob was a regular at the long gone Arco station out on West Napa Street where other good old boys gathered to place bets, drink and shoot the breeze. Retired Catholic priest Father O'Brian also whiled away his hours with the same group, and on religious holidays made an effort to get them over to the chapel at Leonard Duggan's Funeral Home. On one Ash Wednesday he pursuaded Bob to go along, telling him it wouldn't do him any harm. He placed a smudge of ash on Bob's forehead and repeated a blessing. On the day Father O'Brian died, he gave Bob another, but more special blessing. It was the one his own mother had given to him the day he left Ireland. She had lived through famine in Dublin, craving something sweet, and the only clock she had known was the one on the local church. Her blessing represented the pinnacle of her hopes of a better world for her son.

"May you fall into a tub of honey and find a watch."

It's fair to say that the blessing has worked for Bob Cannard—in as huge a measure as one would expect for such a huge man. My final word is to pay tribute to Bob for being rash enough, and brave enough, to have his life examined in public.

If you have known Robert Hiatt Cannard, you will know that you are unlikely to have the last word on any subject. This book is no exception.

PERSPECTIVE.

In 1976, the bicentennial year of the founding of the United State, I was fifty years old and realized that I had lived a quarter of the history of our country. Today I have already lived more than one third of our history.

The country's bicentennial may have opened my eyes but I have always felt to be an integral part of our country's history. My family, and stories about my ancestors tied me to the past and my roots. My mother's father was in business briefly with Buffalo Bill Cody and knew Wild Bill Hickock quite well. He had traveled the West extensively during the latter half of the nineteenth century and met many of the characters of the day. His father had landed at the Port of Bodega, California before the Gold Rush. These stories always gave me a strong connection to the past.

As a boy, I knew many people who were eighty plus years old. Hardly a day went by that I did not quiz them about their youth. This gave me a clear perspective of the middle third of our history. Their parents and grandparents told them stories of the first third of our history. So I have had virtually first person accounts of what went on from George Washington to George Bush.

I can not understand how anyone could think that history is a dry and dusty subject. I knew two Civil War veterans who were grandfathers of two classmates, that told me stories of the battle of Gettysburg. Nothing could entrance a boy more. A teacher, who taught me to read and whose father had voted for Andrew Jackson, had stories that went back to the birth of the nation. I sought these people out wherever I could find them and listened to their account with rapt attention of what was the history of this nation.

During the middle 1930s, I had lunch everyday with a lady who had been a teenager during the Civil War. Her aunt was married to one of the founders of the iron industry in Danville. Grilled her with questions on every phase of life in Danville at the time. She described in detail the effects of the death of A. Lincoln and how they had traveled overnight just to see the train pass carrying his body to New York and then on to Illinois. She gave me a lovely amber glass canning jar with a glass lid that I still have today. Her daughter who was head of nursing at the Geisinger Hospital told many people that my questions had stimulated her mother's mind and that she lived longer and happily because of it.

Life was different during the Civil War than it was in the 1930s and still much more different today.

We are a very young nation. If we lived in Europe our country could be several thousand years old. We live in the United States of America that has hardly yet begun to take its place. We already lead the world in almost every conceivable advancement for mankind. As "Ronnie Baby" (Reagan) said, "The best is yet to come."

As a citizen I have always felt that what happens locally is the most important. If we can not run our towns well how can we hope to run our states and nation well? The same principals and standards that permit a family to succeed will work in our towns and cities. The closer people live together, the greater consideration we must make to others. As America becomes more populated we must give greater understanding to our neighbors. Just as a family must adjust to each other so must we—in our nation and in the world —accommodate others.

I live for tomorrow, realizing what great good fortune has allowed me to live during such a wonderful and exciting part of our nation's history. Having seen and been part of the Great Depression and the tragic suffering of our people who did not have enough to eat, until the year 2005 when opportunity and plenty is available to anyone who is willing to work, I feel blessed and fortunate to live in the only country in the world where the poor people are fat.

My wife and I are the parents of six sons, all of whom are capable of living on into the future as contributors to society. Each one is independent and capable of survival under almost any conditions. There is no doom and gloom in our household. The intellectual left-wingers can talk endlessly but produce very little. Our sons know how to do things and do them well. People seek them out every day. The future is now and they are ready for it.

THE FINAL WORD (Except with my wife)

The wisdom of age comes from a lot of living and a few mistakes. After reviewing all this material, reading the text several times—and looking at all those pictures—I have come to the conclusion that I could have done a better job with my life if I had been more humble and less defiant; if I had respected other people's opinion more, and relied on them rather than myself. But then again, maybe I would not have faced the challenges the way I did.

Sometimes, we must draw the line and definitely stand on one side or the other. My standard has always been—is it good for the public and not just myself? If I can answer this yes, then I believe I am on the right side because personal gain, or gratification, I think is the root of most problems.

As I look back now, I can see big question marks over some of my decisions. But my belief in the natural order of things leads me to reckon that, overall, I am on the positive side of the line.

Edna's preferred title to this book says it all - "A life well lived."

Bob Cannard. July 2005.

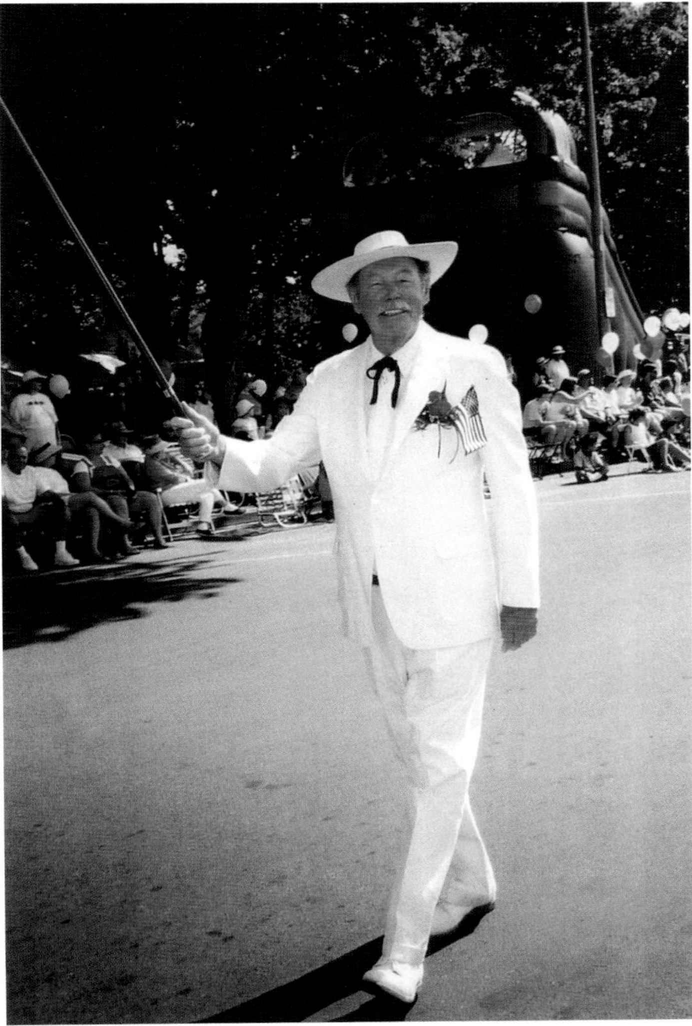

CREDITS

Cover art and computer graphics - Tom Whitworth.

Reproduction of the Carleton Watkins photographs on pages 165 and 183 by courtesy of the Sonoma Valley Historical Society.

Photographs on the following pages are from the Cannard family archives, except where listed below :- 15,17,21,22,23,24,25,26,27,28,29,37,43,49,50,51,52,53, 55,57,59,63,64,70,74,77,85,89,90,91,93,95,96,97,125,128, 150,160,162,163, 164,169,175,177,186,191,192,208, 209,212,213,214,217,219,220,221,232,239.

Photographs on the following pages are by Jeri Lynn Chandler and Tom Whitworth:- 1,11,25(card)26(card)38,43(book)46,52(patch&card)53 (certificate)54,55(certificate)58(tags&badges)59(knife, lighter&hearts)61(certificate)62,63(gold)73,74(cards) 76(cards)78,79,86,90&91(map)94,95(gold)99,105,108,11 7,118,127,129,130,141,145,148,149,150(bottle)151,152, 153,154,155,156,157,159,160(card)164(ring&club)165 (house b/w)168,172,173,185,192(brochure,cross,plaque) 193,194,195,196,197,198,199,200,201,104,205,206, 207(boxes&first two on left)209(duck)210,211,213(oils) 215,216,221(family)222,223.

Photograph at the swimming pool on page 52 courtesy of Eugene Shipe.

Engravings on pages 15, 16 and 45 are taken from *Harper's New Monthly Magazine* Volume XXVI 1862, and the newspaper clipping reproduced on page 48 is taken from a photocopy of a page of *the Danville Morning News.*

The newspaper clippings reproduced on pages 119, 122 and 123 are taken from photocopies of the *Sonoma Index-Tribune* microfilm archives held at the Sonoma County Library, and are reproduced courtesy of the *Sonoma Index-Tribune.* Both Photographs on page 124 and the top photograph on page 125 are owned by, and reproduced courtesy of the *Sonoma Index-Tribune,* who also holds the copyright.

The line and color illustrations on the following pages are by Tom Whitworth:- 1,8,13,31,32,33,35,82,85,87,91,97,98,99,110,139,143,150, 164,181,187,201,203.

The poem "Daybreak" by Liberty Hyde Bailey reproduced on pages 113 and 114 is from *Wind and Weather* by L.H.Bailey, 1916.